GOERING'S GROUND TROOPS

THE LUFTWAFFE FIELD DIVISIONS OF WORLD WAR II

MICHAEL J. STOUT

Naval Institute Press
Annapolis, Maryland

Titles in the Series

Airpower Reborn: The Strategic Concepts of John Warden and John Boyd

The Bridge to Airpower: Logistics Support for Royal Flying Corps Operations on the Western Front, 1914–18

Airpower Applied: U.S., NATO, and Israeli Combat Experience

The Origins of American Strategic Bombing Theory

Beyond the Beach: The Allied Air War against France

"The Man Who Took the Rap": Sir Robert Brooke-Popham and the Fall of Singapore

Flight Risk: The Coalition's Air Advisory Mission in Afghanistan, 2005–2015

Winning Armageddon: Curtis LeMay and Strategic Air Command, 1948–1957

Rear Admiral Herbert V. Wiley: A Career in Airships and Battleships

From Kites to Cold War: The Evolution of Manned Airborne Reconnaissance

Airpower over Gallipoli, 1915–1916

Selling Schweinfurt: Targeting, Assessment, and Marketing in the Air Campaign against German Industry

Airpower in the War against ISIS

To Rule the Skies: General Thomas S. Power and the Rise of Strategic Air Command in the Cold War

Rise of the War Machines: The Birth of Precision Bombing in World War II

At the Dawn of Airpower: The U.S. Army, Navy, and Marine Corps' Approach to the Military Airplane, 1907–1917

The Birth of British Airpower: Hugh Trenchard, World War I, and the Royal Air Force

GOERING'S
GROUND TROOPS

The History of Military Aviation
Paul J. Springer, editor

This series is designed to explore previously ignored facets of the history of airpower. It includes a wide variety of disciplinary approaches, scholarly perspectives, and argumentative styles. Its fundamental goal is to analyze the past, present, and potential future utility of airpower and to enhance our understanding of the changing roles played by aerial assets in the formulation and execution of national military strategies. It encompasses the incredibly diverse roles played by airpower, which include but are not limited to efforts to achieve air superiority; strategic attack; intelligence, surveillance, and reconnaissance missions; airlift operations; close-air support; and more. Of course, airpower does not exist in a vacuum. There are myriad terrestrial support operations required to make airpower functional, and examination of these missions is also a goal of this series.

In less than a century, airpower developed from flights measured in minutes to the ability to circumnavigate the globe without landing. Airpower has become the military tool of choice for rapid responses to enemy activity, the primary deterrent of aggression by peer competitors, and a key enabler to military missions on the land and sea. This series provides an opportunity to examine many of the key issues associated with its usage in the past and present, and to influence its development for the future.

Naval Institute Press
291 Wood Road
Annapolis, MD 21402

© 2026 by the U.S. Naval Institute
All rights reserved. No part of this book may be reproduced or utilized in any form or by any means, electronic or mechanical, including photocopying and recording, or by any information storage and retrieval system, without permission in writing from the publisher.

Library of Congress Cataloging-in-Publication Data
Names: Stout, Michael J. author
Title: Goering's ground troops : the Luftwaffe field divisions of World War II / Michael J. Stout.
Other titles: Göring's ground troops
Description: First edition. | Annapolis, Maryland : Naval Institute Press, 2026. | Series: History of military aviation | Includes bibliographical references and index.
Identifiers: LCCN 2025037239 (print) | LCCN 2025037240 (ebook) | ISBN 9781682479773 hardback | ISBN 9781682479797 ebook
Subjects: LCSH: Germany. Luftwaffe. Felddivisionen | Germany. Luftwaffe—Infantry | World War, 1939–1945—Campaigns—Eastern Front
Classification: LCC D787 .S738 2026 (print) | LCC D787 (ebook)
LC record available at https://lccn.loc.gov/2025037239
LC ebook record available at https://lccn.loc.gov/2025037240

♾ Print editions meet the requirements of ANSI/NISO z39.48–1992 (Permanence of Paper).

Printed in the United States of America.

9 8 7 6 5 4 3 2 1

Maps created by the author and Dr. Alex Mendoza of the University of North Texas.

I did it, Dad. I miss you.

CONTENTS

List of Maps   xi

Acknowledgments   xiii

Introduction   1

1. Creation of the Luftwaffe Field Divisions, Part I   7

2. Creation of the Luftwaffe Field Divisions, Part II   29

3. The First Year of Combat:
   17 September 1942–20 September 1943   49

4. Army Takeover of the Luftwaffe Field Divisions,
   1943–44   73

5. Luftwaffe Field Divisions in the West, 1944–45   93

6. Luftwaffe Field Divisions in the East, 1944–45   117

Conclusion   148

Notes   157

Bibliography   201

Index   217

MAPS

1. Overall Deployment of LwFDs 51
2. Soviet Northern Offensive, 14–27 June 1944 122

ACKNOWLEDGMENTS

I would like to thank Dr. Alex Mendoza, Dr. Michael Leggiere, Dr. Geoff Wawro, Dr. Christopher Fuhrmann, and Dr. Roger Reese for their patience and support throughout this process.

I would also like to acknowledge Dr. Rick McCaslin, Dr. Jennifer Wallach, Dr. Harold Tanner, Dr. Courtney Welch, and Dr. Sandra Mendiola, along with the rest of the history department at the University of North Texas, for their support.

I would also like to thank Dr. Rob Citino, Dr. Dennis Showalter, Dr. R. L. DiNardo, and Dr. Gerhard Weinberg for their support in uncovering this topic and putting this work together.

INTRODUCTION

The Mythos and Reality of the Wehrmacht

The mythical image of the fighting quality of the German army in World War II—as being known for lightning-quick attacks, brutal firepower, ably trained soldiers, and formidable success on the battlefield—has persisted across much of the historical scholarship of the European theater. Historians specifically note general German success against their American and especially their Soviet adversaries.[1] This myth can be easily seen in popular culture. Films disseminated by the former Western allies typically paint the German army as a faceless, emotionless machine that the audience is meant to expect to perform well. This pattern even persists in the few films that try to give the German army a face. In Joseph Vilsmaier's 1993 film *Stalingrad*, which ends tragically with the entire cast dying or being taken prisoner, the German soldiers presented in the film—although starving, freezing, and long since having lost real hope for victory—still were portrayed as holding out against impossible odds.[2] The notion of German military excellence was so confidently persuasive that it resisted investigation by many historians after the war, and only recently have flaws have begun showing in this pristine picture.

The Wehrmacht's true role in the Holocaust, for instance, was largely denied for decades, but contemporary scholars have finally presented the war crimes of the German army for all to see.[3] Likewise, the Wehrmacht's status as one of the greatest armies of the war has also been more thoroughly examined, and historians have found serious flaws within both the German command structure and the officer corps itself, especially the rivalries and tension present in the dysfunctional atmosphere created by the Nazi regime. Further weaknesses have been revealed in the German war economy and the German war effort as a whole.[4] The German panzer divisions and Luftwaffe performed admirably in 1939–41, but while these branches proved revolutionary at first, they suffered notable difficulties as the war dragged on, particularly in the realms of production and resupply.[5] However, the greatest single myth of Wehrmacht excellence, the superior quality of its soldiers, remains largely intact.

German soldiers of World War II are often depicted as well-trained, excellently equipped, and extremely resilient.[6] Outnumbered by the men and tanks of the Red Army in the East and outmatched by the airpower and firepower of the United States and Britain in the West, the Germans still proved stalwart opponents, inflicting heavy casualties and holding back the Allies for years. But behind the veil, German manpower had its problems. As the Germans suffered increasingly heavy casualties, the troops had to be replaced, and often too rapidly for the men to be properly prepared. The fighting quality of the German soldier dropped off considerably as the war progressed, though the fact that the German army was on the defensive for most of the latter half of the war likely helped to hide these deficiencies somewhat. Well-known examples of poorer quality soldiers include the *Ost* battalions of the Western Front: captured Polish, Russian, and other prisoners of war (POWs) forced, often at gunpoint, to man stationary defenses on the Atlantic Wall and within France. An additional example is the *Volksgrenadier* formations from later in the war: divisions of old men, wounded veterans, and survivors from destroyed units put back in service for lack of any other options. Another instance was the eleventh-hour creation of the so-called *Volkssturm*, a peoples' militia consisting of poorly trained and equipped civilians Adolf Hitler threw together at the last minute to try and resist the closing grip of the Allied armies.⁷ One of the largest forces of unorthodox reinforcements, and one that has received considerably less coverage from historians than others, is the Luftwaffe field divisions.

These units remain an anomaly in the historiography of World War II. *Reichsmarschall* Hermann Goering created twenty-two Luftwaffe field divisions (*Luftwaffenfelddivisionen*, or LwFDs) on 17 September 1942 with Hitler's blessing and formed them entirely out of Luftwaffe personnel. These men were trained for service as bomber pilots, ground crewman, cooks, clerks, and other air force support personnel, not as infantry. The first units deployed to the Eastern Front within three weeks, with hardly any time for organizing and equipping the units, much less training them. The divisions predictably proved unprepared for combat, and on the whole, their performance was disastrous. Many of the LwFDs disintegrated while under fire, and more than one German commander considered their creation a serious mistake. Field Marshal Erich von Manstein's personal opinion perhaps summarized this most coherently: given the circumstances behind the creation of the field divisions, it was "sheer lunacy" to have formed them in the first place.⁸

After a year of battlefield failures by the LwFDs, Hitler finally realized their weakness. On 20 September 1943, much to Goering's chagrin, he ordered them reorganized as regular infantry divisions under the control of the army. Yet, incorporation into the army failed to solve most of the problems within the divisions. Regular army officers joined the units and helped to train the Luftwaffe troops, but equipment as well as logistical support remained scarce, and divisional manpower was difficult to replenish upon suffering heavy losses. Often, when a division reached the point that it could no longer perform its function, the army high command (*Oberkommando des Heeres*, or OKH) disbanded it and reattached the survivors to other units. Of the twenty-one deployed LwFDs, fourteen served on the Eastern Front, one in the Balkans, one in Norway, two in Italy, and three in Western Europe.⁹ Several were destroyed outright in various combat actions, with most of the remainder cannibalized for their survivors. Only four of the LwFDs survived the war, and three of them were so mangled that they were divisions in name only by that time.

Despite their significance to the German war effort and to the history of the Luftwaffe, the LwFDs have received little analysis from professional historians. Few secondary sources exist on the subject, and none of them examine the subject in any real depth beyond a general combat history and technical details of divisional organization.[10] There are necessary questions to be answered: Who were these men? What was the overall combat record of the LwFDs? What happened to the LwFDs after the merger with the army in 1943?[11] In addition, three other issues seem crucial. Why did the Germans create these units in the first place? Did the divisions remain ineffective after the army's takeover? What was their overall impact on the German war effort?

The Work

The objective of this book is to answer these questions, while at the same time providing a complete English-language history of the Luftwaffe field divisions themselves. This study will examine the creation, training, combat service, and overall contribution of the formations to the German war effort. In addition, the LwFDs will be firmly placed within the historiography of the German army in World War II as yet one more example of the faltering quality of German manpower in the latter years of the conflict and the chaotic dysfunction inherent within the Nazi regime.

There are a number of issues for historians to deal with in approaching this topic, which might have contributed to the lack of solid scholarship thus far.[12] As with many European military units from World War II, surviving documents can be difficult to locate. Many of the records about the LwFDs themselves are incomplete or missing entirely. There are available records for most of the divisions, as well as a good number of regimental and battalion-level records. One limitation of these archival records is that some of the documents only cover a small timeframe during the war. Researching the documents of larger command units—corps, armies, etc.—is the only real way to possibly fill in the gaps. In addition, a number of German officers' memoirs proved to be quite valuable in discussing the LwFDs, in particular those of Erich von Manstein, Walter Warlimont, and Albert Kesselring.[13] There also are documents available written by a few of the field division commanders, as well as Eugen Meindl, the commander of Division Meindl and the man in charge of assembling, equipping, and training the first wave of LwFDs.[14]

This book is organized into six chapters. The first two will focus on the reasons why the LwFDs were created. In particular, the first chapter will cover the manpower crisis of the winter of 1941–42 and the reasons the Germans lacked a substantial supply of ready replacements, as well as the internal tensions inside the German high command that divided Hitler and his generals. The second chapter will specifically deal with Luftwaffe ground strength during World War II. This will address the LwFDs but in particular will focus on the rest of the units the Luftwaffe controlled during World War II. The point of the chapter is to set up the rest of the Luftwaffe ground forces as a precedent for the creation of the LwFDs in 1942 while also providing a much-needed introduction to another underexamined topic from the war. Chapter 3 will cover the first year of the LwFDs' existence: their organization, training, equipment, major combat actions, and what went wrong. Chapter 4 details the takeover of the LwFDs by the army and the changes made to the divisions, while chapters 5 and 6 analyze whether these changes made any impact on the performance of the LwFDs in combat by tracing the history of the divisions to the end of the war, with chapter 5 covering the Western Front, Italy, and the Balkans and chapter 6 detailing the Eastern Front.

Because there are twenty-one units to follow on virtually every front of the European Theater, much of the combat study will be focused on particular campaigns, bringing in individual LwFDs where appropriate. In the West, these include Operation Goodwood in the summer of 1944, and in Italy, the drive for Rome in mid-1944. With two-thirds of the divisions stationed in the East, this study will focus on several major operations fought between September 1942 and the end of the war in 1945, including the German attempts to relieve Stalingrad in late 1942, the siege of Leningrad, the Soviet northern offensives in January 1944, and Operation Bagration in summer 1944. The LwFDs will also be compared to regular army divisions in similar situations in how they held up or faltered against Allied offensives. The LwFDs were blamed for allowing many of the Russian breakthroughs in the major offensives of January and July 1944. Comparing how the LwFDs, at this point under army control, measured up to other army divisions will be important to understanding whether the army's reorganization of the LwFDs made a difference in their combat performance. Lastly, it should also be noted that one LwFD does not receive much attention in this project—the 14th—simply because it was stationed in Norway, saw no action, and was still there and intact when the war ended in 1945.

The LwFDs' overall impact on the German war effort was largely detrimental. The quarter-million men in the divisions were largely unprepared for action, an issue that was never truly solved by either the Luftwaffe or the Wehrmacht. Though other Luftwaffe ground formations proved successful in action, the weak foundation of a lack of training and equipment led to the destruction or dissolution of the majority of the LwFDs over the course of the war. While some units fared better than others, most LwFDs suffered the consequences of their high command's mistakes, leading to tremendous casualties and a long-lasting stigma of their overall weakness in action. To answer the various questions surrounding these units and properly examine their overall history, however, the first task is to examine why the Luftwaffe field divisions were created.

CHAPTER ONE

CREATION OF THE LUFTWAFFE FIELD DIVISIONS, PART I

The Origins

The Luftwaffe field divisions were born out of necessity, and their creation can be traced to three primary causes. First and foremost was the manpower crisis on the Eastern Front following the winter of 1941–42.[1] The Germans had suffered severe losses since the Soviet counteroffensive started in December 1941, and the German army required replacements. The Luftwaffe appeared to have personnel to spare, and the army looked to the Luftwaffe's ranks for reinforcements. The second factor behind their creation was the internal atmosphere within the German high command, highlighted by Hitler's undermining of the army and the political tension and distrust this caused between the Führer and his subordinates.[2] The third reason was the fact that early Luftwaffe ground units largely performed fairly well, setting a precedent for future formations.

This chapter will focus on the manpower crisis itself and determine how the Germans found themselves in that position. Though the manpower crisis was the basic reason that the Germans needed reinforcements, it does not explain why the new soldiers remained under the Luftwaffe's control.

To explain that, this chapter will also examine the internal situation within the German high command caused by the distrust between Hitler and his army subordinates. This tension mainly stemmed from the growing influence of the Nazi Party over the German military and the resistance from the German army and general staff.

The Wehrmacht's Zenith: 1939–41

The LwFDs were emblematic of how different the Wehrmacht of 1942–43 was from the early years of the war. Since the war began on 1 September 1939, the Germans had launched a spree of successful operations; Poland, Denmark, Norway, the Netherlands, Belgium, and France fell rapidly to them. Following that came lightning drives into the Balkans, along with startling victories in North Africa by the famous *Afrikakorps* under General Erwin Rommel. All of these victories were made possible by the advent of a new unit: the panzer division.

The panzer division was a combined arms formation, linking the speed and power of the tank with motorized supporting infantry and artillery to create a self-contained army within an army. While the Allies were bewildered by the employment of such a formation early in the war, the panzer division perfectly reflected the usual tactics of the German army that stemmed from the Prussian army during the eighteenth-century reign of Frederick the Great. Because of Prussia's and, later, Germany's limited internal resources and precarious position on a continent surrounded by enemies, German commanders always aimed for wars to be *kurz und vives*, or "short and lively." A long attritional conflict was something to avoid, as the country would always be at a disadvantage due to its enemies' superior resources.[3]

To accomplish this, the German army followed a doctrine containing two crucial elements: *Bewegungskrieg*, or "the war of operational movement," and *Auftragstaktik*, or "mission tactics." To fight *Bewegungskrieg*, the German army moved aggressively, always striving for greater mobility than their adversary. The ultimate goal was to catch the enemy in a great *kesselschlacht* ("cauldron battle"), surrounding and decisively defeating them to end the war. *Auftragstaktik* was more complex, but just as important. The literal translation is "mission tactics," but it is perhaps better explained as "the independence of the subordinate." The German officer corps was allowed to think and act independently, rather than conducting operations under strict orders as so many of their opponents were trained to do. While this sometimes led to disaster, many of the greatest Prusso-German victories were due not only to the quick thinking of the commanding general in charge but also to a smart independent move by one of his subordinates who had spotted an opening and moved without orders to take advantage of it.[4]

Frederick II earned his moniker "the Great" by winning a string of victories in the Seven Years' War using these tactics. Further, the Prussian army used this formula to great success against Austria in 1866, crushing the main Austrian army at Königgrätz and essentially deciding the war mere days after it began. They did so again against the French in 1870–71 when Emperor Napoleon III was surrounded and forced to surrender at Sedan, virtually ending the conflict. However, World War I and the trench stalemate on the Western Front ended the string of successes. The Germans could not recover from the three-year stalemate and ultimately lost the war as a result.[5]

The advent of armored vehicles opened immense possibilities for modern warfare, and every modern nation investigated this potential during the interwar period. Yet, while Britain, France, and other nations examined tanks as a brand-new weapon, Germany saw them as a means to an end. The German solution for how to use armor was the panzer division, and its entire purpose was to simply restore the traditional German way of war: utilizing modern mechanization to restore the *Bewegungskrieg* lost in World War I.[6] The panzer division married the modern technologies of armor, mechanized infantry, and mechanized artillery to traditional tactics and doctrine, and the Germans further combined the new unit with close airpower support. Tanks, artillery, and airpower blasted holes through enemy defenses while the infantry supported the initial assault, and then the fully mechanized unit could quickly speed through the gaps in the line and break through to the enemy flank and rear.

The panzer divisions allowed the Germans to run roughshod over every opponent they encountered in the early stages of World War II. Poland fell in twenty-eight days. France took thirty-eight, though the battle was truly won in the first three days of the operation. Denmark fell in just four hours. Yugoslavia collapsed in twelve days, during which time the Germans demolished an army of a million men, captured over 250,000 Yugoslav troops, and suffered barely 600 total casualties in return. The blitzkrieg into Greece was likewise over rapidly; in eighteen days, the Germans inflicted 340,000 casualties, including 280,000 captured, at a cost of just 5,000 casualties of their own.[7] Despite these impressive results, the assault on the Soviet Union was to prove a great challenge for the Germans. They underestimated the greatest Soviet advantages: the Soviets had plenty of space and numbers to trade for time, which would draw the Germans into their worst fear, a war of attrition.[8]

Operation Barbarossa, the German invasion of Russia, began early on the morning of 22 June 1941.[9] Three giant army groups, North, Center, and South, began a full offensive of more than three million troops spearheaded by more than 3,300 tanks. The Germans caught the Soviets completely unprepared and inflicted unbelievable losses upon the Red Army. The German progress was dizzying. The Soviet air force (*Voyenno-Vozdushnye Sily*, or VVS) was nearly destroyed outright by the Luftwaffe on the first day. Army Group North covered half the distance to Leningrad within the first five days of action. Army Group Center, commanding fully half of the German armored forces under General Hermann Hoth and General Heinz Guderian, had even greater success, stampeding through initial Soviet defenses and bagging massive prisoner totals in pockets in Minsk and Bialystok simultaneously as well as in Smolensk. Army Group Center by itself captured nearly 900,000 Soviet troops within the first two months of the invasion.[10]

In light of the success, on 3 July, General Franz Halder, chief of the general staff, went so far as to famously write in his diary, "It is no exaggeration when I say that the campaign against Russia was won in fourteen days."[11] Between them, the German army groups seized city after city, encircling the Russian defenders in over a dozen giant *kesselschlachten*. The huge pockets of Soviet forces trapped within Minsk, Bialystok, Kyiv, and other cities yielded millions of prisoners and large amounts of captured material. Historian David Glantz estimates that in the first six months of Operation Barbarossa, 229 Soviet divisions were lost, either destroyed outright or taken prisoner by the German army. By December the Soviets had suffered over four million casualties.[12]

By the end of 1941 the Germans surrounded the city of Leningrad in the north, a siege that would last nine hundred days, and also had nearly reached the gates of Moscow. However, the rapid nature of the advance severely stretched German supply lines to a point far beyond their capacity to support the Wehrmacht in continuing the massive offensive. The Germans underestimated both the distance involved and the equipment and manpower reserves of the Red Army. The main Soviet battle tanks, the T-34 and KV-1, outmatched the vast majority of their German counterparts and also most German antitank weaponry. The Soviets were able to quickly replace divisions lost in combat, albeit clumsily and at great cost to themselves. The campaign in France had covered about 150 miles, whereas Army Group North had to advance 490 miles to reach Leningrad. Army Group Center had to travel over 600 miles to get to Moscow. The assault against Moscow quickly bogged down in the face of supply shortages and the onset of the Russian winter. While the panzer divisions were barely able to cover the distance, regular infantry divisions had to attempt to keep up at a murderous pace. This was certainly hard on the men and especially bad for the several hundred thousand horses transporting their equipment.

The speed of the German advance likewise contributed to the problem; the Wehrmacht moved so rapidly that their logistics simply could not keep up. To get around this, the Germans sacrificed most supply concerns in favor of fuel and ammunition in order to launch one final drive against Moscow. It failed, and the Germans paid for their gamble. Supplies were low, and the Germans lacked winter clothing. With their tanks and other vehicles breaking down as the weather grew wet and cold, the Germans were in an extremely precarious position to fight the counteroffensive launched by the Red Army on 5 December 1941.[13]

The sudden weight of facing seventeen fresh Soviet field armies caught the Germans flat-footed, and the Wehrmacht was driven back hundreds of miles while suffering hundreds of thousands of casualties. With the Wehrmacht virtually immobilized due to the lack of fuel and the quality of the roads, stopping the attack would prove difficult at best. Hitler himself deserves some credit for saving the German army via his controversial

Haltbefehl, or "stand-fast order," which commanded the Germans to hold and fight for every inch of land. While decried both at the time and since, the reality of the situation went Hitler's way.[14] Retreating would have caused much greater losses, especially in equipment and material. The Soviets troops, though fresh, were badly equipped for a prolonged offensive. The Red Army, still reeling from the disaster of the past six months, was relying on its own last reserves of strength: vast waves of bodies. Such a tactic could only last for so long.[15]

The Germans barely managed to hold, while the Soviets in turn exhausted themselves and were unable to continue the push westward. Though the front tentatively stabilized by early March 1942, the cost of the fighting proved severe for both sides.[16] Since the start of Barbarossa, the Soviets had suffered an incredible 6.1 million casualties, including 3.6 million killed or missing. While Soviet losses were exceptional, the Wehrmacht's own casualties of just over a million proved perhaps relatively worse.[17] The heavy toll was in sharp contrast to the relatively bloodless blitzkrieg campaigns of 1939–40, and the losses proved much more difficult for the Germans to replace than for the Red Army. Moreover, the bulk of the German army was now fixed in the east, ultimately doomed to remain fighting there for the rest of the war.[18]

German Manpower Crisis, 1941–42

Thanks to an immense prewar training effort, the Soviets had more than fourteen million reservists with at least rudimentary military training available at the time of the German invasion. This gave them the manpower pool needed to survive the destruction of more than two hundred divisions in the first six months of the campaign. The Soviets were able to call up 5.3 million men by the end of June 1941, and by spring 1942 at least fifty new field armies had been deployed to the front lines.[19] While the Red Army still had to overcome equipment losses and other serious issues, they at least had the manpower necessary for short-term survival.

In contrast, the German prewar training program had been constrained by both the Treaty of Versailles and the organization of army high command. Versailles reduced the interwar German army (the Reichswehr) to a mere 100,000 men, and although the Germans did a great deal to circumvent the restrictions under the leadership of Hans von Seeckt, the Reichswehr remained greatly unprepared for a major war.[20] In particular, the Germans had a very small navy, no air force, and no pool of reserves. The latter point was perhaps the harshest—retraining a pool of reserves from scratch would take time, and World War II broke out too soon for much progress to be made.[21]

Adolf Hitler's rise to power in 1933 allowed the Reichswehr to begin rebuilding, and in 1935 rearmament began in earnest. It became clear that the army was ill-equipped to properly handle the process. The main directives given to the organization branch of the army general staff in 1935 were immense. The branch was to expand the army far beyond the 100,000 men of the Reichswehr, including through the reinstitution of conscription, the expansion of the officer corps and high command to provide proper leadership, and the creation of new branches of the military for previously forbidden weapons such as tanks and heavy weapons as well as the Luftwaffe. In addition, the organization branch had to handle the procurement of weapons, ammunition, and other supplies from a nonexistent armament industry as well as the construction of training and barracks facilities for the vast new army. In the face of this monumental task, other great issues of preparing the army for war—particularly setting up logistics, equipping the new units, and, most importantly, organizing the reserves—were initially relegated to the background.[22] The organization branch was poorly staffed to handle such an immense mission. When war broke out in 1939, the branch consisted of just fifteen officers and another fifteen aides, and it is quite possible that these massive prewar responsibilities were undertaken by an even smaller number of personnel.[23]

Despite the use of many expedients to further the tasks along, the process was slow and incomplete.[24] The Reichswehr had called up classes of just ten thousand men per year for a twelve-year service term. Beginning in 1935, Germany began calling up entire age classes for two-year terms. However, that meant that it took until 1937 to begin organizing reserve and replacement units. In 1939 only a few fully trained classes were available to call up, compared to as many as twenty classes for each of Germany's adversaries.[25]

Expanding the officer corps also proved difficult. The Reichswehr had only 4,000 officers among its 100,000 men, and increasing those numbers became a major project. To expedite the process, officer training was shortened, and a number of Reichswehr noncommissioned officers (NCOs) were promoted. Additionally, officers discharged in 1918 were brought back into service, and some police officers were transferred to the army. Those officers no longer fit for duty with front-line units were given administrative positions within the army command structure.[26]

German industry likewise was having issues keeping up with the buildup, and by 1939 the production of ammunition, armored vehicles, and other war-making materials was at barely acceptable levels. The German army may have invaded Poland and France spearheaded by its cutting-edge panzer divisions, but those divisions were mostly equipped with Panzer Mark Is and IIs. The Mark I was a glorified armored car, while the Mark II was still a light tank. The Allies, and the French in particular, possessed far tougher vehicles. German General Burkhardt Müller-Hillebrand noted that the only reason these issues did not impact the Wehrmacht earlier in the war was because of how quickly the early campaigns ended. Poland fell easily, there was an eight-month period of waiting and buildup before the operations against Scandinavia and France, and another year elapsed before Germany began the invasion of Russia.[27] Even so, the Wehrmacht's panzer divisions were still lacking in strength. In June 1941 most German tanks invading Russia were Mark IIs and IIIs, neither of which could match the Soviet T-34 or KV-1. While there were twice as many panzer divisions in 1941 as there had been in 1939, this was only accomplished by cutting a division's standard tank strength in half—essentially, doubling the number of units without increasing the number of vehicles.[28]

Despite the efforts of the high command to expand the army, at the outbreak of war the German army only had 1.1 million trained reservists, amounting to just 38 percent of those eligible for service. To this figure can be added the approximately 1.7 million reservists between the ages of thirty-six and forty-five, but these men had last received training in 1918. Thanks to these prewar efforts, when war broke out the German army was able to rapidly expand to a force of 3,754,000 men. Meanwhile, the German replacement army, the portion of the army responsible for making up immediate losses, numbered just 989,000 men in 1939, and that number had only decreased by the start of Barbarossa.[29] While the early blitzkrieg campaigns against Poland, France, and the Balkans had been relatively bloodless for the Wehrmacht, these paltry reserves failed to cover the losses sustained in Russia, and by early 1942 the Germans were scrambling for trained reinforcements. While the Germans had additional manpower to draw upon from their population, they did not have the trained reserves available to match the Red Army in the winter of 1941–42.[30]

Much of the German army at the outbreak of war was classified into "waves" characterizing the quality of their personnel. Panzer divisions and specialized units such as paratroopers and mountain divisions largely were top-notch and well-equipped, but it was a very different story for the German infantry. While divisions of the first and second waves were based on the recently trained reservists, a sizeable amount of personnel within the third- and fourth-wave divisions were World War I veterans, many of whom were over forty years of age. The German army of 1939 had a total of fifty-one first- and second-wave infantry divisions numbering about 865,000 troops, but the third- and fourth-wave divisions numbered thirty-five and counted nearly 590,000 men.[31] This meant that from the outset, the lightning-quick *Bewegungskrieg* machine that was the German army already heavily utilized older soldiers—men who, while trained, were of a poorer quality than most historians tend to picture within the victorious early-war Wehrmacht. The quality of the available personnel pool would only degrade as the war grew harsher.[32]

Increasingly, especially on the Eastern Front, the Germans would sacrifice the quality of their infantry units in favor of maintaining the mechanized and panzer forces, both of which were more mobile and thus more flexible than their infantry counterparts. The Germans were trying to hold a two-thousand-mile front line in the Soviet Union, and the panzers were effectively the only reserve units that could be quickly utilized to counterattack against enemy breakthroughs. When they were first formed, the Luftwaffe field divisions were designated static units, meaning they were meant to simply hold the line, not launch an offensive. Both Hitler and Luftwaffe commander Hermann Goering wanted them deployed to quieter sectors instead of where the fighting was heaviest.[33] The LwFDs were just one example of the German army cramming infantry bodies into a defensive position in the latter stages of the war. Another such example was the *Ost* battalions on the Western Front, which were composed of Russian, Polish, and other POWs who were forced to man the Atlantic Wall at gunpoint.

Luftwaffe Personnel as a Solution

The Luftwaffe of early 1942, in sharp contrast to the army, appeared to have personnel to spare. This disparity was due to both its organization and the personal whims of the man in charge of it. The air force was organized as an independent branch of the OKW (*Oberkommando der Wehrmacht*, or armed forces high command). This independence allowed Goering to directly place as much as he could under his control. This included not just air operations forces but also Germany's antiaircraft batteries, paratroopers, many signal units, the camp guards for ten Luftwaffe-run POW camps for captured Allied airmen, and even the state forestry department (of which Goering was also in charge as the Reich's "chief huntsman").[34] As a result, the Luftwaffe mustered considerable size. By 1941 it had more than 1.7 million men under arms, fully 20 percent of German manpower strength in that year. Only 588,000 served in flying units, which included pilots, ground crews, and also paratroopers. Signal troops numbered close to 285,000 men, while the antiaircraft branch listed over 571,000.[35]

In addition, the Luftwaffe's air arm had suffered heavy losses from June 1941 to March 1942. Initial air operations on the Eastern Front had proved just as exceptional as the ground invasion. The onset of cold weather drastically decreased the effectiveness of German air support and took its toll on equipment readiness. In addition, the actual strength of the Luftwaffe on the Eastern Front had greatly diminished. The Luftwaffe during the campaigns in 1939–40 had primarily been a support arm for the panzer divisions, providing close air support and dominating opposing air forces. The offensive in the Soviet Union had proven much larger and more difficult than previously imagined, and the Luftwaffe's air arm was not equipped well enough to take on the task. According to General Erich von Manstein, the Luftwaffe had taken on operational commitments in Russia "for which, as had since turned out, it was unable to find sufficient numbers of either air-crews or machines."³⁶ The Luftwaffe's fighting strength had faltered significantly after the defeat in front of Moscow. Aircraft broke down in the cold winter months, and as the VVS began rebuilding and getting back into the fight, combat attrition was catching up with the German fliers as well. Of the 2,750 aircraft stationed in Russia for the German summer offensive of May 1942, less than 50 percent were still operational by October, the month that the LwFDs were first deployed.³⁷ With the Luftwaffe in such a weak position, Manstein commented that it had the men available "and could have spared them long ago."³⁸

Hitler exacerbated the problem by withdrawing most of an entire air group, *Luftflotte* 2, from the east in mid-November to support the Mediterranean theater.³⁹ Supply issues, primitive airstrips, the worsening weather, and a slowly recovering Soviet air force only worsened the issue. These heavy losses left the Luftwaffe with an apparent surplus of flight personnel, giving the branch an even larger pool of personnel that the army wished to tap into. On 12 September 1942 OKH requested the transfer of naval and Luftwaffe personnel to help replace the army's losses in Russia.⁴⁰ Hitler initially agreed to the transfer, but Goering then stepped in.

The Meeting of 12 September 1942

At this point in the existing scholarship on the Luftwaffe field divisions, the reader finds a blanket statement. Goering did not want to relinquish control of his "good National Socialists" and offered to create his own divisions of Luftwaffe personnel instead, which the Wehrmacht could help supply with equipment the Luftwaffe lacked. To the utter disbelief of the army, Hitler agreed. The army argued that to deploy these units would be to invite disaster, but Hitler's mind was made up.⁴¹ While this has been the usual description of the event, the actual account of a meeting also yields additional details that must be acknowledged.

Walter Warlimont, the deputy chief of OKW's operations staff, provides the primary account of the OKW meeting that spawned the LwFDs. As the fighting continued in 1942, Hitler ordered the swapping of worn-out divisions in the east with fresh ones from the west, and Warlimont noted that over time, "this frequently resulted in divisions being moved to the Eastern

Front which were neither equipped, trained nor in any way ready for deployment in that theatre." On top of that, Warlimont also lamented that German long-term planning was "wrecked" due to their lack of reserves. OKW's operations staff attempted to fix the personnel issue, though they initially got "no support from OKH." Warlimont's staff, "after much urging," finally instilled some courage in the head of OKW, General Wilhelm Keitel, and convinced him to submit an order to Hitler requesting the transfer of 100,000 Luftwaffe and 20,000 Kriegsmarine personnel to the army. Keitel cut the number of requested personnel in half to just 50,000 airmen and 10,000 naval personnel, possibly to placate an anticipated ferocious reaction from the Führer.[42]

At the next OKW briefing, on 12 September 1942, Luftwaffe chief of staff Hans Jeschonnek approached Warlimont and "agitatedly" asked him whether he was the originator of the transfer order. Upon Warlimont's affirmation, Jeschonnek chuckled, remarking, "Then you'd better get ready for something!" Shortly after the exchange, Goering stomped in, with Hitler himself making "as though he knew nothing about it," though Warlimont was sure that this was a staged moment between Hitler and Goering. Goering went up to Hitler and declared that he was not going to let his "good young National Socialists" be dressed in the gray uniform of the "reactionary" army. Instead, he was "quite prepared" to raise divisions of his own, provided that they consist solely of Luftwaffe personnel.[43] Hitler at once agreed and even demanded twice the number of Luftwaffe men as originally ordered. Warlimont protested but received no support; Keitel saw this as the end of the matter, and General Alfred Jodl, chief of the OKW operations staff and Warlimont's direct superior, seemed to believe that "none of this had anything to do with him personally." Warlimont continued, "And so the bells tolled for the birth of the unfortunate 'Luftwaffe Field Divisions.'"[44]

Tension in the German High Command: Nazis vs. Traditionalists

Warlimont's despair coincided with another problem within the German high command that enabled Goering's scheme to work. While the army's manpower needs explain why Luftwaffe personnel were to be transferred to ground units, the reason why the new recruits remained with Goering reflects the growing tension between the army high command and the increasing level of Nazi control over the armed forces. Hitler's relationship with the army is a well-known element of his rise to power in 1933. He did not have the full backing of the army during this period; rather, he had to carefully manipulate his way around whatever objections the army may have had against his policies.[45]

At first, there was good news for both sides. On 3 February 1933, just days after being elected chancellor, Hitler met with his generals and told them his basic goals for his regime and the role he wanted the army to play within it. In particular, the Führer stressed crushing dissent from Marxist and pro-democratic groups, the rearming of the military and the Nazi Party's full support for the German army, and the need to militarize the German people. Most of the army was fine with these ideas, as Marxism and democracy were seen as major threats, and the effort to rearm the military was most welcome. Some officers might have had their misgivings, but they kept them to themselves.[46]

One thing the army was particularly wary of was Hitler's force of paramilitary thugs, the SA (*Sturm-Abteilung*) organization under Ernst Röhm, who openly wanted to replace the regular army with his men. As the SA outnumbered the Reichswehr thirty to one, there was ample chance that this could be done. Hitler recognized this issue, and his removal of Röhm and the neutralization of the SA in the "Night of the Long Knives" (30 June–2 July 1934) earned the army's approval.[47] The death of Weimar president Paul von Hindenburg in 1934 removed the last obstacle to Hitler seizing full control of the government, and the army was content with its new leadership. The Nazi government's economic programs and the resulting stimulation of the German armaments industry and regrowth of military strength were helpful to the army as well.

The army's contentment did not last. As the Führer and Nazism continually gained influence over the army, elements within it increasingly protested.[48] In 1933 Hitler appointed Werner von Blomberg as minister of war, but Werner von Fritsch, the commander in chief of the army, and many other officers saw Blomberg as a puppet of Nazism.[49] On 5 November 1937 Hitler finally revealed his true war aims regarding Lebensraum and his initial plans for the annexation of Austria and Czechoslovakia to his military and diplomatic advisors.[50] Blomberg and Fritsch, among others, raised their doubts, which only earned them both Hitler's resentment. In January 1938 Hitler's cronies Heinrich Himmler and Reinhard Heydrich orchestrated a political scandal against Blomberg and Fritsch that led to their removal. Instead of replacing Blomberg, Hitler reorganized the entire German high command structure by creating OKW, which he headed. He appointed Wilhelm Keitel to run the administrative sections of OKW and made Walther von Brauchitsch commander of the army.[51]

These appointments definitely suited the Führer more than the general staff. Appointing Brauchitsch was meant to placate the army's objections; the man favored neither Nazism nor the stiff traditionalism of the general staff and was thus trusted by both as a neutral figure.[52] Keitel, meanwhile, seemed to try every which way to avoid being given his new role, suggesting multiple alternatives for the position, including Goering, but Hitler rejected all of them. Keitel's role lacked any real value, as Hitler assumed the role of commander of OKW. To keep his job, Keitel had to become increasingly subservient to Hitler's whims. In Keitel's own words, his new job made him "miserable," and his resulting dour mood was taken for weakness by many of his fellow officers.[53]

In the years leading up to the war, tension continued between Hitler and the generals. Chief of the general staff Ludwig Beck was dismissed in 1938 following open condemnation of Hitler's policies regarding the takeover of the Sudetenland in Czechoslovakia.[54] His replacement, Franz Halder, worked very well with Brauchitsch, but the two still could not stand up to Hitler's will. The spectacular successes in France and Poland catapulted Hitler's influence and gave him even greater authority over the army. Brauchitsch was removed after Operation Barbarossa foundered outside Moscow in December 1941, and Halder would be removed in September 1942 after one too many disagreements with the Führer. Hitler assumed full command of the German armed forces following Brauchitsch's removal, and throughout the rest of the war, maintained an overbearing influence over strategic decisions.[55]

Claus Schenk Graf von Stauffenberg, the man who later tried to assassinate Hitler on 20 July 1944, provided one of the best descriptions of the German high command situation in 1942. Speaking to a new class of general staff candidates in December 1941, then-Major Stauffenberg stated, "Our high command organization... is more idiotic than the most capable general staff officer could invent, if he received the task to create the most senseless wartime high command structure he could."[56] Hitler's establishment of OKW created a chaotic mess of a power struggle between competing services and personalities, with Hitler firmly at its center. All interservice requests, such as the transfer of personnel from the Luftwaffe to the army, had to pass through OKW, and thus usually required Hitler's approval. This was particularly devastating to the army's authority. It shoved OKH to the sidelines and limited the army's focus to purely operational matters. OKW even removed the army high command from commanding the army itself; by late 1942 OKH only had authority over the Eastern Front, with OKW running the rest of the war. With no authority over the navy, Luftwaffe, or Waffen-SS (the combat branch of the Nazi Party's paramilitary *Schutzstaffel* [SS] organization), the request to transfer Luftwaffe personnel to the army had to go through Hitler (and Keitel) in September 1942.[57]

In addition to seizing control over most of Germany's strategic decision-making, Hitler also actively moved to subvert the German general staff. The goal was to change it, and the officer corps in general, from the traditional Prussian elitist branch to a unit theoretically more based upon individual performance in combat but, more importantly, upon openness to National Socialism. Hitler, as a former *Frontkämpfer* (front-line fighter) of World War I, held an intense disdain for and distrust of the army general staff.[58] He had fought through four years of the trench stalemate during the Great War and heavily distrusted the generals whom he felt had failed him and his fellow troops during the conflict.[59] He constantly complained that the army was nothing but "tradition here, tradition there," and that it was to him the "least reliable element in the state, worse even than the Foreign Office or the judiciary," two of his least favorite departments in the government.[60] The general staff had maintained an elitist image and exceptionally high standards since the end of the Napoleonic Wars, and even the exponential increase of the officer corps in the 1930s and severe losses withstood on the Eastern Front failed to dislodge that mindset.[61] In Hitler's mind, the general staff was a "special caste of particularly snobbish, pretentious airheads and destructive vermin . . . no imagination, full of sterile fertility, cowardice, and vanity." Hitler even went as far as to call the general staff "more repugnant than the Jews, since the Jews at least fully acknowledge to themselves that they never want to be soldiers, while the generals claim that entitlement only for themselves."[62]

Hitler's seizure of the supreme command of the army was completed when he appointed his chief adjutant to the Wehrmacht, Rudolf Schmundt, to head the army personnel office on 1 October 1942. Placing his ally Schmundt in the position gave Hitler undue influence over all officer promotions within the army, allowing him to remove top commanders who did not agree with him and to influence the rise of junior officers who did.[63] This move served to further silence opposition from the general staff, and the army increasingly fell under the influence of Hitler and the Nazi Party. This is turn created an air of great mistrust between the generals and the Führer, which had dire implications for the war effort.

The Luftwaffe fared differently from the army. It was separate from the other branches of OKW and thus not under the army's control. This was Hitler's doing, and he did so for primarily political reasons. On the one hand, it provided his sycophantic toady, Goering, an important platform of state service from which he could continue increasing his own power. In addition, keeping the Luftwaffe independent and under Goering's control gave the Nazi Party a branch of the armed forces under its direct influence and outside the institutions of the old Prussian system that still held fast in the army.[64] Hitler repeatedly defended the Luftwaffe's independence, though the isolation from the other services increasingly led to strategic and communication problems that detrimentally influenced the war effort and particularly the Führer's relationship with Goering.[65] One such ill effect regarded the deployment of Luftwaffe ground units. Though deployed in an army theater of operations, all Luftwaffe troops, including Flak (antiaircraft) units, paratroopers, and eventually the LwFDs, technically answered to Goering above everyone else, including whichever commanders the formations were currently serving under. This led to numerous difficulties in the field, as army commanders often had to go through the Luftwaffe in order to redeploy air force ground units.[66]

This link between Nazism and the Luftwaffe directly ties back to Goering's proposal of creating the Luftwaffe field divisions to protect his men from the clutches of the army. Warlimont's account gives a derisive description of the reaction of others present at the 12 September meeting. Both Keitel and OKW operations chief of staff Alfred Jodl failed to interject, with Jodl, despite being Warlimont's superior officer, pretending it had nothing to do with him. Warlimont objected, but his arguments went unsupported even by other OKH officers present. Field commanders like Erich von Manstein did strenuously voice their objections after hearing the news, but the level of ignorance displayed by Hitler's leadership at the meeting further proves how silenced OKH had really become in the military hierarchy. Warlimont also noted that Hitler demanded double the number of men from Goering. That number would be doubled yet again; eventually, the divisions would consist of over 200,000 men.[67]

The relationship between the Nazi Party and the Luftwaffe has been debated. One suggestion is that while a Nazi-controlled Luftwaffe was perhaps the aim, it was not very successful as "officer recruitment and traditions were not all that different between the army and air force."[68] Though Goering kept tight control over the Luftwaffe, his subordinates largely remained free of Nazi influence. Luftwaffe chief of staff Hans Jeschonnek, though certainly pro-Hitler, was not, strictly speaking, a Nazi. Under Jeschonnek and his successors, the Luftwaffe general staff prevented the party from ultimately gaining a strong foothold within the Luftwaffe hierarchy, though the party managed to interfere with air force affairs. This argument is punctuated by the example of Heinrich Himmler, who in late October 1944 reacted to this steadfast resistance of the Luftwaffe command staff to Nazi influence by attempting to persuade Hitler to establish an SS air force so that the party would have some sort of air formation under its direct control. Goering and the Luftwaffe general staff were able to counter this and maintain control over the full strength of Germany's air arm, though this suggests conflict existed at least at some level between the Luftwaffe and the party.[69]

These notions are undoubtedly false, especially in the case of the LwFDs. If true, this would fly in the face of the fact that Goering sold his argument to create the LwFDs to keep "good National Socialists" from the control of the "reactionary" army "still steeped in the traditions of the Kaiser." Every secondary work written thus far on the LwFDs has used this reasoning, and what truly drives the point home is the unity of facts between primary sources.[70] The Nazi Party was largely responsible for the establishment of the Luftwaffe. With Goering in charge, this did lead to greater ties between the party and the air force, in contrast to the openly critical army. Luftwaffe field marshal Albert Kesselring openly admits that the Luftwaffe "was guided by Nazi principles from the outset."[71] The Luftwaffe general staff and the air force officer corps might not have been as supportive of Nazism as Goering wanted, but this fails to address the actual troops that formed the field divisions. Soldiers of the supposedly "reactionary" army were inundated with Nazism even as their commanders tried to combat the spread of its influence. As the war dragged on, the army suffered increasingly heavy losses. Early in the war, German troops had excellent esprit de corps, but the massive losses eventually cost the army this internal cohesion. Surviving veterans often could not connect with young, raw recruits, and morale began to falter as unit cohesion collapsed. Nazism became a prime factor that filled the void and gave the troops some semblance of solidarity.[72]

Given the closer relationship between the Luftwaffe and the Nazi Party, it is conceivable that Nazism affected Luftwaffe personnel in much the same way as their army counterparts. The vast majority of Luftwaffe troops who joined the LwFDs volunteered for the service, which at least indicates a sense of loyalty toward the German cause, if not entirely that of the Nazis. Most important of all is the fact that the Luftwaffe answered to Goering, not its general staff. Goering was a Nazi and for the majority of the war was even designated as Hitler's heir. For all intents and purposes, historians can assume a sustained link existed between Nazism and the Luftwaffe.

Another element to be considered is Hitler's own focus on military loyalty to himself. Goering was offering to create units specifically loyal to National Socialism, and thus to Hitler. The way Goering sold the argument, the Führer likely found it attractive. The LwFDs were hardly unique in this instance. Throughout the war, Hitler created large numbers of elite forces loyal only to him. The chief example was the Waffen-SS, which eventually grew to the strength of thirty-eight divisions and over 800,000 men. The *Volksgrenadier* divisions were another such force, and to prove the point, the remnants of more than a few LwFDs were incorporated into *Volksgrenadier* units when their parent formations were dissolved.[73] Moreover, the LwFDs were not even the first Luftwaffe ground units deployed to action; among others, paratroopers, Flak divisions, and the Hermann Goering Parachute Panzer Division had all seen combat prior to the field divisions' existence. Goering's promise would also certainly be in keeping with the continued desire for control over the German armed forces that Hitler had actively striven for since he had risen to power and had largely acquired by late 1942. If the Luftwaffe was not in some way influenced by Nazi ideology like the SS, Hitler possibly would have turned down Goering's request.

Hitler and Goering

The notion of direct loyalty to Hitler leads to one other factor in this discussion: the personal relationship between Goering and Hitler. This is obviously important to the creation of the field divisions but is one of the hardest to understand. Looked upon from the outside, the shock felt by army leaders when Hitler agreed to the creation of the LwFDs is quite understandable, not just because of the likely military consequences but also because of Goering's track record. The Reichsmarschall had a long history of promising things he could not provide. Goering's control of the Luftwaffe tended to deal with his personal vanity as much as it did Germany's war needs. "Leave it to my Luftwaffe" became a favorite boast.[74]

A former fighter ace in World War I, Goering was among Hitler's earliest supporters, even as far back as the failed Beer Hall Putsch in 1923. Goering's relationship with the Führer was by far the predominant element of his character. His rise to power was intrinsically linked to Hitler's, and the potential fall of the latter would certainly lead to the Reichsmarschall's own collapse. Goering became Hitler's right-hand man. Whatever the Führer wanted done, Goering did. This arrangement began to implode on the Reichsmarschall over time. In their biography of Goering, Roger Manvell and Heinrich Fraenkel perhaps explain this best: Goering, while gaining glory in a subordinate role, compensated for it by "indulging in displays of self-glorification that were to become increasingly childish."[75]

Going into the war, Goering increasingly was blamed for all manner of the Wehrmacht's problems. For instance, army chief of staff General Franz Halder blamed Hitler's order to halt the panzers outside Dunkirk in 1940 and allow the Luftwaffe to finish off the trapped Allies as a vain attempt at glory-hunting by Goering. The Luftwaffe failed to destroy the Allies at Dunkirk, and a string of botched operations followed.[76] Goering was easily excited by General Kurt Student's idea to use a pure paratrooper force to take Crete, and the resulting Operation Mercury in May 1941 was fully under the Reichsmarschall's command. Though a victory, it cost Germany heavily and ultimately led to the permanent grounding of Germany's airborne infantry.[77] The Luftwaffe's efforts against Britain and Malta in 1941–42 led to little success, and the offensive against Malta only began to show some results when Hitler had Goering shift additional airpower from the Eastern Front to the Mediterranean in late 1942. This in turn severely weakened the Luftwaffe in Russia at a time when the Red Army and VVS were beginning to recover from the disastrous losses suffered during Barbarossa.[78] Most grievous of all of Goering's boasts would be the aerial resupply efforts to surrounded German pockets. This worked at smaller points such as Kholm and Demiansk during the winter crisis of 1941–42, but the much larger and more important efforts to resupply Rommel's troops in North Africa and the Sixth Army at Stalingrad cost the Luftwaffe dearly and proved little more than additional broken promises from Goering.[79]

In light of Goering's consistently frustrating actions, Hitler's actual trust in the Reichsmarschall has to be called into question. As early as January 1938, when Blomberg and Fritsch were removed from their positions, Blomberg suggested that Goering be his successor as minister of war. Hitler flatly refused, stating that Goering "was neither patient enough nor diligent enough for the job."[80] Throughout 1942 Goering's position grew weaker. The consistent disappointments from the Luftwaffe in 1942 were bad enough, but the impact of the first serious Allied bombing raids, particularly the first thousand-plane raid over Cologne on the night of 30–31 May 1942, drew Hitler's ire, and Goering bore the full brunt of the Führer's anger. Over the course of 1942, as Germany's position in the war took a turn for the worse and with Goering's Luftwaffe repeatedly falling short of his boastful claims, it is easy to see why the Reichsmarschall himself felt his influence over Hitler sharply waning. At his trial at Nuremburg, Goering himself admitted that "the chief influence on the Fuhrer, at least up to the end of 1941 or the beginning of 1942, if one can speak of influence at all, was exerted by me. From then until 1943 my influence gradually decreased, after which it rapidly dwindled."[81]

According to Manvell and Fraenkel, the Reichsmarschall spent the winter of 1942–43 "in the shadows." He made "a desperate bid for reinstatement in Hitler's favor" by proposing the Stalingrad airlift, which failed disastrously.[82] The dates involved here are very important in the case of the Luftwaffe field divisions. Goering ordered them created on 17 September 1942. By his own admission, this places the event near the end of the period Goering held some degree of influence over Hitler. There can be little doubt that the Reichsmarschall's long list of broken promises eventually caught up with him, given the bevy of intense criticism aimed at him and his Luftwaffe by Hitler and other party members. It is questionable how much Hitler could trust Goering in September 1942 to come through with yet another promise. With that in mind, it should be noted that though Hitler had initially agreed to the army's request to transfer the Luftwaffe personnel in the first place, he actually changed his mind in favor of Goering. Goering's idea to create the LwFDs, according to Erich von Manstein, was not surprising, as "Goering had always done things on an extravagant scale in his own domain."[83] Given this sentiment, Hitler's decision to side with the Reichsmarschall after dealing with his failures for nearly two years rightfully shocked the army.

Richard Overy describes Hitler's continued confidence in Goering as "the most difficult thing to explain" about the latter stages of the war.[84] As late as 1945, propaganda minister Joseph Goebbels noted in his diary, "Everything the Führer says about the Luftwaffe is one long indictment of Goering, yet he cannot bring himself to take a decision about Goering personally."[85] Overy believes that an "uncertain and unchronicled sentimentality" stemming from the strength of Hitler and Goering's early relationship kept Hitler from sacking Goering even in the last days of the war.[86] If nothing else, Goering consistently remained loyal to the Führer, and that may have been all that mattered. Between a group of discontented army officers

Hitler was actively subverting on the one hand and a blundering but loyal Nazi colleague on the other, Goering might have simply been the stronger choice for the Führer.

The heart of understanding both the existence and future problems in combat of the LwFDs is the German army's manpower crisis in 1942. Prewar training programs failed to prepare the army for the breakout of war in 1939, and by December 1941 German reserves were exhausted. After several months of scraping by, the German high command attempted to alleviate the problem by taking personnel from other branches, only to have their efforts thwarted by a bombastic performance by Hermann Goering. That Hitler agreed to Goering's proposal to form Luftwaffe ground divisions is an obvious reflection of the power struggle that existed within the German high command since the Führer gained power in 1933. Hitler subverted the control of the general staff for years before, and by 1942 he had nearly gained full control over German armed forces. Keeping a force of troops under direct control of a Nazi subordinate certainly appealed to Hitler.

Crucially, this was not the first time in the war that this was done, nor would it be the last. The Luftwaffe field divisions joined the Waffen-SS, *Volksgrenadier* divisions, and other such "private armies" that made up a significant portion of German strength by the end of the war. In addition, the LwFDs were not the first Luftwaffe ground formations to be created and see combat. Germany's antiaircraft units and paratroopers, historically praised for their combat prowess in World War II, were under the direct control of the Luftwaffe as well. The air force even fielded its own panzer unit, named for the Reichsmarschall himself. Even beyond the more specialized units, the Luftwaffe field divisions were still not the first of their kind. Luftwaffe personnel volunteered for infantry service in the army back in late 1941 and served with varying degrees of distinction throughout the winter crisis. There were plenty of ancestors to the field divisions, and their contributions to the war also need to be addressed.

CHAPTER TWO

CREATION OF THE LUFTWAFFE FIELD DIVISIONS, PART II

The Luftwaffe in the Ground War, 1939–42

While German manpower needs and the relationship between the army, Hitler, and Nazism have been covered by historians, a third cause for the creation of the LwFDs has yet to be properly addressed: the role of the Luftwaffe in the ground war. The LwFDs were not the first air force units to be involved on the ground. Two units in particular that have been well researched in the scholarship of World War II are paratroopers and antiaircraft units. Germany's paratroopers (*Fallschirmjäger*), the elite airborne infantry that spearheaded the famous blitzkriegs of 1940–41 into Scandinavia, the Low Countries, France, and the Balkans, were technically part of the Luftwaffe and answered to Goering. The Flak formations also were under the Luftwaffe's control. Not only were they key to Germany's air defense, but also Flak artillery, especially the 88-millimeter (mm) gun, became an exceptionally effective antitank weapon on all fronts of the war.

The involvement of the Luftwaffe on ground-level operations went far beyond paratroopers and Flak units, however. The Luftwaffe already possessed huge numbers of personnel: over 1.7 million by 1941. When the idea of transferring Luftwaffe troops to the army was first discussed in September 1942, Hitler's agreement bewildered the army officers present. The army argued that to deploy these units would be to invite disaster, but Hitler's mind was made up.

Despite making a decision that has since been characterized as varying degrees of lunacy, in Hitler's mind, there was some reason to trust Luftwaffe troops in combat. It is important to distinguish that Luftwaffe personnel were not an example of "scraping the bottom of the barrel"; in fact, after the Waffen-SS, the Luftwaffe had first pick of the best new military recruits. Though they were not trained for infantry combat, the Luftwaffe men to be transferred to OKH were among Germany's best and brightest. With proper training, many German commanders felt that the Luftwaffe troops could conceivably perform quite well.[1] This concept was not new to the war, either: Luftwaffe units were already fighting in the east, and in early 1942 air force troops were already becoming an important component of Germany's ground forces. By the end of the war, the air force fielded an impressive list of ground formations, including not only twenty-two field divisions but also eleven paratrooper divisions, thirty-one Flak divisions, an entire panzer corps (the "Hermann Goering" formation), and a wide array of technical detachments, auxiliary formations, and special security units. By August 1944 the Luftwaffe mustered 2.8 million personnel. Given that it was by that time drastically weakened in the air, this only further shows the enormous size of the Luftwaffe's ground complement.[2] With this force accounting for between sixty and seventy divisions, the Luftwaffe's contribution to the ground war deserves analysis and its own place in World War II historiography.

Fallschirmjäger and the Early War

Two of the basic Luftwaffe formations were paratrooper and antiaircraft divisions, and both already played key roles in the war effort. *Fallschirmjäger* had been on the forefront of many of the famous German blitzkriegs of 1940–41. At the start of the war, there were two units of airborne infantry, the 7th *Flieger* (Air) Division (later renamed the 1st *Fallschirmjäger* Division) and the 22nd *Luftlande* Division (glider-borne troops). The

7th *Flieger* Division led the assault into Denmark and Norway in April 1940 and also dropped ahead of the panzer divisions during the offensive into Belgium and the Netherlands that May, most notably seizing the major fortress of Eben-Emael. The unit also served as the vanguard for Operation Mercury, the German invasion of Crete that lasted from 20 May to 1 June 1941.[3]

Parachute infantry was a new weapon of war, however, and the Germans saw mixed success. In many cases, dropped paratroopers incited panic among the Allied forces and secured vital locations, but in others, the *Fallschirmjäger* were too few or too scattered to capture many of their targets. Norwegian resistance at Dombås from 14–19 April 1940 destroyed a single company of 160 paratroopers deployed to take the town, with the survivors forced to surrender.[4] The town was a junction of one of only two communications routes that linked Oslo with Trondheim. Located two hundred kilometers south of Trondheim, Dombås seemed an ideal strategic target, which Hitler enthusiastically made a priority for the operation. Yet, the operation was doomed from the outset: the aircraft transporting the paratroopers ran into bad weather, Allied antiaircraft fire struck several aircraft, and the German commander, an *Oberleutnant* Schmidt, was killed in the first engagement with the Norwegian defenders. Of a force of 15 aircraft and 160 men, only 7 planes returned home, and Norwegian forces captured just 45 surviving paratroopers. Despite the failure, the swift defeat of the rest of the Allied forces in Norway led to their release soon enough.[5]

Likewise, paratroopers played a key role leading the German Case Yellow (*Fall Gelb*) offensive into France and the Low Countries beginning on 10 May 1940. Paratroopers secured a number of key areas ahead of the advance, shutting down strong points and securing strategic junctions, but not all of them were successful. In the Netherlands, elements of the 7th *Flieger* Division were deployed to capture the airfields around The Hague, which in turn would allow additional German troops to land by air transport and possibly capture the Dutch royal family. When the offensive began on 10 May, the paratroopers were unable to secure more than one of the airfields, and the Dutch defenders shot down many German transports as they tried to land on hostile runways. The Dutch royal family escaped. The Luftwaffe would be the key to the quick Dutch surrender, but it was due to a massive bombing campaign against the city of Rotterdam, not the actions of the paratroopers.[6]

The Battle for Crete in May 1941 proved the most significant for the *Fallschirmjäger* units. The assault was the first-ever invasion by primarily airborne infantry against an enemy target. The 7th *Flieger* Division and accompanying glider-borne forces would again lead the way, preparing a beachhead for incoming seaborne reinforcements. The Germans ultimately underestimated the size of the Allied defense force on the island. The incoming paratroopers were outnumbered nearly three to one by the Allies on the island, and they also lacked heavy weapons support for the initial drops.[7] As a result, the paratroopers suffered heavy losses facing the entrenched Allied defenders.[8] Though the Germans eventually prevailed, the high cost of the operation convinced Hitler that paratroopers no longer had any usefulness, and they would never again launch a major airborne operation in the war.[9]

Paratroop jumps in World War II were often inaccurate, a particular difficulty the Allies would later contend with in Sicily and Normandy, and ground-based infantry with heavier equipment could easily mop up the sometimes-isolated pockets of airborne soldiers. The Germans recognized that paratroopers were valuable as light infantry and would continue to train them until the end of the war as elite ground units. Yet, the inherent weaknesses with early paratroop drops, coupled with the high cost to transport aircraft that the Germans increasingly could ill afford to lose, turned the German high command away from further combat jumps in the war. Ironically, Crete was also the point where the Allies began heavily investing in their own paratroop units, observing their impact on early war German operations.

One particular Luftwaffe commander involved in Operation Mercury would be key to the Luftwaffe field divisions later in the war. Major General Eugen Meindl was a former artillery officer who had transferred to the Luftwaffe in 1940 and was put in command of an elite Storm Regiment (*Sturmregiment*) of combined paratroopers and air-landing troops for Operation Mercury.[10] On 20 May 1941, the first day of the assault, Meindl's group of approximately 2,300 men was to seize an important airfield at Maleme, but the drop was a disaster. Most of Meindl's heavy weapons were destroyed and his men were scattered. The Allies in the area were much stronger than had been estimated, and two British heavy tanks in particular gave the Germans fits. Meindl himself was wounded twice on 20 May but was able to maintain control over his regiment until late in the afternoon. He eventually would be airlifted out of Crete. Meindl would be moved to the Eastern Front once he recovered, and he played a major role in actions perpetrated by Luftwaffe ground units, including the first true Luftwaffe field division. He would do well enough that he would be put in charge of organizing and training the rest of the LwFDs in late 1942.[11]

Though they were kept out of the sky, German *Fallschirmjäger* became highly valuable as infantrymen. The Germans would raise eleven divisions of paratroopers during the war, though the vast majority of them only saw action as infantry. During Operation Barbarossa, the paratroopers of the 7th Flieger Division were attached to Army Group North and in the fall of 1941 had helped halt Soviet counterattacks in the region south of Leningrad.[12] Later on, the 7th *Flieger* Division fought against the Western Allies in Sicily and would remain in the Italian theater for the rest of the war. Germany's paratroopers, now hardened veterans, were among the best-equipped and best-trained infantry in the German armed forces. They would continue to serve throughout the war and consistently gave a good accounting of themselves in combat. Paratroopers would provide some of the most potent resistance against the Western Allies in Normandy following the landings in summer 1944.[13]

Flak Formations in a Ground Role

In addition to the airborne infantry, Germany's antiaircraft formations also answered to the Luftwaffe and had played a major role early in the war. The German army as late as April 1941 had argued that it needed its own antiaircraft force for coordination and logistics purposes, but Luftwaffe officers decried the idea. In their view, army antiaircraft units would never be trained to a satisfactory level without Luftwaffe involvement, and the division of antiaircraft units between the army and air force would only complicate matters of command and logistics. Dealing with such problems was the reason the army had for suggesting the idea in the first place, but in the end the question went to Hitler, and he decided in favor of the Luftwaffe. The air force maintained control of the vast majority of German antiaircraft units but also was to support the army during ground operations. The army did maintain a few antiaircraft battalions of its own, but normally these units only consisted of Flak machine guns rather than heavier weapons.[14]

While designed as antiaircraft artillery, Flak units rapidly became useful in an antitank role on the ground. The primary German antitank weapons at the start of the war were light pieces, firing only 37- and 50-mm rounds. These failed to stop the heavier tanks used by most of the Allies. Early in the war, the French Char B-1 tank actually performed quite well against the Germans despite the German victory in France, with German antitank rounds simply bouncing off the hulls of the tanks. In Operation Barbarossa, the Germans faced much more serious resistance in the form of the Soviet KV-1 and T-34 designs that, like the B-1, proved impervious to lighter antitank weapons. The Luftwaffe came to the rescue in these cases, and their antiaircraft weapons provided the necessary firepower to deal with the heavier Soviet armor. By early 1942 eight full Flak divisions were on the ground in Russia. In particular, their Flak-36 88-mm antiaircraft guns had quickly proved valuable in an antitank role against the superior Soviet T-34 and KV-1 tanks.[15]

Flak units saw huge success in an antitank role. In North Africa, the two Luftwaffe Flak battalions assigned to General Erwin Rommel's *Afrikakorps* had shot down forty-two Allied aircraft, but they had also tallied a total of 264 kills against enemy tanks. Flak units in the Balkans had not only destroyed thirty bunkers and several Allied tanks during the campaign but also disabled a tank production facility.[16] It was in Russia that Flak units truly earned their keep. In a report of 28 February 1942 to Goering himself, the Luftwaffe liaison with the army assessed that "employment in ground combat against Russian tanks and ground targets increasingly became the primary task of flak artillery of all calibers."[17] By the end of 1941, just six months after the start of Operation Barbarossa, Flak units had accounted for nearly 1,900 aircraft, 926 tanks, and 583 Russian bunkers destroyed.[18] Edward Westermann states this was actually a mixed success. As the Eastern Front degenerated into a battle of attrition, the army relied increasingly on Flak units. This in turn drew German antiaircraft defenses from within Germany itself, weakening the country's internal antiaircraft defensive capabilities. In addition, a full third of the German ammunition budget was devoted to producing antiaircraft munitions in the last half of 1941, thus leading many historians to argue that Germany sabotaged itself later in the war by devoting so many resources to the Flak arm early on.[19] However, while Germany may have been more susceptible to the Allied air offensives, the Flak units attached to the army certainly made their impact known for the rest of the war.

Flak formations from a division down to battalion level could vary in strength, but in general all possessed excellent firepower. An antiaircraft battalion usually consisted of three heavy and two light batteries of guns. A heavy battery consisted of four to six 88s or heavier 105- or 128-mm guns, while a light battery consisted of between twenty-one and thirty-six 20- and 50-mm guns. Two additional 20-mm guns were attached to each heavy battery. Three to five battalions made up a regiment, and two to five regiments completed a full Flak division.[20] By the end of 1940 the German antiaircraft branch consisted of 791 heavy batteries and 686 light batteries manned by over half a million men.[21] By the end of the war, the antiaircraft branch had fielded thirty-one full Flak divisions armed with 31,559 guns, including 12,169 heavy pieces. This firepower made Flak units a powerful and important support force for the regular army.[22] Looking at the key roles of both the paratrooper and Flak formations, it is important to remember that though they were usually attached to army commands, they were in fact under Luftwaffe control and made up of well-trained Luftwaffe personnel.

Luftwaffe Armor: The Parachute Panzer Division "Hermann Goering"

A third well-known Luftwaffe ground unit was the famous "Hermann Goering" Division, although that designation is actually a misnomer.[23] The unit began its existence as a Berlin police detachment in 1933, but following the Night of the Long Knives and the removal of the SA in 1934, Goering transferred the unit to the Luftwaffe and renamed it "Regiment General Goering." In 1935 part of the regiment was transferred out to become the 1st *Fallschirmjäger* Division, which is why the later units included *Fallschirm* in their designations. In 1936 the Regiment General Goering became a bodyguard force for Goering and would remain so for the rest of the decade. It participated in the annexations of both Austria and Czechoslovakia in 1938. In 1940 the regiment took part in the offensive against France, and in 1941 it was attached to the 11th Panzer Division and heavily involved in Operation Barbarossa. In particular, the unit saw action against the trapped Soviet pockets at Bryansk and Kyiv.[24] In July 1942 the regiment was upgraded into a brigade and finally in October 1942 was reformed into a *Fallschirm-Panzer* Division, the "Parachute Panzer Division 'Hermann Goering.'" While the designation elicits fantastic visions of German tanks being airdropped into combat by parachute, in reality it was a regular panzer unit, albeit under Luftwaffe control. The division was sent to North Africa following the British victory at El Alamein, but the majority of the men were captured along with 250,000 other Axis personnel at the surrender of Tunis on 13 May 1943.[25]

A core group of officers escaped the surrender, and the unit was reformed as "Panzer Division Hermann Goering" in Sicily. The unit served impressively in Sicily, facing the American Seventh Army's landings at Gela and continuing to provide heavy resistance against the British. Following the British capture of Centuripe, the division fell back to Messina and managed to escape to Italy before U.S. Gen. George S. Patton's forces took the town.[26] The division continued to fight in Italy for the rest of 1943 and into the following year, in particular participating in the Battle of Salerno in September 1943. The division's panzers nearly drove the Allies back into the sea during that engagement but were repulsed by Allied naval bombardment.[27]

Following the armistice signed between Italy and the Allies on 3 September 1943, the Hermann Goering Division participated in Operation Axis, the violent disarmament of the Italian army by the German forces in Italy. Nearly 30,000 Italian troops were killed as the Germans attacked their positions, and the Italian military as a whole was taken prisoner, with the country itself falling under German occupation.[28] In April 1944 the unit was redesignated again as the "Parachute Panzer Corps Hermann Goering," becoming a full-fledged panzer corps. Following the fall of Rome on 4 June 1944, the formation moved back to the Eastern Front, where it would serve for the rest of the war. On 24 January 1945 the corps was assigned to Army Group Vistula, defending the Warsaw pocket against the Red Army. Most of the force was destroyed during the battle, though some elements survived until the end of the war.[29]

The Hermann Goering formation was noted for being skilled in combat. Unlike most of the men of the Luftwaffe field divisions, the men of the Hermann Goering were largely trained infantry. The unit was largely composed of *Fallschirmjäger*, whose capabilities in combat had already been established, and the vehicles and equipment used by the division were among the best Germany could field. The unit is also notable for the commission of several grotesque war crimes over the course of the war. In particular, about eight hundred soldiers of the unit participated in quelling the Warsaw Uprising that took place between August and October 1944. Polish witnesses to the action accused the unit of putting civilians in front of their tanks as human shields while advancing against the insurgent barricades.[30]

Luftwaffe *Alarmeinheiten* and *Bandenbekämpfung*

The prior three examples are the most easily recognized instances of Luftwaffe ground forces in action, but additional Luftwaffe units were also involved on the ground. As the Wehrmacht advanced into Russia, the Luftwaffe established new bases and supply depots. As all army personnel were needed at the front lines, the Luftwaffe organized ad hoc *Alarmeinheiten* (emergency units) of volunteers to defend these new positions against Russian partisans. Though poorly equipped and trained, these units gave a surprisingly good accounting of themselves. One of their most notable performances came during the winter crisis of 1941–42. A hodgepodge force combining *Alarmeinheiten*, a company from the *Luftlande Sturmregiment*, the glider-borne troops who were veterans of Crete, and scattered paratroopers, Waffen-SS, and army personnel came together under the command of the glider troops' commander, Luftwaffe General Meindl, and managed to hold out against heavy Red Army attacks at the important Yukhnov airbase, located in the central front southwest of Moscow, between mid-January and early February 1942. The force, designated "Luftwaffe-Gruppe Meindl," proved capable of not only defending the airbase but even launching local attacks to keep supply routes open and evacuate wounded soldiers.[31]

The *Alarmeinheiten* took on an expanded role as the war went on, in particular facing off against the bands of partisans that constantly harassed the rear areas of the German front line in the east. The Luftwaffe in particular would be employed in an anti-partisan role in Poland. The German policy of *Bandenbekämpfung* (combating banditry, meaning partisans) was essential for Nazi plans for future state-building: clearing the conquered areas of the east of partisans, Jews, and any other undesirables to make *Lebensraum*. On 18 August 1942 Hitler issued Directive 46, which relabeled the partisans as "bandits," making an important distinction: it allowed the Germans to ignore the hitherto international recognition of partisans as enemy combatants who must be dealt with fairly. Labeling them as mere bandits allowed the Germans to simply shoot partisans on sight.[32]

Hermann Goering's commands included the Reich Forestry Department (*Reichsforstamt*, or RFA), which as early as March 1940 deployed units of sharpshooters to "secure" the Białowieża Forest in eastern Poland against pockets of Polish resistance fighters as well as the occasional child "illegally hunting" to support their family. In April 1940 the RFA raised the Forest Protection Corps (*Forstschutzkorps*, or FSK) to serve as a makeshift commando unit in charge of securing the Polish forests for German exploitation.[33] Along with partisans, the unit was also to deal with any Jews located in the area.[34] The Luftwaffe and FSK forces in eastern Poland were under the command of *Oberforstmeister* (Senior Forester) Walter Frevert, who personally directed a long list of anti-partisan and anti-Jewish operations alongside an SS battalion and a police bicycle battalion, and Frevert himself commanded a company of huntsmen from the FSK. From 24 to 31 July 1941, Frevert deported more than seven thousand people from thirty-four villages in the Białowieża Forest. The Germans subsequently pillaged the villages and kept everything of value, including livestock. This in turn crippled the local economy. Several days later, on August 9, the SS unit serving with Frevert's men killed nearly six hundred Jewish men over the age of fifteen, with the women and children deported to a ghetto in Kobryn, near Brest-Litovsk.[35]

As the Germans advanced farther into the Soviet Union, partisans became an increasingly serious problem. The assassination of SS security chief Reinhard Heydrich on 4 June 1942 brought the matter to a head. Though he was actually killed by a British-trained team of Czech exiles, the Germans falsely linked the assassins to two Czech villages. Hitler ordered a brutal response against the villages, leading to the massacre of over 1,300 people and the deportation and imprisonment of almost 13,000 more.[36] Heydrich's death and the growing partisan menace in the east inspired a retooling of German efforts at security in the rear areas of the Eastern Front. Directive 46 not only reclassified partisans as common bandits but also gave authority for combating the bandits solely to Heinrich Himmler and the SS. However, as the Luftwaffe was already involved in the fighting, Goering worked out details with Himmler that allowed the Luftwaffe to continue working in an anti-partisan role.[37] On 5 September 1942 an additional ten thousand Luftwaffe troops under Major Emil Herbst were deployed to combat partisan activity in the rear areas of the Eastern Front. These units, known as the "boys in blue" in reference to their blue Luftwaffe uniforms, were well-equipped light infantry and performed quite efficiently.[38]

The Luftwaffe and the RFA were ordered to reinforce the areas threatened by these "bandits," and by summer 1942 a full-strength battalion of foresters and Luftwaffe troops was created: the Luftwaffe *Sicherungsbataillon* (LwSB, or security battalion), on station in the Białowieża Forest. The unit possessed 11 officers, 69 NCOs, and 406 enlisted personnel. Extra companies were raised even as late as November 1942. In 1943 the LwSB was replaced by the *Jäger-Sonderkommando Bialowies der Luftwaffe* (JSKB), a battalion comprised of the former LwSB and RFA foresters. The JSKB reached a peak strength of 14 officers and 621 men in November 1943 and was well equipped with small arms, light field artillery, a signal detachment, and even a light reconnaissance plane with pilot and mechanic. The Luftwaffe troops, though slated for police duty, were heavily armed, having been issued regular army weapons, including the standard-issue Mauser Kar98k carbine, the MP40 machine pistol, and MG34 light machine guns.[39] The chain of command ran directly from Goering through his adjutant, Luftwaffe Colonel Bernd von Brauchitsch (the nephew of Field Marshal Walther von Brauchitsch, the chief of the army until 1941), and on to Frevert's and Herbst's units. The supply and administrative support for the JSKB and the forester units were in the hands of *Luftgau* (Air District) 1, based out of Königsberg in East Prussia.[40]

Luftwaffe *Alarmeinheiten* typically were trained to protect airfields and other installations. Police duty had not been in their training, and fighting in the forests of eastern Poland could easily degenerate into close-range or even hand-to-hand combat. To correct the weakness, the Wehrmacht had devised the Jagdkommandos, or hunting commandos, who adapted tactics typically used for hunting wild game and paired them with a version of the tactics often used by partisans themselves: small teams supported by skilled trackers that set ambushes, exploited weak spots, planned ruses, conducted sabotage, and so forth. Using these tactics, the JSKB and other Luftwaffe units began to be quite skilled at their activities.[41] In addition to their skill, their ruthlessness began to show as well, often thanks to the actions of their commander, Major Herbst. He often conducted public executions, labeling those convicted of being "Bolshevik" agents, agitators, and the like. With direct authority from Goering, Herbst answered to no court system; he had the power to decide guilt or innocence himself.[42] He did not always pronounce guilt, though his "mercy" could leave much to be desired; one particular incident on 28 September 1942 at the Polish village of Roczkowka proves the point. Accusing the villagers of harboring and supporting bandits, Herbst and several *Jagdkommandos* surrounded the area and forced more than five hundred civilians to dig their own grave pits, with Herbst beginning on-the-spot questioning of the townsfolk. As the men of Roczkowka stood before the pits ready to be shot, Herbst abruptly changed his mind and rescinded his order for punishment. Herbst concluded in his report that the likely traumatized village would now be hostile to any bandits who possibly wandered in.[43]

The number of people killed by the JSKB and other Luftwaffe units in the area is difficult to determine. Significant numbers of Jews were killed on sight. For partisans, Herbst reported that between July 1942 and March 1943, approximately 92 bandits were killed and more than 280 other executions and reprisal shootings took place. Few members of the LwSB or JSKB were killed; their units' diaries reported a total of thirty-nine killed and forty wounded.[44] The JSKB collapsed in July 1944 during the Red Army's summer offensive. Lacking adequate heavy weapons, the battalion was overwhelmed by front-line Soviet armored units. Those men who escaped were reassigned to the *Fallschirm-Panzerkorps* "Hermann Goering."[45] This was not the only area the Luftwaffe fought against partisan units, either: the 11th LwFD would spend much of its combat service facing partisans in Greece and Yugoslavia.

Luftwaffe Field Regiments and the Kholm Pocket

Luftwaffe ground service went even beyond *Alarmeinheiten* and security units. As early as October 1941, the army had begun to scour Germany for additional manpower, and a number of Luftwaffe troops volunteered to help. By January 1942 they had been organized into seven Luftwaffe field regiments (*Feldregimenter der Luftwaffe* [FR der Lw] 1–5, 14, and 21), hastily trained by paratrooper instructors, and they were scattered, often by battalion, across the Eastern Front as needed.[46] A major concentration of these troops would center on the twin pockets of Demiansk and Kholm in the northern theater. Kholm's 5,000 defenders had been surrounded since 22 January, while six full divisions and 96,000 men of the German II Army Corps were likewise trapped in Demiansk on 9 February. Elements from several Luftwaffe regiments took part in both the defense and relief efforts.[47]

Kholm was a strategically important communications junction, located at the confluence of the Kunya and Lovat Rivers on the German Army Group North's right flank. It offered the only real crossing point over the soft, marshy ground that covered the area. As the Soviet offensive continued in January 1942, the 3rd Shock Army, part of the Kalinin Front, launched an assault that hammered the German XXXIX Panzer Corps, under the command of General Hans-Jurgen von Arnim. As the Germans fell back through Kholm, von Arnim decided to deploy a garrison in the town to hold the strategic location. The defenders of Kholm were known as *Kampfgruppe* (Battle Group) Scherer after their commander, Major General Theodor Scherer. General von Arnim thought that Kholm would be surrounded only briefly and that the Germans would quickly reform and launch a counterattack. This proved to not be the case, and Kholm would be under siege for three and a half months. During this time, three German infantry regiments, the 65th Reserve Police Battalion, a smattering of minor forces (including a handful of drivers from the Kriegsmarine), and a late-arriving Luftwaffe field battalion had to hold against the full strength of the 3rd Shock Army.[48]

The garrison was cut off from supplies and at first had no antitank weapons. The first serious Soviet assaults began on 23 January 1942, just two days after the Germans were surrounded. Lacking antitank capabilities, the only defense the Germans had was a simple explosive device triggered by an engineer and a fuse. Fortunately, the device destroyed the lead tank in the Soviet column that day, which caused the rest to fall back.[49] The perimeter measured barely two kilometers and shrank further as the siege continued. Though the Luftwaffe attempted to airdrop supplies and the defenders attempted to build a small runway to receive planes, Kholm was a very small target area. Many of the drops landed behind Russian lines. The Luftwaffe lost 25 aircraft during the siege—a fairly high rate considering the town was surrounded for 105 days—and resorted to using gliders at points to deliver supplies. While this was more accurate, it also meant that wounded could no longer be airlifted out of the pocket.[50]

At first, the Germans in Kholm numbered around 3,500 men, but another 1,500 reinforcements would come in over the course of the siege. The garrison received some antitank weapons and also managed to capture some Russian equipment, even turning a disabled T-34 tank into a gun emplacement. In addition, as German relief forces got closer to the pocket, German artillery could be called in via radio to aid in the defense.[51] The reinforcements that reached Kholm included a machine-gun battalion that had been cut off and fought their way through Red Army lines to join the Kholm garrison in late January. In addition, a Luftwaffe field battalion was airlifted into the town. Two others would support XXXIX Panzer Corps' relief effort.[52]

The Luftwaffe battalions had gotten off to a rocky start prior to the surrounding of Kholm. After arriving at the German base at Staraya Russa on 20 February 1942, the Third Battalion of FR der Lw. 1 (III./FR der Lw. 1) found itself ill-equipped for the brutal winter and also under sporadic fire from Russian Katyusha rocket batteries. The battalion suffered heavy losses in its first engagements but fared better when it was airlifted into Kholm to reinforce the garrison.⁵³ The Red Army's attacks continued, but the Russians attacked in predictable patterns around the perimeter. This greatly helped the German defenders; the Russians would hit the same sectors the same time of day, which allowed the Germans to stop each assault in turn.⁵⁴

Though surrounded, Scherer maintained radio communications with General von Arnim and XXXIX Panzer Corps. Von Arnim began putting together a relief operation in early February 1942, while Scherer deployed two detachments from his group to the west side of Kholm. Part of von Arnim's force included two additional Luftwaffe battalions from FR der Lw. 5 that were stationed northeast of the pocket in blocking positions, protecting the German relief effort. Once XXXIX Corps began its assault, Scherer's men would simultaneously move out to meet the relief group. Scherer's men temporarily seized two nearby hills from the Russians, but sniper fire and heavy artillery drove the Germans back into Kholm. Likewise, von Arnim's relief assault failed, and the Germans in Kholm remained under siege. The only bright side of the failure was that German artillery was now in range to support the defenders in Kholm.⁵⁵

On 23 February 1942 the Soviets celebrated Red Army Day by launching a major offensive against the pocket spearheaded by a huge wave of tanks. Scherer's forces only barely held, backed by supporting artillery and Luftwaffe air support. As the siege continued through March and April, the situation grew more precarious. The Kholm pocket slowly shrank by half, reduced to a perimeter of just five hundred by two hundred meters.⁵⁶ Scherer had suffered more than three thousand casualties, with little chance of reinforcement outside of a full relief by XXXIX Panzer Corps. General von Arnim's corps finally tried another push toward Kholm that would last through April, drawing ever closer to the besieged pocket. Kholm was finally relieved on 5 May by a column from XXXIX Panzer Corps. In a 105-day siege, the garrison had suffered over 3,700 casualties. Of the nearly 5,000 men remaining, only about 1,200 were still fit for action. However, the men had withstood multiple attacks from six Soviet infantry divisions and two tank brigades. Though they suffered as heavily as the rest of the garrison, the deployed Luftwaffe battalions did their part in holding and relieving the town.⁵⁷

The Demiansk Pocket and Division Meindl

Simultaneously with the siege of Kholm, the Soviets besieged another German pocket at Demiansk, approximately sixty miles to the northeast. Compared to Kholm, the Battle of Demiansk was a much larger conflict. The town was situated in heavily forested terrain and was key to the Soviet goal of driving into the rear of Army Group North, where they planned to seize the towns of Staraya Russa and Velikiye Luki. Holding the town was thus paramount to securing Army Group North's position. Heavy Soviet forces, including the 3rd Shock Army, 34th Army, and 1st Guards Rifle Corps, encircled the German II Army Corps in Demiansk on 9 February 1942. Though technically labeled a corps, the II Army Corps was highly over-strength, containing five infantry divisions, the 3rd SS "Totenkopf" Division," and a number of other units. The Germans numbered 96,000 men, all under the command of General Walter von Brockdorff-Ahlefeldt. Attacks against the beleaguered garrison lasted nearly three months, and fighting continued around the city for nearly a year.[58]

Demiansk was surrounded by elements of the Soviet 3rd Shock Army, the same force besieging Kholm, along with the Soviet Northwestern Front and part of the Kalinin Front. Also present were the Soviet 11th and 34th Armies, 1st and 4th Shock Armies, and 1st and 2nd Guards Rifle Corps. Demiansk was nearly surrounded during the initial Soviet push, but at first the pocket was not a Red Army priority. The commander of Northwestern Front, General P. A. Kurochkin, had initially been told to drive for the German rear, taking the strategic German staging areas at Staraya Russa and Velikiye Luki. However, Kurochkin was wary of leaving such a large German force in his own rear and requested permission to take out the II Army Corps before moving onward. While the Soviet high command agreed and transferred several major units to Kurochkin's control, the net result was that the Northwestern Front was attacking two targets at the same time and ultimately lacked decisive superiority in either area. Weak coordination and German air superiority also hampered the Soviet efforts, and the offensive quickly bogged down.[59]

Though the Soviet offensive exhausted itself, the Germans in Demiansk were completely surrounded by 21 February 1942. The key to the pocket turned out to be two airfields controlled by the Germans inside the city. This opened the door for the Luftwaffe to resupply the city by air to a much greater extent than in Kholm, where the small size of the pocket severely limited the accuracy and size of German airdrops. On 22 February Hitler ordered Demiansk to be turned into a fortress pocket that perhaps could be used to relaunch an offensive against Moscow and ordered the Luftwaffe to begin resupplying the pocket. The Luftwaffe was responsible for bringing in a daily quota of 270 tons of supplies to keep the II Army Corps fighting.[60] Not only was the Luftwaffe successful in doing so, but also the air resupply operation of the Demiansk pocket would inspire the Germans to try a similar approach to supplying the German 6th Army that would be trapped in Stalingrad in November 1942. That effort would fail, however.[61]

The Germans immediately began organizing a relief effort, code-named Operation *Brückenschlag* (Bridge-Laying), under the command of Major General Walter von Seydlitz-Kurzbach. The effort to break the siege of Demiansk was extensive, involving six German divisions and two additional corps, and within them fourteen Luftwaffe battalions. One Luftwaffe battalion, II./FR der Lw. 3., took part of the thrust toward Demiansk itself, while the remainder, joined in three ad hoc regiments, held the exposed right flank of the operation against both Russian partisans and regular Red Army forces. The assault was not scheduled to begin until 21 March 1942, which essentially meant that Seydlitz and Kurochkin were racing each other to Demiansk, and the Red Army had a very small window to try and destroy the II Army Corps.[62]

Russian operations began on 6 March 1942. Kurochkin had underestimated by half the size of the German force in Demiansk. He ordered the attacking forces to proceed at "an offensive tempo of not less than ten kilometers a day" in order to quickly destroy the pocket.[63] Because of Kurochkin's inaccurate estimates of German strength in Demiansk, he believed the Germans had very few troops within the city itself. Kurochkin felt that if he dropped an airborne force of about ten thousand paratroopers directly behind German lines, they could disrupt the German rear areas enough to destabilize the perimeter for Kurochkin's main assault to break through. In particular, the paratroopers were to capture the airfields that allowed the Germans to be easily resupplied. The Soviet 1st Airborne Corps was chosen for the operation. The mission was extremely risky; the paratroopers would only be carrying three days' worth of supplies for a mission that was supposed to last seven to ten days, with their only real chance of resupply coming from airdrops until a link could be established with the Russian ground forces.[64]

This mission recalled the riskiness of paratroop drops: light infantry, dropped into isolated positions, with the only hope of reinforcement coming on the ground. A similar operation from a Western Allied perspective would be Operation Market-Garden in the Netherlands in September 1944. That operation essentially was the same basic plan and exhibited the same weaknesses as the Soviet drop on Demiansk: Allied paratroopers would jump behind German lines and hold their positions until relieved by British armor. Just as the Soviets did in Demiansk, the Allies both underestimated the German defenders and made mistakes of their own, resulting in terrible losses for the paratroop forces.

Considering the Germans had twice the number of troops as the Soviets thought, the paratroopers would be landing among vastly stronger German defenses. The German defenders not only picked up on the landings of the Russian airborne forces, but they also spotted some of the early resupply efforts by Russian aircraft. Instead of a few disorganized rear-area defenders, the entire 3rd SS Totenkopf Division was posted to defend the airfields. Soviet paratroopers were constantly under fire from German artillery and aircraft and quickly began suffering heavy casualties. The Germans were easily able to counter the initial assaults, and their efforts soon switched from defending against an airborne assault to preventing the now-trapped Russian troops from breaking out. The entire 1st Airborne Corps was virtually destroyed in the debacle.[65]

The drive to Demiansk began on 21 March 1942 and slogged for several weeks against heavy Russian resistance. Seydlitz's force moved en masse, operating in close proximity to push its way toward the city. Because the divisions involved were moving so closely, the flank of the force suddenly had wide gaps under watch by largely understrength units. One of the units protecting Seydlitz's flank was a formation known as Division Meindl, the first true Luftwaffe field division and named for its commander, General Eugen Meindl.[66] Following his defense of Yukhnov, General Meindl had been assigned on 29 February 1942 to take control over the scattered Luftwaffe field regiments, but due to their dispersal he was unable to organize his force before June. The formation consisted of four Luftwaffe regiments (FR der Lw. 1–4) combined with the command staff of Meindl's *Luftlande-Sturmregiment* to create the first formal Luftwaffe division. The unit was lightly armed and lacked a proper artillery regiment and trained crewmen. Instead, it only had a few captured Russian 76-mm guns and gunners trained for antiaircraft pieces rather than field artillery. The division would not receive a conventional artillery component until March 1943. Meindl's unit was positioned opposite the full strength of the Soviet 1st Shock Army. Despite the weakness, Meindl's troops displayed the same skill and tenacity as at Yukhnov in holding the gap between Demiansk and Kholm in swampy, terrible terrain.[67]

As Seydlitz's relief force moved against Demiansk, the forces within the city began to plan a second assault to try and break out to meet the relief effort. The assault force included the 3rd SS Totenkopf Division and a combined regiment of several detached battalions from the other formations trapped within the city. The operation, code-named *Fallreep* (Gangway), began on 14 April. However, the besieging Soviets caught wind of the effort and poured artillery fire into the city. The Demiansk forces only began to make progress on 17 April. They reached the Lovat riverbank two days later, and upon crossing the river on 20 April made first contact with Seydlitz's approaching force. Upon finally linking up with troops of the II Army Corps at the town of Ramushevo, the effort moved to reestablish a land route to the city itself. The link was made on 1 May. After the success of the relief operation, it now became crucial to hold the supply routes open.[68] Four days later, the Kholm gap to the southwest was also liberated, but the Germans were in a precarious position. The relief operations had stretched the Germans thin, and there was a wide hole in the line between the two relieved areas.

Holding the ninety-kilometer gap between Kholm and Demiansk fell to Division Meindl. After protecting Seydlitz's flank during Operation *Brückenschlag*, the division maintained that position following the relief of Demiansk.[69] Its primary duties included operations against large concentrations of Russian partisans that had gathered in the nearby swamps. The division did so well that it was even cited in an OKW dispatch of 23 June 1942 for its "distinguished" service in defending "the seriously threatened front lines" during the winter of 1941–42.[70] Division Meindl also fought in the successful Operation *Winkelried* (28 September–10 October 1942). With the Russians still pressing against Demiansk, Division Meindl and three other divisions launched an offensive to widen the bottleneck keeping the fortress supplied. The operation was successful. Two divisions, the 5th *Jäger* and the 126th Infantry, trapped the Russian 1st Guards Rifle Division at the Lovat River, while Division Meindl and the battle-hardened remnants of the 3rd SS Totenkopf Division outflanked it, crossing the Redya River and forcing the Russian unit's surrender.[71] In December 1942 the unit would be redesignated the 21st Luftwaffe Field Division.[72]

Division Meindl was the first Luftwaffe infantry formation of divisional strength to serve on the front, and it performed excellently. While the Luftwaffe field divisions as a single topic may appear to be an anomaly, this fails to take into account the huge commitment made by the Luftwaffe toward the German ground forces. German paratroopers fought on the front lines for almost the entire war, earning a reputation for skill in battle. Flak units, along with their role of protecting the skies above the German army and the German people, likewise became highly valuable in an antitank role in all regions of the European theater. Goering already had a personal unit of soldiers from as early as 1933 in the Hermann Goering formation, which grew in strength and importance as the war continued until it was a full panzer corps. Luftwaffe security units protected many of the rear areas of the front lines and actively participated in combating partisans as well as engaging in atrocities against Eastern Europe's Jewish population. Luftwaffe ground units possessed at least a serviceable combat record, helping to hold the pockets at Demiansk and Kholm and fighting on the front line as 1942 continued. The general success of Division Meindl, together with the Flak units, paratroopers, and security formations, other full-strength Luftwaffe divisions may have appeared conceivable to Hitler in September 1942.

CHAPTER THREE

THE FIRST YEAR OF COMBAT

17 SEPTEMBER 1942–20 SEPTEMBER 1943

"Sheer Lunacy"

The first year of deployment for the Luftwaffe field divisions was an unmitigated disaster. They were thrown into action completely unprepared and suffered grievous casualties as a result. The three main issues facing the LwFDs were a general lack of training, a lack of experience, and insufficient equipment. The field divisions were put together far too rapidly, in some cases being deployed less than three weeks after Reichsmarschall Hermann Goering ordered their creation, and as such did not receive much training at all. What training they did receive exacerbated the issue: these men were instructed not by experienced trainers but by Luftwaffe officers who themselves had not received proper training.[1] The LwFDs were further burdened by an inconsistent number of weapons and manpower across all of the divisions. Each division varied in manpower strength, most battalions lacked any weapons besides small arms, and all of the divisions were severely lacking in heavy weapons, particularly artillery.[2]

These weaknesses reared their heads when the first LwFDs reached the front lines in the east. Men would break quickly under fire from Soviet armored formations, and, in general, the field divisions earned a poor reputation among the rest of the German army. Many German generals had scoffed at the idea of the LwFDs when they had first heard of it, and every time one of the field divisions collapsed in combat, their skepticism was justified.[3] Between 17 September 1942 and 20 September 1943, the men of the LwFDs suffered 90,000 casualties out of an initial strength of around 200,000 men, and several of the divisions did not survive that first year in action. For most German generals, this first year of the divisions' existence essentially determined their overall mark on the war effort. Several German generals discuss the LwFDs in their memoirs, usually devoting just a mournful snippet to their lack of training and general ineffectiveness.[4]

This sparse depiction of the field divisions as a disastrous one-shot error is far too basic to be a complete picture of the history of the units. Many questions remain to be answered about this first year of action. Why were the organization and training of the LwFDs so poorly handled? Had it been done differently, could they perhaps have been more successful in action?

Organization and Training of the Luftwaffe Field Divisions

Five specific LwFDs are representative of both the major deficiencies and the wide array of experiences that all of the Luftwaffe units faced during their first year of deployment. In the center, the 2nd LwFD was stationed in the Rzhev salient, a dagger-like bulge that pointed from the German lines directly toward Moscow and was consequently an object of great concern for the Soviets to deal with. During one of the largest attempts to close the pocket, Operation Mars in November 1942, the 2nd LwFD would face the brunt of a Soviet assault and would have a very disastrous experience during the battle. To the south, the 15th, 7th, and 8th LwFDs were linked to Erich von Manstein's forces and his attempt to relieve the Stalingrad pocket and break the German Sixth Army out of its encirclement. Thanks to intelligence failures, all three divisions faced repeated Soviet assaults over the winter of 1942–43, leading to their quick dissolution. Farther south, the 5th LwFD faced heavy fighting in the Caucasus but, unlike the other four LwFDs, actually survived the year, and elements of the unit even received commendations for their service in combat. These five units are

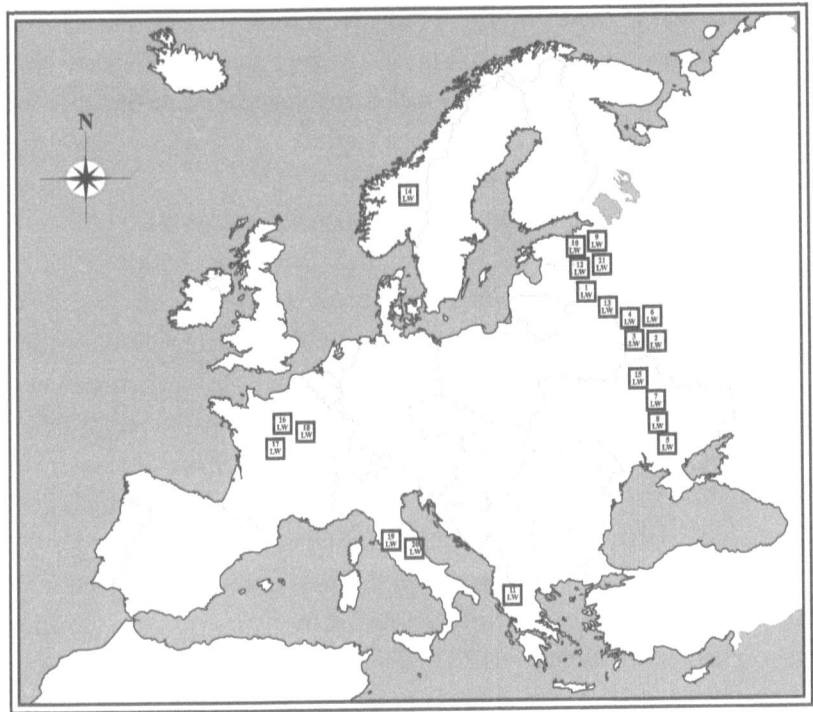

MAP 1. Overall Deployment of LwFDs

also representative of the whole experience of the Luftwaffe units for the first year of the formations' deployment.

Hitler's consent to Goering's creation of the LwFDs had stunned German army leaders who had argued against such units. The generals wanted the Luftwaffe troops transferred to the army to be properly equipped and trained before being sent out to reinforce existing units already at the front. To them, Goering's idea was ludicrous. F. W. von Mellenthin's *Panzer Battles* contains the standard opinion of the LwFDs during the period of October 1942 to September 1943. He notes that though the LwFDs were given "excellent human material" and the "best of equipment," their training was woefully inadequate. They were commanded by men "who knew nothing about land fighting" and were essentially "a creation which had no sound military foundation—the rank and file paid with their lives for this absurdity."[5]

The LwFDs were staffed with Luftwaffe personnel who offered their service in response to a call for volunteers Goering issued on 17 September 1942. Goering's order specifically called for "volunteers," stating that "he who voluntarily joins this corps must do it with a strong heart and without hesitation. However, he can expect special considerations for courageous service, including promotion and decoration." Goering's order also notified the Luftwaffe personnel office to direct these men to him so that he could personally approve them for the new divisions.[6] One member of the 7th LwFD recalled that the members of his unit came from all sorts of different prior assignments, including cooks, armorers, barbers, drivers, and clerks. In addition, bomber pilots and ground crewman notably joined the divisions, and Luftwaffe Flak units were attached to each unit as well.[7]

In addition to forming the LwFDs, Goering created four Luftwaffe field corps (Luftwaffenfeldkorps or LwFK) as higher administrations for the field divisions, and each operated under the combined jurisdiction of the Luftwaffe general headquarters as well as the various army commands the units became attached to. I and IV LwFK were initially deployed to Luftflotte 4, working with Army Groups A and B in the southern sector of the Eastern Front, while II LwFK was sent to Army Group Center and III LwFK supported Army Group North. This deployment would change over time; the eventual deployment of the field corps was as follows. I LwFK (5th, 7th, 8th, and 15th LwFD), II LwFK (2nd, 3rd, 4th, and 6th), and III LwFK (1st, 9th, 10th, 12th, 13th, and 21st) were deployed to the Eastern Front to Army Groups South, Center, and North respectively. IV LwFK (16th, 17th, and 18th) was sent to France. In addition, the 19th and 20th were stationed in Italy with XIII *Fliegerkorps*, while the 14th and 11th LwFDs were deployed respectively to *Luftflotte* 5 in Norway and to the commander in chief, Southeast, in Greece.[8]

Getting the volunteers and setting up a chain of command aside, the initial organization of the field divisions themselves was disorganized and badly mismanaged. This discussion must begin with the man in charge, Luftwaffe General Eugen Meindl, the namesake for Division Meindl.[9] Putting Meindl in charge of organizing the field divisions was an obvious choice in hindsight. Based on the performance of his *Luftlande-Sturmregiment* in Crete, an ersatz formation he organized and commanded in the successful defense of the Yukhnov airbase in the winter of 1941–42 and the success of Division Meindl for most of 1942, there was no reason to expect that he would try any less hard with this new assignment.[10]

Despite the optimism, Meindl was thrust into what became a highly frustrating situation. His original mission was to assemble twenty-two Luftwaffe field divisions and have them ready for combat by the winter of 1942. He asked for, and Hitler initially agreed to provide, three months to train each division, but this did not prove to be the case.[11] The actual schedule for the organization of the new units barely gave any time to sort out personnel and draw equipment, let alone train for combat. Goering ordered the LwFDs created on 17 September 1942, but just eleven days later on 29 September ordered that the training of three divisions (2nd, 3rd, and 4th) be completed by 10 October, while the 1st and 5th through 10th LwFDs had until 1 November.[12] This meant that the first ten field divisions had less than a month of overall training after their creation, with three of them getting just under two weeks. Within six months, all twenty-two divisions were formed and equipped. Their deployment was equally rushed: in Meindl's own words, "once one had been formed, but in no way trained, it was transferred and committed at whatever sector of the front it was deemed necessary to hold. I fought against this, but it was in vain, as were all of my warnings."[13]

More grievous than the brevity of the training was its extremely poor quality. Goering had wanted all of the personnel in the divisions to come from the Luftwaffe, including the officers, even though none of them were trained for infantry combat. As a result, many of the officers who were supposed to train their men had no idea what they were doing themselves. One man, a former Flak crewman, recalled utter chaos when he joined his unit, the 7th LwFD: "What horror! My comrades had no idea about weapons, even some of the officers did not. . . . All these people were from different assignments—cooks, armorers, barbers, drivers, supply and administrative clerks. . . . [S]ome of them immediately requested to be returned to their original units." His commander further asked him to take over machine-gun training because the officer in charge had no idea how to work the weapon. The soldier also noted he was deployed with only three days of training on the gun, "then we were shipped to Russia."[14]

The organization of the divisions with all-Luftwaffe personnel was heavily scrutinized and was the basis for most of the negative depictions of the LwFDs. Erich von Manstein notably commented that the entire idea was "sheer lunacy," which summed up the general opinion of other German officers on the subject. Manstein continued, wondering where the divisions would receive training, battle experience, practice working with other formations, or even quality divisional, regimental, and battalion commanders.[15]

Even Goering appeared to understand the divisions' probable limitations in combat. On 12 October 1942 he issued Basic Order Number 3, stipulating that the LwFDs were to be used only in "defensive missions on quiet fronts."[16] Goering's concern was echoed by Hitler himself. In a meeting with Luftwaffe chief of staff Hans Jeschonnek on 1 February 1943, the latter wanted to transfer an additional 70,000 men to the LwFDs. When Hitler asked why, Jeschonnek stated that it was to keep the units from collapsing; Hitler merely remarked that such a thing had always been an issue with those units anyway.[17] More telling, Hitler also had told General Meindl when the latter had been assigned to train the divisions that the LwFDs were intended to be "sort of a 'fire-brigade' behind the front, equipped as well as possible, made mobile for winter movement, and well trained."[18] This did not last; the divisions did not receive any of those things, and Goering's order was not closely followed. Four of the first LwFDs were deployed immediately to the southern sector of the Eastern Front to aid the offensives aimed at the relief of Stalingrad. There is no evidence that Goering's Basic Order Number 3 was acknowledged in any respect. Why had the army done this, especially considering the fact that these generals who had complained so much about the divisions' formation surely knew of their potential weaknesses?

The German Army's "Maelstrom of Misorganization"

Burkhart Müller-Hillebrand's postwar work on the decision-making of the German general staff places the LwFDs into a much larger organizational problem within the German army that grew in importance as the war dragged on. As manpower became increasingly critical, the German army went to extreme lengths to recover losses. Transferring Luftwaffe and naval personnel to the army was just one method used; others included increased conscription from occupied territories, employing some women in factory service and the signal units to free up men for combat duty, and granting fewer replacements to noncombat units. Some of the remedial measures had little (or even a negative) effect on the units involved. As the war dragged on, destroyed units were often lumped together into ad hoc combat groups of such varying strength that their combat value was severely impacted. Müller-Hillebrand comments that the LwFDs should have been disbanded and given over to army command in early 1943, as it was clear that their combat value was minimal. Instead, they ended up being lost in the "maelstrom of misorganization" plaguing the German army. Further non-army combat units such as the *Volksgrenadier* divisions, increasing numbers of Waffen-SS units, and even some naval infantry battalions formed in early 1945 ultimately left army units neglected and severely understrength, left to be sacrificed on the front line.[19]

A further issue with the LwFDs was their chaotic logistics situation. The divisions answered to the Luftwaffe in terms of administration and logistics but were tactically under the Wehrmacht's control. This divide in command and control also caused tactical problems. German generals such as Albert Kesselring and Erich von Manstein had trouble issuing orders to Luftwaffe units under their command. Kesselring's situation is most interesting, as he was a Luftwaffe officer. While commander in chief south (*Oberbefehlshaber Sud*) in Italy, Kesselring effectively controlled all ground forces, and even he had trouble issuing commands across the military branches. A move as trivial as redeploying a Flak battalion to allow more adequate antitank coverage could cause great friction.[20] Command and control problems, in turn, affected the logistics situation. Supply lines for units such as the LwFDs were intermingled between the army and Luftwaffe commands, which helps to explain the shortage of heavy weapons and supplies that exacerbated the weakness of the field divisions.

The Allied powers, especially the Soviets, also indirectly influenced this situation. Part of the myth of the German army's excellence in World War II is the equal assumption of the inferiority of the Red Army in comparison. The myth infers that Soviet numbers won the battles more than anything else, simply smashing bodies into the Germans. This myth has been broken in recent decades, but the historiography of the LwFDs in particular still lags behind this breakthrough. The Soviets may definitely have outnumbered the Germans in most battles in the east, but there was much more to the Red Army than numbers. Superior Russian intelligence operations are certainly one part of the true picture of the Red Army, which by late 1942 was beginning to grow out of the operational funk it had suffered since Barbarossa the year before. While equipment, manpower, and training were core issues to consider, the plight of the Luftwaffe field divisions was at least partially linked to a general German deficiency in intelligence operations as well.

Soviet *maskirovka* (misinformation and deception tactics) notably fooled the Germans repeatedly over the course of the war. The Soviets' most famous success probably was prior to their summer offensive of June 1944, but successful use of *maskirovka* also pertains to the case of the Luftwaffe field divisions.[21] In the fall of 1942, OKH correctly assessed that the Red Army possessed seventy-three reserve rifle divisions and eighty-six reserve tank brigades, along with a host of other forces available already on the front line. Meanwhile, the same office also asserted that no major Soviet offensives were due in the southern sector for late 1942, while in reality, the Red Army was actively planning moves against both Stalingrad and the Rzhev salient. *Maskirovka* was at least partly responsible for this assertion; Soviet deception using a mix of deliberately unencrypted messages and coded transmissions fooled OKH into believing that the troop concentrations forming opposite the Third Romanian Army on the flanks of the Stalingrad position were only there for shallow attacks against the railroads leading into Stalingrad, when in fact the Romanians would be one of the first formations smashed by Operation Uranus, Red Army Marshal Georgi Zhukov's counteroffensive around Stalingrad.[22]

Faced with such comforting, albeit incorrect, estimates, it is not difficult to understand why the Germans, all the way up to Hitler himself, underestimated the threat. The deployment of several LwFDs to the supposedly "quiet" southern sector makes much more sense from that regard. The LwFDs being sent to the south were supposed to temporarily relieve a few veteran panzer divisions stationed behind the lines at Stalingrad so the panzers could receive reinforcements. As the Germans planned to move their own panzer units back from the line, the LwFDs and the rest of the German forces faced at least 660 Russian tanks in just the four spearhead Soviet tank corps, with plenty more coming in behind. The 2nd LwFD would be hit head-on by no less than five Russian tank divisions and ten rifle divisions near Rzhev during Operation Mars. With such absolute Soviet dominance in the penetration sectors, it is difficult to picture an understrength and poorly trained division holding up to the pressure.[23]

The Luftwaffe troops that joined the field divisions were in fact trained for war, but for a different kind. Having been recruited as airmen and air support personnel, they were now being thrust into the front against Red Army armor and expected to hold their positions. General Meindl lamented that "these were the best men we had, and they went to the front without any training," leading to "terrific" levels of casualties without any real success on the battlefield.[24] Meindl also felt that the Germans likely would not have lost any more than they actually did in 1942–43 had the Luftwaffe divisions been appropriately trained and not deployed piecemeal across the front lines. Meindl directly blamed Hitler and the German high command for the disastrous errors made regarding the LwFDs, noting that they were "men who did not have the slightest idea of events at the front" and that he "was disgusted at their lack of intelligence." Meindl often complained about how powerless he and other subordinate officers felt when "dealing with the cliques at Hitler's headquarters," noting further that "it was increasingly obvious that we no longer thought for ourselves. Strategic ideas and politics were the exclusive concern of the High Command; we had only to obey and carry out the orders without compromise."[25]

Divisional Strength Discrepancy

In addition to the general lack of training, there was a wide discrepancy in divisional strengths, and the LwFDs often mustered only half the manpower of a standard army division. The field divisions generally were given from four to six infantry battalions in two regiments and one artillery regiment of varying strength. Compared to a German army division's standard three regiments containing nine battalions with a full artillery complement, the LwFDs were far weaker than their paper strength indicated.[26] Though the listed strength of each LwFD was 12,500 men, that figure was rarely achieved.[27] The 1st LwFD, for instance, had just 6,429 officers, NCOs, and enlisted men.[28] Attached support personnel brought the total to perhaps 8,000 men. Some units were stronger: the 11th LwFD contained over 10,000 men, while the 21st mustered over 16,000 due to an incomplete 22nd LwFD being added to its complement. The general manpower of an LwFD remained below that of an army division, though, and its artillery component was severely lacking.[29]

A good comparison of the strength of an LwFD would be to a Soviet rifle division. Russian units tended to be smaller than their German counterparts, primarily to help with command and control within a Red Army that in late 1942 was still suffering from the losses taken the previous years. While an LwFD was small by German standards, it was often even smaller than the Russian units they faced. The full on-paper strength of a Soviet rifle division listed around 11,000 men, about a third of whom were armed with automatic weapons, backed by 573 machine guns, 52 tanks, 24 76-mm and 36 122-mm guns, 48 light artillery pieces, 111 mortars, 72 antiaircraft guns, and over 1,500 motorized vehicles. A Luftwaffe field division, meanwhile, numbered on average less than 10,000 men, nearly all armed with rifles, and backed by perhaps 500 machine guns, up to 24 pieces of artillery, a varying number of handheld antitank weapons, a couple hundred bicycles, and around 2,700 horses.[30] There was a wide gap in firepower between an LwFD and any unit it had to fight, and in many cases on the Eastern Front the Luftwaffe units individually had so much front line to cover that they would be facing multiple enemy divisions at a time. This situation almost invited the catastrophes suffered by so many of the LwFDs over the course of their combat history.

In addition, because the divisions answered to the Luftwaffe rather than to the army, replacements for losses were difficult at best to organize, as there was no logistical system in place to handle it. The Luftwaffe largely did not provide replacements for the divisions after the initial volunteer group, and neither did the army. LwFDs frequently rebuilt their strength by incorporating the shattered remnants of other field divisions. For example, the survivors of the 2nd and 3rd LwFDs would eventually help replace the losses of the 4th and 6th, while the remainder of the 7th and 8th formed the core of the 15th LwFD when the latter unit was initially created. When the 15th itself collapsed soon after, its remnants too were sent to reinforce the 5th LwFD.[31]

The Destruction of the 7th and 8th LwFDs

The resulting combat performance was abysmal. Despite the initial intention for the LwFDs to be a sort of substitution force, being deployed in quiet areas to possibly allow more elite units to either move elsewhere or fall back and reinforce, the Luftwaffe soldiers often were thrust into heavy fighting.[32] The units attached to Army Group North remained fairly quiet, but the divisions in the other two sectors saw very heavy action. Between December 1942 and January 1943, the 7th and 8th LwFDs with *Armeeabteilung* Hollidt in the south were the first two LwFDs to be destroyed, having collapsed during the operations to relieve the German 6th Army trapped in Stalingrad.[33] The 2nd LwFD was blasted almost to pieces during the Soviet assaults on the Rzhev salient in November 1942. The 5th LwFD suffered heavy losses during Seventeenth Army's retreat in the Caucasus, and the 15th LwFD, which had absorbed the remnants of the 7th and 8th, served with the Fourth Panzer Army in a bloody clash near Rostov. Despite actually receiving a commendation for its actions at Rostov, the 15th was forced to withdraw to recuperate due to heavy losses.[34]

The 7th and 8th LwFDs are among the units most widely cited by contemporary sources as examples of the issues faced by the field divisions.[35] The 7th LwFD was formed in November 1942 at the troop training ground at Grossborn. The unit was one of the first field divisions to see action, but it immediately showed alarming problems. The original strength of the division included only three infantry battalions rather than the usual four that already made the Luftwaffe units weaker than their army counterparts. A fourth battalion was not added to the 7th until a month later when the division was already at the front, and that battalion was only comprised of ground crews, supply personnel, and other Luftwaffe forces behind the lines on the Eastern Front. The 7th found itself attached to

XXXXVIII Panzer Corps, one of the principal units of Army Group Don under Erich von Manstein and thus part of the relief effort against the Stalingrad pocket. The 7th Division was deployed to the front line barely three weeks after its formation, which allowed for only rudimentary training. Despite these problems, the 7th did have the advantage of possessing a slightly stronger artillery complement than the usual LwFD, mustering three batteries including eight 105-mm artillery pieces and five StuG-III assault guns. This theoretically gave the division a better chance at stopping an enemy armored assault than many of its fellow Luftwaffe units.[36] However, the 7th's thirteen artillery pieces were outgunned nearly five to one by a standard Russian rifle division's artillery complement.

The 8th LwFD, meanwhile, got its standard four infantry battalions when it was formed in late October 1942 at the East Prussian training ground at Mlawa. It too was deployed after only a few weeks of training. On 25 November it was assigned to *Armeeabteilung* Hollidt as part of Army Group Don. The Germans were preparing for Operation *Wintergewitter* (Winter Storm), a targeted relief effort against Stalingrad itself. The 7th LwFD with XXXXVIII Panzer Corps was tagged as one of the support units for the push, while the 8th was to be placed in a blocking position.[37]

Wintergewitter was plagued from the start. Facing Soviet pressure against his flanks, Manstein had to redeploy two panzer divisions on 3 December 1942 to help stabilize the front line of the Romanian Third Army. This left XXXXVIII Panzer Corps with just the 11th Panzer Division, the 7th LwFD, and the 336th Infantry Division. The relief offensive rapidly ground to a halt, with the Luftwaffe troops being forced into defensive operations, suffering heavy casualties in the process. The Germans slowly had to withdraw, with the 7th LwFD taking a defensive position facing the Don River for several weeks before Soviet pushes forced the Germans to retreat from the Don entirely.[38]

The 8th LwFD fared even worse. Almost immediately after detraining in the small town of Morozovsk, the 8th LwFD next moved straight toward the village of Nizhne Chirskaya. Expecting to find retreating German troops, the 8th instead ran headlong into a Soviet armored column. Only twelve men from the division's advance elements survived. The 8th spent the next week retreating and suffering heavy losses.[39] The unit took up positions around the important Luftwaffe airfield at Tatsinskaya in mid-December 1942. Although reinforced by the 15th LwFD at the airbase, the two units faced the full strength of the Soviet 24th Tank Corps, which had been attrited to a division-sized formation but still mustered nearly 160 tanks. Tatsinskaya was incredibly important to the success of *Wintergewitter*, as it was one of the main airbases for German transport aircraft trying to keep the German Sixth Army supplied and fighting in Stalingrad.[40]

On 24 December 1942 the Soviet 24th Tank Corps blasted through the two LwFDs defending the airfield and began attacking the transport aircraft on the runways. The 8th LwFD's infantry was cut in half, reducing its four battalions to two, and the division's antitank unit was destroyed. Manstein was able to send reinforcements, which in turn were able to drive the 24th Tank Corps back out of Tatsinskaya on 26 December, but at least seventy-two valuable transport aircraft were destroyed—nearly 10 percent of the transport capability of the entire Luftwaffe at the time.[41] Moreover, the 8th LwFD was a shell of its former self at that point. The remnants of both the 7th and 8th were transferred to replace the losses of the 15th LwFD, and thus were the first two LwFDs to be dissolved—just months after their initial creation.[42] Neither the 7th nor the 8th received any compliments for their service; in the case of the 7th, even the Romanian forces that served alongside the unit resented and scorned the hapless nature of the Luftwaffe formations. Considering the generally low German opinion of their own allies during World War II, having those same allies scorn the Germans is a measure of how poorly the Luftwaffe personnel were stigmatized.[43]

The failures of the 7th and 8th divisions in particular show how ineffective the LwFDs were in combat in their first year of service.[44] The image of a field division simply collapsing and being routed within a short time is a repeated scene in the sources.[45] There is truth to that description; the 8th LwFD was decimated in a matter of hours while conducting its assault toward the town of Nizhne Chirskaya near the confluence of the Don and Chir rivers, while the 7th was crippled within days supporting Operation *Wintergewitter* with XXXXVIII Panzer Corps.[46] On paper, the 8th LwFD in front of Tatsinskaya was supposedly still well armed. In reality, it was down to barely anything save its rifles; many of its so-called heavy weapons had been scrounged by taking the twin 20-mm cannons off of some unusable fighter planes. The Red Army had also managed to catch part of the division out of position, cutting through and causing havoc in the rear areas of the German line.[47]

The Plight of the "Luckless" 2nd LwFD

While the southern LwFDs suffered from severe limitations and consequently took heavy losses facing down Soviet offensives, one division with Army Group Center might just be the exemplar of the difficulties facing the LwFDs when they were first deployed. The 2nd LwFD, assigned to the German Ninth Army in the Rzhev salient, was crushed by a strong Russian offensive on 25 November 1942. Though reinforcements held the line, much of the blame for the debacle was placed on the novice unit, and the 2nd was subsequently transferred to II LwFK at Vitebsk to serve in what was supposed to be a quieter sector.

The 2nd LwFD was formed at Grossborn in late September 1942 and had a similar core strength to the other Luftwaffe field divisions already described. It possessed just four infantry battalions upon its creation, along with a single understrength artillery battalion of three batteries and one company each of antitank guns, Flak, and assault guns.[48] As with other early LwFDs, the 2nd was barely above brigade strength when it was formed. In mid-November, the unit was deployed to the Rzhev salient in the central sector of the Eastern Front, attached to Ninth Army. The division was positioned in line alongside the 246th Infantry Division, approximately ten miles south-southwest of the town of Belyi.[49] Contrary to the intent of Goering's Basic Order Number 3, the front line was not a quiet one. The Rzhev salient had already faced several major offensives in 1942, and Zhukov was preparing his largest attempt yet: Operation Mars, due to launch on 25 November 1942.

The Rzhev salient had been formed in the wake of the failed Soviet offensives of the winter of 1941–42. The salient was pointed like a dagger toward the Soviet defenses around Moscow itself, which meant that the Red Army remained focused on dealing with the threat and the Germans likewise had to maintain it to continue threatening the capital. The German Ninth Army held Rzhev, and attempts to eliminate the salient had already lasted most of the year. In November the Red Army was ready for another major offensive. Operation Mars was designed to push in at the base of the salient from two directions, ideally with the goal of linking the two offensives, surrounding Ninth Army, and destroying both it and the salient all at once. The Soviet attack from the eastern edge of the salient was to penetrate through the German defenses at Velikiye Luki and meet with the Red Army forces that just so happened to be targeting Belyi on the western edge. Red Army General I. S. Konev was in overall command of the operation.[50]

Mars may be remembered today as "Zhukov's greatest defeat," though it certainly did not appear that way at first.[51] The Soviet 41st Army led the way at Belyi, with ten rifle and five tank divisions crashing right through the 2nd LwFD's position south of the city. A second push by the Soviet 22nd Army north of Belyi also broke through the German lines, nearly surrounding the city and trapping the defenders within. By all accounts, the Luftwaffe personnel simply evaporated in panic in the wake of the assault. In comparison, their neighbor on the right flank, the 246th Infantry, managed to hold their own position for almost three more weeks. The Germans also had an ample armored reserve of seven panzer divisions in the Rzhev salient, and the arrival of the 12th Panzer, 19th Panzer, 20th Panzer, and *Grossdeutschland* Divisions sealed off the Soviet gains around Belyi. The Soviet push at Velikiye Luki did not see much success either. The city itself was surrounded, and though it did fall in mid-January 1943, the Soviets managed no further penetration.[52]

The 2nd LwFD's collapse at Belyi led to the division being largely blamed for the faltering of the front line. That the division remained in action into 1943 is a surprise when considering the fates of the 7th and 8th LwFDs, but enough of the division remained viable. The Germans in January 1943 kept the 20th Panzer Division immediately behind the unit in the new front line to lessen the chance of another Russian breakthrough. On 25 May 1943 the division was transferred to the northern part of Army Group Center's front line, a "quieter" spot on the line, and attached to XXXXIII Army Corps. On 17 July 1943 the 2nd was grouped with three other LwFDs into a new II Luftwaffe Field Corps. The LwFK was also composed of the 3rd, 4th, and 6th LwFDs, none of which had had particularly distinguished starts to their service. On 14 September OKH shifted the boundary of Army Group

Center south of Nevel, which ultimately left the four LwFDs of II LwFK covering the border between Army Groups Center and North, potentially leaving a highly vulnerable target for the Soviets.[53]

The Red Army took advantage by launching a powerful assault on Nevel on 6 October 1943. The offensive targeted right between the 2nd and 6th LwFDs, and again the 2nd broke quickly, leaving a ten-mile gap in the front line that the Soviets poured through. Nevel was retaken by the Soviets, with the survivors of the 2nd LwFD only barely getting out of the city. By taking Nevel, the Soviets now threatened the northern flank of Army Group Center around the city of Vitebsk, which is where the II LwFK remained stationed for what would become the rest of its existence. By January 1944 the 2nd LwFD was disbanded, its survivors added to the German LIII Army Corps.[54]

The unit's collapses at Rzhev and then at Nevel marked its reputation as a "luckless" formation, with several army divisional and corps commanders calling the Luftwaffe troops "gutless." This comment most likely reflected the sheer panic shown by the men of the inadequately trained unit as it faced down multiple attacking Soviet formations. This panic is clearer when examining the disparity between the comparably light personnel losses and the horrendous material losses sustained by the division during the breakdown and rout. From 6–12 October 1943 in front of Nevel, the 2nd LwFD lost 722 men, but material losses added up to over 2,600 rifles, 550 machine guns, 26 antitank guns, and 42 Flak guns. The general conclusion based on the disproportionate equipment losses can really only be that the men of the 2nd had simply thrown down their weapons and run away. Goering himself was said to have been furious at the ineptitude of this division making him lose face.[55]

The Luftwaffe personnel of the 2nd LwFD probably were not truly cowards, especially considering they had already been trained for service in the air war. Despite this, they had not been properly trained in ground combat before they had to face down multiple Soviet offensives in the Rzhev salient and at Nevel. Putting even trained military personnel into a situation similar to that faced by the 2nd LwFD would not have made much of a difference if that unit was insufficiently equipped and trained. In the face of overwhelming Soviet superiority at the assault point, the division could not stop the enemy from breaking through. Over the rest of the war, many other German infantry divisions, both Luftwaffe and regular army, would do the same in similar situations, though the singular collapse of the 2nd LwFD is much more clearly linked to its deficiencies in training and equipment.

The 5th and 15th LwFDs in Southern Russia

While the 2nd, 7th, and 8th LwFDs disintegrated quickly, two other LwFDs on the southern front suffered from similar difficulties yet managed to overcome these issues—at least temporarily. The 15th LwFD was a unique unit, formed completely from so-called excess personnel from *Luftflotte* 4 in southern Russia: ground crewmen and the like. The first commander of the 15th LwFD was General Alfred Mahncke, a longtime air force officer who had begun his flight career in World War I and returned to the Luftwaffe in 1935 after a stint commanding police forces in the interwar period. By all accounts a talented air force officer, his only infantry experience was a brief period as a company commander twenty-five years earlier in 1917. By his own admission, he was not a great choice to command a ground division—not due to a lack of his own skill but due to his obvious disinterest in what he considered a foolish idea: "Here was a task I knew I could handle, but circumstances proved to be stronger than my personal preferences." As for his opinions of his orders: "Dreamed up at a comfortable desk in a warm office, the order's outlines were easy to understand. But the writer ignored that we were 4,000 miles from Berlin, in the Caucasus steppe, at the onset of winter, expecting to be called to the front at any time. ... we often wished we had those clever chaps from the offices at home with us to prove how stupid their idea of creating a *Luftwaffenfelddivision* really was."[56] Mahncke's own comments on his involvement with the 15th LwFD are completely in keeping with the general view of German officers on the idea of all-Luftwaffe infantry units. In particular, he mentions that it was only after the war that he found out why the divisions were created: "a concession to Goering's vanity" and "a botched attempt from the start."[57]

The 15th LwFD was created almost on the run. The division was to be allocated to LVII Army Corps and the German relief effort against

Stalingrad, but it would not be ready for several weeks. As of December 1942 the division had yet to be deployed. In the rush to field the unit, Mahncke could not get his artillery battalion equipped, thus leaving only a few Flak guns for heavy support. The division's actual artillery contingent would not arrive until May 1943, and to say it was outdated does not do that term justice. The Germans had resorted to at least partially equipping the division with nineteenth-century French 150-mm field guns taken from museums, complete with bronze barrels.[58] The deficiencies did not end there. When the 15th finally moved forward on 31 December 1942, Mahncke had to disarm one of his infantry regiments in order to fully equip the other. That meant only one regiment was filling in for the entire division's place in the line at the town of Proletarskaya, just southeast of Rostov. The virtually unarmed regiment was kept in reserve until replacement equipment could come in. Putting the final touch on this chaotic situation was that on 2 January 1943, General Mahncke was replaced, having been ordered to take over a *Flieger* division to the north. That meant the still-organizing division, just half of which had just reached the front line, had a brand-new commander who had to try and make sense of this mess.[59]

On 15 January 1943, just two weeks later, a Soviet offensive broke through the line at Rostov. The 15th LwFD was forced to fall back to Taganrog and was soon reassigned to the V Army Corps on 3 February. Despite numbering five divisions, the corps was worse for wear; the five units amounted to just 11,000 men.[60] In March the remnants of the 7th and 8th LwFDs were added to the 15th, and the division was again reassigned to XXIX Army Corps as part of the new German Sixth Army, replacing the army of the same designation lost at Stalingrad. The commander of Sixth Army, General Karl-Adolf Hollidt, noted that XXIX Corps as a whole was down to just over 8,700 men, facing nearly 70,000 Russians on the line. All told, Sixth Army only counted 31,000 men, facing over 136,000 Soviets.[61] In May 1943 the 15th finally received its 1870s-era artillery regiment, giving it another small transfusion of firepower, but ultimately not enough to bring the division anywhere near full strength.

In the aftermath of the German failure at Kursk, in late July 1943 the Soviets launched an attack against the weak lines of the Sixth Army, blasting through the positions of XXIX Corps and forcing the 15th LwFD to make a fighting withdrawal. At one point, the division was completely surrounded at the mouth of the Mius River near Taganrog but managed to break out. Despite this, the division had nearly been bled out. The ancient artillery pieces had to be left behind, leaving the unit without artillery support yet again. One of the two regiments had been reduced from 2,600 men to less than 400 following the offensive. The remnants of the division were moved to Melitopol and placed just north of the town.[62]

The fate of the 15th LwFD was tied to the final field division deployed to the southern sector in the East, the 5th. The 5th possessed just four infantry battalions and one artillery battalion when it was assembled in late September 1942, but unlike other LwFDs the 5th's artillery only consisted of two batteries of *Nebelwerfer* rocket launchers, leaving it with a severe lack of heavy fire support. The unit's antitank battalion was mostly equipped with captured French weapons that proved wholly inadequate for the Russian front. It only received about five weeks of organization and training prior to shipping out to the Eastern Front, being stationed southwest of the city of Krasnodar on the Kuban River, just off the Black Sea coast. The Luftwaffe troops were intermixed with the Romanian Cavalry Corps on the front line and were one of four German divisions sent to reinforce the position.[63]

On 11 January 1943 the Soviet 56th Army launched an offensive aimed at Krasnodar. Both the Romanian and German positions were badly hit by the assault, with the 5th LwFD actually broken into two contingents, one under the German First Panzer Army and the other with Seventeenth Army. The Russian offensive forced the First Panzer to retreat north, while the Seventeenth Army retreated westward toward the Taman Peninsula. By April the Germans were able to launch an attack aimed at closing the main gap in the German front line and also relieving the pressed 97th Jäger Division, which was bearing the brunt of the Soviet offensive around the town of Krymskaya. An assault gun battery attached to the 5th LwFD's antiaircraft battalion proved extremely useful in closing the gap, and the commander of the 97th Jäger, General Ernst Rupp, actually thanked the Luftwaffe personnel and the other German troops from V Army Corps that supported them in a divisional communiqué dated 17 April 1943.[64]

The 5th LwFD continued to perform well in holding the line, although it suffered severe losses in doing so. By June 1943 the division was transferred across the Kerch Straits into the Crimea and even began received additional artillery support. In September 1943 the division was transferred to Melitopol, alongside the 15th LwFD. A Soviet offensive against the city began on 26 September, and by the third week of October the Soviets finally broke the German lines, cutting off the Crimea and driving the LwFDs into the lower Dnieper River region. Most of the 15th LwFD was destroyed defending Melitopol, and the 5th absorbed the remainder of the 15th into its ranks.[65] The 5th LwFD managed to survive to be absorbed by the army in November 1943.

"Solutions" and Stigma

The prevalent opinions of the ineffectiveness of the LwFDs are valid for the first year of their deployment. When they saw real combat, the divisions were often scattered and cast aside. Morale in these units suffered as a result of their deficiencies. Tossed into combat without proper training or leadership, they were completely unprepared for its rigor. General Meindl summed up the heavy casualties and difficulties suffered by the LwFDs in his report of 15 May 1943. He maintained that the men in these divisions thought of themselves as merely sacrificial pawns, a far cry from the glory promised to them by Goering.[66]

Meindl's report noted several major issues facing the Luftwaffe divisions due to their depleted manpower: the front lines were stretched very thin, with few reserves behind to support them. The men were exhausted, their morale clearly shaken, and with it their confidence in their leadership. They "felt neither like fliers or soldiers."[67] Meindl quickly pointed out that 80 percent of these soldiers were volunteers, who performed their duty even in poor conditions. If they felt like sacrificial pawns in pointless Luftwaffe units, they would likely transfer out of the Luftwaffe to serve in the army or other services. Meindl also noted that unless the manpower situation was solved quickly and on a long-term basis, the twenty-two field divisions and also other units that relied on Luftwaffe volunteers, such as the Hermann Goering Division and the various *Fallschirmjäger* units, would see their overall fighting quality drop precipitously.[68] Given that a major reason the LwFDs even existed was due to Goering and the Luftwaffe wanting their own ground divisions, this became a major topic of discussion for *Oberkommando der Luftwaffe* (OKL) over the second half of 1943.

General Meindl wanted to consolidate the LwFDs into higher-quality units such as *Luftlande* or *Sturm* divisions, which were better trained and more mobile and could work alongside the spearhead panzer divisions. Four to five other LwFDs could form two air assault units that could serve as airborne or glider divisions. By incorporating the personnel of the LwFDs into formations trained by soldiers with more experience in combat, Meindl wanted to maximize the effectiveness of the remaining troops in the divisions. He had been the one to train the majority of the field divisions and thus hoped to reorganize them so as to not waste the remaining manpower that had been allocated to the units.[69] Meindl in particular emphasized the cooperation of these new airborne units with panzer divisions, noting that he "saw the opportunity to damage the enemy locally on a smaller scale, so he has not the peace to prepare himself for a new offensive ... even in the instance of a hostile breakthrough, the joint use of tanks and airborne troops in a counterattack is a valuable reserve."[70]

Meindl had support for the general idea of reorganizing the field divisions; Erhard Milch, the main organizer of the German aircraft industry during the war and a close associate of Hitler himself, affirmed that paratrooper units could draw on the LwFDs for replacements and stated that it was desirable to reorganize the LwFDs into stronger units. Another opinion came from General Hermann Ramcke, commander of 2nd *Fallschirmjäger* Division in France, who felt that the men of the LwFDs, given some additional training, would make good replacements for the German paratroop units.[71]

To pull the nearly twenty remaining field divisions out of the front line and convert them into new units would require the approval of OKW, and OKL was concerned that instead of transforming the LwFDs into better units, Hitler would simply transfer the LwFDs over to the army. Members of the Luftwaffe, especially Goering, did not want this. Hans Jeschonnek met with Goering on 26 June 1943 at Goering's country home to discuss what to do with the LwFDs. Jeschonnek was quite clear about his opinion: should the field divisions be transferred to the army, the army would "destroy" them, and OKH chief General Kurt Zeitzler "had already confirmed" this. Zeitzler and the army wanted to "extract" personnel from the LwFDs to reinforce army formations—in essence, exactly what the army had always planned for the Luftwaffe personnel before the LwFDs were ever created. Jeschonnek backed any suggestion that did not involve sending the LwFD troops over to the army, recommending both Meindl's ideas and also those of General Erich Petersen, the commander of IV LwFK, to consolidate the existing divisions down to a total of fifteen units.[72] Frankly, though consolidation was a viable option, this would not have strengthened them to a significant degree; at the time only nineteen divisions were still functional, and most of them were already understrength. At least that option would keep the LwFDs under Luftwaffe control. Goering, for his part, simply said that he would discuss the matter with Hitler.[73]

Despite the various attempts to keep the LwFD personnel in the Luftwaffe, Hitler made up his own mind. His faith in the Reichsmarschall had been shaken enough that he decided to remove the LwFDs entirely from the Luftwaffe. On 20 September 1943 Hitler chose to order the LwFDs to be transferred to the army with the effective date of 1 November. This gave the Luftwaffe almost six weeks to try and change Hitler's mind, but events on the front line during that time forced the issue. The previous July, the Germans launched what would become their last major offensive on the Eastern Front, Operation Citadel, against the salient at Kursk. The failure of that operation provoked a number of Red Army counteroffensives, including the assaults against the positions of the 2nd LwFD at Nevel and those of the 5th and 15th LwFDs at Melitopol in October 1943, the month of transition for the LwFDs to the army. The Soviet actions that October resulted in the utter collapse of the 2nd LwFD, the dissolution of the 15th, and the fighting retreat of the 5th, and immediately preceded the full absorption of the LwFDs into the army. In the face of his divisions' difficulties, even Goering, though still reluctant to give up his men, acknowledged that the army might do a better job of providing replacements and equipment.[74] This decision went along smoothly with army leaders, who had wanted this to be the case from the time the LwFDs had been proposed.[75] By the time the units were absorbed, several more LwFDs were gone. The year had seen four Luftwaffe divisions lost in their entirety: the 2nd, the 7th, the 8th, and the 15th, with heavy casualties among many of the others.[76]

The remaining LwFDs were absorbed into the army on 1 November. At least some of the men in the divisions perhaps looked upon this as a good thing; the men of the "luckless" 2nd LwFD received a positive message from the division's commander on 24 October 1943: "In the heaviest and the worst fighting . . . you have proven yourself. . . . I know you will fulfill your duty. . . . I wish you luck and a healthy homecoming."[77] The army undertook a massive overhaul of the divisions, reorganizing them along army lines. However, despite the army takeover of the units, the stigma of the first year of their service in combat never truly went away. This shows in the fact that Manstein, Mellenthin, and other contemporaries failed to acknowledge the Luftwaffe units beyond the fall of 1943. Even when changes were made to the divisions, most German army officers still thought of them as the wastes of manpower they had always seemed to be. This stigma would make German generals move these units to truly quiet sectors, to keep these supposedly weaker units from causing problems like the 2nd LwFD had in the Rzhev salient. That so many contemporary German sources simply stopped examining the LwFDs after their absorption into the army in 1943 is notable evidence of how pitiful the officers at the time considered these units overall.[78]

An earlier quote from F. W. von Mellenthin's *Panzer Battles* requires a second look. He notes that though the LwFDs were given "excellent human material" and the "best of equipment," their training was woefully inadequate. They were commanded by men "who knew nothing about land fighting" and were essentially "a creation which had no sound military foundation—the rank and file paid with their lives for this absurdity."[79] There is certainly truth to this description. The rapid demise of the 7th and 8th LwFDs shows the exact "absurdity" being suggested by Mellenthin being played out.

That said, Mellenthin is also incorrect, at least in one key part. The LwFDs certainly did not contain the best equipment. The divisions were hardly equipped outside of their rifles, with only rudimentary artillery support and little to no mechanization. In terms of weapons technology, the Luftwaffe divisions were largely still stuck in World War I, and in the case of the 15th LwFD, its nineteenth-century artillery complement was even older than that. Aside from that disparity, Mellenthin is fairly correct. The divisions' own commanders, going all the way to the highest level, drastically hindered them in no small way. Goering and Hitler creating the divisions had more merit than previous authors have considered, as there were multiple reasons discussed in the previous two chapters to suspect that Luftwaffe personnel could make an impact on the ground at the front. Instead, the divisions' lack of training, hasty organization, poor equipment, and in some chances even their deployment derailed any real chance at success.

For the most part, the Germans did send the LwFDs to what were supposedly quiet front lines, but the Soviets had fooled them in the south. Soviet military deception being as effective as it was against the Germans, several LwFDs were caught up in some of the larger Soviet offensives of 1942–43 when they clearly should not have been in that position in the first place. Marked by poor and hasty training, inconsistent armaments, and a number of poor decisions made by German commanders at all levels, the men of the Luftwaffe field divisions suffered mightily in the first year of action. While the army did eventually take over the divisions and implement changes, those changes and whether the condition of the Luftwaffe units actually improved in the wake of their disastrous first year of service are still in question.

CHAPTER FOUR

ARMY TAKEOVER OF THE LUFTWAFFE FIELD DIVISIONS, 1943–44

The Army Takes Over, 1 November 1943

The Luftwaffe field divisions' catastrophic first year of deployment forced both the Luftwaffe and the army to question their combat value and to come up with solutions to the problems at hand.[1] Ultimately, on 1 November 1943, the divisions were absorbed into the regular army on Hitler's orders. These remaining LwFDs were redesignated *Felddivision (Luftwaffe)* or FD (L).[2] The *Heer* undertook a massive overhaul of the divisions, reorganizing them along army lines. On paper, each unit's strength was increased to three regiments from two, thus containing six total battalions rather than four. In addition, the artillery complement was finally upgraded to match that of a regular army division. Army officers and personnel were assigned to the divisions to improve their training and leadership, and many of the original Luftwaffe officers were also further trained in infantry tactics.[3]

Though the army did improve the units, many problems remained, especially in terms of logistical support. The divisions remained dangerously undermanned, and furthermore, what reinforcements the army gave the units often consisted of either men who were too old for service or forced

Russian "volunteers" (*Hilfswilligen* or *Hiwis*) captured on the Eastern Front.[4] While the field divisions received replacements, training, and officers, they also lost a good number of troops and other elements at the same time, mainly due to the fact that the Luftwaffe high command resented the seizure of their ground units by the army. Nearly every FD (L) lost its Flak battalion, as the Flak units from each unit remained under Luftwaffe control. Other personnel were transferred to other Luftwaffe units for additional training or even a complete transfer of service. Though the army did improve the fighting capabilities of each Luftwaffe unit on paper, the field divisions mostly spent the next few months in a state of flux. Elements coming in, elements going out, a near-total replacement of officers within the divisional hierarchy, and the ultimate confusion resulting from all of the changes left many of the personnel remaining in the units disheartened and with poor morale.[5]

This chapter will focus on two major themes. First, the reforms undertaken by the army to revamp the Luftwaffe field divisions need to be explored in terms of specific improvements and numbers. Along with what the units gained from the army, the tally must also include what they lost back to the Luftwaffe. The loss of the divisional Flak battalions and sometimes up to thousands of men possibly offset whatever improvements the army made to the units. Second, to assess all of these changes to the field divisions, this chapter will examine each of the remaining field divisions assigned to the Eastern Front, the Western Front, and the Mediterranean theater.

Personnel Changes: Gains and Losses

The condition of the Luftwaffe field divisions varied greatly at the time of the army takeover. Despite the given on-paper strength of the formations, there was no standardization of equipment or manpower across each unit. The 1st LwFD, on the southern portion of Army Group North's sector around Leningrad, reported its strength on 28 October 1943 at around 6,400, with just 2,779 fighting personnel.[6] The 6th LwFD, stationed around Vitebsk at the northern sector of Army Group Center's front line, reported a strength of 7,400 men. The three divisions stationed in France all numbered under eight thousand. Meanwhile, the 21st LwFD, formerly Division Meindl but now redesignated and serving with Army Group North, had double the strength of a regular division at 16,000 men. The 21st counted four infantry and two artillery regiments, thanks to the unit absorbing the manpower of the never-completed 22nd LwFD. Equipment varied widely across each unit as well, especially in regard to artillery. Instead of the relatively standardized equipment of regular German infantry divisions, the Luftwaffe artillery regiments primarily were armed with captured French and Russian pieces of varying calibers, which only served to increase the logistics issues within the divisions.[7]

The army instituted several changes to the LwFDs, the most basic of which was redesignating them as *Felddivision (Luftwaffe)*. The main goal of these changes was to standardize the strength, equipment, and personnel of the Luftwaffe divisions. Nearly the entire chain of command in each Luftwaffe division was to be replaced, with army officers put into positions previously held by Luftwaffe ones. The structure of each division was reorganized as well. In general, each division now had three regiments with a total of six battalions. The artillery component was also restructured so that each FD (L) had three light battalions and one heavy battalion. Each division was granted a reconnaissance battalion as well as a battalion of pioneers.[8] These were overall good changes and, on paper, certainly made the divisions stronger.

However, a number of circumstances made actually attaining the overall goal of increasing the divisions' strength quite difficult. Of particular importance was the divide between Luftwaffe and army leadership over what to do about the field divisions. Goering's command, though it had lost control of the divisions themselves, retained control of the Flak units assigned to them. As such, nearly every Flak battalion was withdrawn from each FD (L) to be deployed elsewhere under Luftwaffe command. The Luftwaffe also transferred additional personnel out of the units to reinforce other Luftwaffe formations. This resulted in varying changes for every division's manpower strength, leaving several of the divisions arguably weaker than prior to the army takeover. For instance, the 11th FD (L) gained 1,250 replacements from the army, mostly older recruits with little training, but this failed to make up for the 11th losing its Flak battalion on top of another 1,100 men who were retained by the Luftwaffe, either because of their specialized training or due to their volunteering for paratrooper service. The

16th FD (L) in France lost more than two thousand personnel back to the Luftwaffe, leaving its strength at just 60 percent of its complement, with the average age of soldiers in the division being over thirty years old.[9] Overall, ten thousand men from the LwFDs were transferred into paratroop service, and six thousand other specialty personnel were redeployed to other Luftwaffe units.[10]

None of the changes to the divisions came easily for their personnel. The loss of many officers, fellow soldiers, and Flak units had a disastrous effect on the already low morale within the field divisions. Each unit already suffered from the stigma of the previous year's performance at the front, their poor morale already detailed in General Meindl's report of 15 May 1943, and these changes did not help the atmosphere within the divisions.[11] Many of the replacements delivered to the field divisions were substandard, either older recruits or, in the case of the 17th FD (L), two battalions of captured Russian *Hilfswilligen* who "agreed" to serve in the German army. These units were known in France as the *Ost* (East) battalions and are notable within World War II historiography for their overall unreliability outside of the simple act of mustering a static defense.[12] In essence, the newly reorganized FD (L)s were being transformed into what the army referred to as static (*Bodenstandig*) divisions, virtually immobile units that could put up resistance but lacked any means of rapid movement.

The net results of the reforms implemented to the LwFDs were essentially a compromise between what the army wanted and what the Luftwaffe suggested to do to the units considering the difficulties they faced in combat. While the army had wanted to just dissolve the units and send their personnel where they were needed, the Luftwaffe had advocated reequipping and retraining the divisions to form more specialized formations. Hitler's orders, as well as the situation on the front lines, had resulted in only middling changes to the units. The divisions stayed together and gained army leadership, replacements, and training, but they also lost a great deal back to the Luftwaffe.

These changes likewise manifested themselves to a varying degree across each of the field divisions. Following the 5th LwFD's retreat from Melitopol, the unit moved with Army Group A to a defensive position south of Nikolayev, near the mouths of the Bug and Dnieper Rivers. It had suffered heavy losses in the previous battle and was greatly understrength when taken under army control, having had to entirely disband three infantry battalions and one artillery battalion, as well as losing large elements of its pioneer and signal companies. Though it received some army officers, the only replacements the division got were the remnants of the dissolved 15th LwFD.[13] The unit's position was one of several points struck during the Red Army's Dnieper-Carpathian offensive (24 December 1943–17 April 1944). Soviet assaults beginning on 20 March enveloped the entire left flank of the German Sixth Army, trapping it against the Black Sea. The 5th was caught up in the retreat, suffering heavy losses again; although it escaped the trap, the division was in bad enough shape that it had to be disbanded in May 1944, with its survivors sent to four separate infantry divisions.[14]

The lifespan of the 5th LwFD deserves further analysis. The 5th performed better overall in combat, despite its deficiencies, when compared to its fellow LwFDs. Even while incurring heavy losses and constantly fighting understrength, the unit endured, even earning some commendations from other divisions serving alongside it. Chiefly responsible for this was the performance of the division's officers and men. The addition of the remnants of the 15th LwFD to the unit also gave the 5th a much-needed boost of reinforcements following the retreat from Melitopol. The unit's assault gun battalion also deserves some credit for holding back a few Soviet pushes during the division's combat history. The 5th could be considered one of the better Luftwaffe divisions organized, but this might also be considered an anomaly in the face of the difficulties faced by nearly every other LwFD in 1942–43. The 5th had virtually the same problems as other units, including a lack of manpower, obsolete artillery, and little training but managed to adequately perform in combat and maintain its composure when it had to retreat. Despite this fact, while the 5th certainly appears to have been a better unit than the 2nd, 7th, or 8th LwFD, its performance was still merely "adequate" overall in comparison to the standard German infantry division.

FD (L)s with Army Group North, Eastern Front

Meanwhile, the six FD (L)s attached to Army Group North in the East largely had seen only minor action thus far in the war. Thus, the period of

November 1943 to January 1944 is crucial to understanding these units' conditions prior to the Soviet northern offensive that began on 14 January 1944, and several of these formations had severe weaknesses prior to facing down a major offensive. Army Group North, a relatively quiet theater that had lacked a major offensive since the siege of Leningrad began in 1941, was the ideal place to deploy the Luftwaffe divisions.

The 1st FD (L) was formed over a mere nineteen-day period from 19 October to 7 November 1942. Training was obviously lacking in the unit, but more crucially, the division had one artillery battalion instead of an artillery regiment, meaning it had only one-third the heavy weapons of a standard field division. The 1st FD (L) was deployed to Novgorod in mid-November 1942 to relieve the battered Spanish "Blue" Division on the front line, and the 1st remained positioned immediately north of the city.[15] Though it greatly lacked training and experience, the division would have more than a year to become accustomed to the constant artillery exchanges and infantry probes each side sent at the other on the line.[16]

Despite being in a so-called quiet sector, the division remained heavily engaged against Red Army probes, and some of those attacks were stronger than others. One report dated 25 March 1943 detailed the division's losses for just the previous week of combat at 617 casualties, including 156 killed.[17] A later report from 8 April 1943 provides a breakdown of those March 1943 casualties and some additional ones suffered since: 34 *Offiziere*, 137 *Unteroffizieren*, and 431 men. This is also especially revealing in another respect: in the past weeks of combat, the division's officers suffered nearly a quarter of the casualties sustained by the formation as a whole.[18] In the German army, it was not uncommon for officers to suffer higher casualty rates than the men; officers led from the front, personally fighting alongside their men and taking part in many of the riskiest elements of combat.[19] It speaks volumes about these Luftwaffe men that they were willing to act in a similar manner, but in a unit that suffered the problems of a poorly trained and organized Luftwaffe field division, heavy officer losses could not have helped the unit's integrity much.[20] It is also notable that despite the division's losses, the Soviets suffered far more; divisional battle reports from 15–23 March 1943 typically estimate Soviet casualties at several times that of the Germans for each engagement, with more than seven thousand in total.[21] While these German estimates could, and likely should, be taken with a grain of salt, it is still clear that the 1st FD (L) was standing firm on the line against Soviet attacks.

Though the division appeared to be holding its own against the Red Army in the Leningrad sector, it was not receiving replacements to cover its combat losses. Beginning in November 1943, a moment when the 1st stood at an effective strength of only 6,429, the reorganization process continued to weaken the unit. The Luftwaffe pulled the Flak battalion from the division, which seriously hampered its already thin artillery component. The unit's assault guns had been withdrawn to help arm another field division. The division also lost another 1,300 men to reinforce the paratrooper units.[22] When the next major Soviet offensive opened on 14 January, the 1st FD (L) was seriously understrength and had just fifteen antitank guns and their three batteries of artillery available to cover their entire front line. The only advantage the unit had at the front was that it was defending behind the Volkhov River, but that was frozen solid on 14 January.[23]

Other divisions with Army Group North faced similar circumstances to the 1st. The 9th and 10th FD (L)s were the first two Luftwaffe divisions formed that had regimental headquarters units to control their infantry battalions; the first eight field divisions formed did not have that level of organization, just individual battalion commands. The 9th and 10th also had one other advantage over previous units: each had a total of six infantry battalions, rather than the usual four, giving those two divisions more manpower than the standard Luftwaffe division. The two divisions were deployed to the Eastern Front in mid-November 1942 and stationed side by side holding the eastern edge of the Oranienbaum pocket, a small cluster of trapped Soviet troops just west of the besieged city of Leningrad. Both divisions covered a long section of the front line, with the 9th on an eleven-mile front and the 10th covering seventeen miles.[24]

This likewise was a quiet sector of the front line for much of the war. The 9th mainly had to deal with Russian partisan activity in the area between the Oranienbaum and Leningrad pockets. The division had to form a four-company *Jagdkommando* to help deal with the guerrillas, actually gaining reinforcements in the form of two Ost battalions of Russian *Hiwis* to help with that objective. The 9th was equipped well enough in terms of small arms to fight partisans, with over 18,000 rifles allocated to the unit as of 23 May 1943. Much like the 1st FD (L), though, while the 9th had small arms, it lacked heavier weaponry. In January 1944, on the eve of the Soviet offensive, the 9th had only 110 mortars, 37 machine guns, and fifteen antitank guns, and its artillery only had enough ammunition for a five-minute barrage.[25] The divisional Flak component likely could have helped with antitank capabilities, but in November 1943 the Luftwaffe pulled the Flak battalion as part of the shift of the field divisions over to army control. This meant that the 9th FD (L) now covered its front line with thirty-six fewer guns.[26]

The 10th had a slightly less active front line than the 9th, facing fewer partisans than the 9th had to deal with, although in January–February 1943 two battalions of the 10th were shifted to reinforce the front line at Krasny Bor, near the city of Kolpino, just south of Leningrad itself. This was due to a major breakout attempt by the Soviets trapped in the city. The Luftwaffe battalions were part of an ad hoc battle group put together around the Spanish Blue Division and German 212th Infantry Division. The offensive was bloody and fierce, lasting from early January to the end of February 1943 and resulting in heavy Soviet casualties. Following the battle, the battalions from the 10th were returned to the division. The state of the 10th remained the same for the rest of 1943, with only the loss of its Flak battalion as part of the army takeover in November. Like the 9th FD (L), this division too lacked antitank weapons, only having eleven of them on the eve of 14 January 1944.[27]

Another unit attached to Army Group North, the 13th LwFD, was in much worse shape. The division was formed with six battalions of infantry and a four-battalion artillery unit, although its artillery was entirely horse-drawn, making it the only field division deployed to the Eastern Front that had to deal with such an issue.[28] The 13th was deployed just north of the 1st FD (L), near the city of Chudovo behind the Volkhov River. Though the 13th saw only light action for much of 1943, the army changes in November ended up weakening the unit rather than strengthening it. The reforms were merely window-dressing; the unit gained some army officers and some reorganization, but the division lost not just its Flak battalion but also two infantry battalions, dropping its strength to four. The division only had twelve antitank guns as well, and the formation had to cover a fifteen-mile section of front line behind the Volkhov. Like the 1st FD (L), the 13th was in dire straits on the eve of the Soviet offensive in January 1944.[29]

Standout Formations: The 12th and 21st FD (L)s

Despite the difficulties faced by four of the six divisions in Army Group North, two of them actually appeared to come out ahead: the 12th and 21st FD (L)s. The 12th was formed over a longer period of time than other LwFDs in 1942, beginning its formation in October but not deploying until December. This gave the division several more weeks of training than other field divisions. While still suboptimal, it was far more training than some of its fellow formations received. The unit contained six infantry battalions rather than the usual four, with a better complement of automatic weapons and heavy weapons in comparison to the armament of the previously mentioned units. The 12th LwFD was equipped with 141 machine guns, 18 flamethrowers, and 36 mortars to augment its small arms, and its artillery regiment contained 24 captured French 75-mm artillery pieces, along with an antitank company armed with 12 75-mm antitank guns and 10 StuG-III assault guns: 75-mm artillery pieces mounted onto the chassis of a Panzer Mk III. Its artillery complement was a bit lighter than it should have been; the third battalion in its artillery regiment was in reality its Flak battalion.[30]

The 12th LwFD did not see action until March 1943, when it was assigned to the Kirischi bridgehead, just south of Lake Ladoga and just to the north of the 13th LwFD's position in the theater. The division would remain in that spot for nearly nine months, engaging in artillery duels and facing off against the occasional Red Army probing attack. The unit remained very static for the rest of 1943, seeing little in the way of heavy action.[31] When the LwFDs were absorbed by the army in November, the 12th lost its Flak unit but gained some decent replacements in the form of two additional artillery battalions containing four German 105-mm pieces and twelve captured French 155-mm howitzers, giving the unit a much heavier artillery complement than its fellow FD (L)s. In a report issued by Army Group North on 19 December 1943, the 12th FD (L) was listed as one of the stronger units in the army group; specifically, it was designated as a category III formation, one capable of offering a full defense against an enemy assault. Only six other divisions in the Army Group received that designation.[32] While this might say something about the state of Army Group North's units at the time, it also shows that the 12th was in fact a much better-equipped division than many of its fellow units.

The other division that appeared to come out ahead in the army reforms was the 21st LwFD. The sixth and final field division assigned to Army Group North, the 21st began its existence as Division Meindl in February 1942. The manpower of this unit thus had a different origin than the other LwFDs, as Division Meindl's roots were the better-organized and -trained Luftwaffe personnel who volunteered for ground combat service in the wake of the winter crisis of 1941–42. Around the same time the LwFDs were originally ordered to form, Division Meindl also participated alongside the 3rd SS *Totenkopf* Division in the successful Operation *Winkelried* along the Demiansk front line.[33]

In December 1942 the division was redesignated the 21st LwFD. The greatest single changes adopted as part of the transition were a change of position and a proper allocation of artillery. Division Meindl had operated consistently without proper artillery support, having just a single battery of captured Russian 76-mm guns. It took until the summer of 1943, but the 21st eventually contained a full artillery complement of four battalions, one of them Flak, equipped with fully motorized artillery pieces: German 105-mm and French 75-mm and 155-mm guns. In addition, the Germans evacuated the Demiansk salient from 17 to 26 February 1943, consolidating their position south of Lake Ilmen and actually managing to create a small reserve of units that were to be used in holding the salient.[34]

The 21st possessed a much larger antitank component than other LwFDs, with one source stating that as of October 1943 the division fielded over fifty antitank guns and ten assault guns.[35] This dwarfed the complements of other Luftwaffe divisions with Army Group North. In October 1943 the division faced down not one but two major Red Army armored thrusts against their position and passed the tests easily. When the 21st was inducted into the army the next month, the division lost its Flak battalion but gained an extra battery of French artillery pieces. The division did lose over 1,100 men to the paratrooper units, but it did not matter in the long run. The 22nd LwFD, planned for completion in late 1943, was cancelled, and its personnel added to the 21st FD (L). This brought the latter's manpower to four infantry regiments, twice that of any other field division, with over 16,000 men. Coupled with the heavy artillery and antitank components, the 21st was easily the strongest of all the Luftwaffe field divisions at the end of 1943.[36]

Dire Straits: The FD (L)s of Army Group Center

In sharp contrast to the varying stance of the six Luftwaffe units in Army Group North, the three field divisions assigned to Army Group Center were uniformly in very poor shape following the army's reforms. All three of these FD (L)s, the 3rd, 4th, and 6th, were stationed as part of Third Panzer Army around Vitebsk, at the northern point of Army Group Center. The 3rd LwFD was deployed in early November 1942. The division was very understrength upon its deployment, consisting of just four infantry battalions, a single artillery battalion with three batteries, and a company each of Flak, antitank weapons, signal troops, and engineers. The 3rd, along with the 2nd, 4th, and 6th LwFDs, were assigned to the II *Luftwaffenfeldkorps* in December 1942. The II LwFK was positioned at the northernmost point of Army Group Center; in essence, the field divisions were the link between Army Groups North and Center.[37]

Upon its deployment, the 3rd LwFD was assigned to two months of training in the rear areas of Army Group Center. The unit primarily handled anti-partisan duties during this time, protecting towns, depots, and rail tracks. The rear area behind the II LwFK was heavily infested with Russian guerrillas, and the German army allocated the 3rd LwFD to reinforce the police, SS, and *Alarmeinheiten* units fighting the partisans. In February 1943 the Luftwaffe troops played a major part in an assault against a partisan stronghold at Surazh Rayon, located between Vitebsk and the front line where the II LwFK was stationed. This attack was moderately successful, killing around 3,700 of the partisans. This ultimately did not solve the guerrilla problem, as the offensive only really succeeded in driving the partisans into the more heavily wooded areas behind the lines.[38]

The 3rd LwFD received some reinforcements to its artillery component in the summer of 1943. Three artillery battalions were added, along with upgrading the Flak and antitank companies to full battalion size. Though the division's artillery regiment on paper was now overstrength, each of its four battalions only had two batteries apiece. That said, the divisional artillery component became one of the stronger elements of the unit in comparison to its light infantry strength.[39]

Heading into the fall of 1943, the II LwFK was aligned to the north of Vitebsk, in front of the town of Gorodok. The 3rd LwFD was squarely in front of Gorodok, flanked by the 4th and 6th LwFDs. Just to the north was the 2nd LwFD, near Nevel. On 6 October the Red Army launched the offensive that broke the 2nd completely and drove a deep wedge in the German line, though support from the 3rd held the line. A second offensive would follow on 24 December against the 3rd's position at Gorodok, but in between the two battles, the Luftwaffe divisions were absorbed into the army. The 3rd lost its Flak battalion and ultimately would not have time to receive much in the way of army reinforcements.[40]

The following Soviet offensive on 24 December blasted into the German lines around Gorodok, inflicting heavy losses on the 3rd FD (L) and several other units and ultimately forcing the German units to fall back toward Vitebsk. The Soviets broke through the line between the 129th Infantry Division and 6th FD (L), just to the north of the 3rd. This collapsed the German line, forcing a retreat by all three of the Luftwaffe divisions to the south. The Soviet forces, led by the 5th Tank Corps, veered to the south as well, ultimately halting about eighteen miles behind the Luftwaffe position, trapping the three FD (L)s in a salient just north of Vitebsk. The Red Army renewed its offensive on 9 January 1944, hurling about sixty infantry divisions and twenty-two tank brigades against the Third Panzer Army's eighteen divisions, focusing on the small salient containing the FD (L)s. The 4th and 6th were driven back toward Vitebsk, suffering heavy losses but maintaining cohesion. Meanwhile, the 3rd utterly collapsed under the assault. The Soviets called off the offensive on 17 January after their advance stalled, but the damage to the 3rd was severe enough that the division was dissolved just five days later. The remnants of the 3rd were added to the 4th and 6th.[41]

The 4th and 6th FD (L)s survived the winter assaults around Vitebsk and Gorodok, but neither division was in great shape going into 1944. The 4th, like the 3rd, was deployed quite understrength, originally having been organized with four infantry battalions and a sorely lacking artillery component. The divisional artillery battalion possessed five assault guns and two batteries of *Nebelwerfer* rocket launchers but had no regular field pieces, leaving the division without effective fire support. The division also contained the usual Flak battalion, signal company, pioneer company, and antitank battalion. The division was assigned to II LwFK with Third Panzer Army around Vitebsk in late October 1942. The 4th then settled into a long period of exchanging artillery fire with the Soviets and fighting off the occasional infantry probe. During the summer of 1943 the 4th received two additional artillery battalions, bringing the divisional battery total to twelve. This improvement was then slightly offset by the loss of the Flak battalion when the division was taken over by the army.[42]

As with the 3rd and 4th, the 6th LwFD was also deployed to the Eastern Front understrength, with four infantry battalions and a better-equipped artillery battalion. The 6th at least received a bit more training than either the 3rd or 4th, not deploying to the front lines until early January 1943. The unit was assigned to the II LwFK around Vitebsk but began its service deploying forward to the front line just south of Velikiye Luki. This was not a quiet sector for a field division to serve; this was the same area in which Division Meindl had mainly served. About 7,500 German soldiers remained in the city, but as of December 1942, only two strong points inside the city were still in German hands. The 6th LwFD was one of the units meant to help relieve the city, but its inexperience in combat proved a great hardship. Velikiye Luki fell to the Soviets on 16 January 1943, and the 6th had to fall back to a position in front of Gorodok, just north of the 3rd LwFD. The final Soviet assault on the city blasted through the lines of the 6th LwFD, and it took ten other German units reinforcing the line to even halt the Red Army's push.[43]

Once in the line north of Vitebsk, the 6th participated in anti-partisan operations behind the lines. One battalion from the division participated in Operation *Maigewitter* (May Thunderstorm), targeting partisans around the Gorodok highway supplying the front line. The operation was successful in keeping the roads clear of partisans for the time being. In the summer of 1943, the division's artillery component was reinforced, expanding from a single battalion to a full regiment. This would be later offset by the loss of the division's Flak battalion when the army took over the unit in November, but the division could at least count on forty-eight pieces of artillery, including eight French 155-mm and four German 150-mm howitzers.[44]

The men of the II LwFK held a front line fifty miles long in the fall of 1943. The 6 October 1943 offensive that scattered the 2nd LwFD to the north also hit the 6th hard. The division suffered heavy casualties and was driven backward toward Vitebsk, conducting a fighting retreat from 7 to 25 October. The Soviets launched additional assaults on 26 November and 9 December, taking several key towns and opening a twelve-mile gap in the line between Army Groups North and Center. The Germans quickly sent additional troops to close the gap, but this only temporarily stalled the Red Army.[45]

On 24 December 1943 thirty-seven Soviet infantry divisions and fifteen tank brigades blasted through the positions of the 3rd FD (L), forcing a general retreat by the II LwFK to the south. The Red Army offensive only lasted four days but was renewed on 9 January 1944 with even greater strength.[46] The 6th FD (L) initially held its ground, but on 13 January more than two hundred Soviet bombers began striking the division's position. Only the arrival of army reinforcements, including a full antitank battalion, allowed the 6th FD (L) to hold its position. The steadfast resistance offered by the 6th garnered awards for some of its personnel, including its commanding officer, General Rudolf Peschel, who was awarded the Knight's Cross.[47]

The 3rd FD (L) was dissolved following this offensive, and the 6th gained elements of that unit. That helped to replace some of its losses, even allowing the division to form a third infantry regiment. The divisional engineer and signal companies were also increased to battalion size when the 6th absorbed the men of the 3rd FD (L).[48] The reinforcements were only a temporarily fix, however. By March 1944 the situation around Vitebsk had degenerated into artillery duels, positional struggles, and near–trench warfare, and the 6th FD (L) spent the next several months being continuously bled white in small engagements. By summer 1944 the division was down to just 436 combatants, with little to no chance of gaining reinforcements at this stage of the war.[49]

The FD (L)s in France

The army reforms undertaken after November 1943 affected the formations in the West to varying degrees, just as they did the divisions in the East. The three divisions in France were originally formed in the wake of the German disaster at Stalingrad in February 1943. Two days after the German Sixth Army surrendered in the city, Hitler announced a plan to rebuild the German army. A total of twenty-six divisions were to be refitted or rebuilt. Sixteen of these reequipped units were divisions that had been destroyed in Stalingrad, but in each case a cadre of rear area personnel had managed to escape the Stalingrad pocket. Along with refitting those twenty-six divisions, an additional fifteen new static divisions were sent to France over the course of 1943. This would allow better-quality units to move from the west to the Eastern Front. The static divisions sent to France included the 16th, 17th, and 18th LwFDs.[50]

The three Luftwaffe field divisions in France differed greatly from the other static divisions deployed westward, most notably because the average age of their recruits was thirty years old versus nearly forty in other static divisions. This was due to the LwFDs being established from a core group of top-tier personnel from the Luftwaffe who had volunteered for ground service. The fact that these men were being assigned to a mere static division was cause for major concern from many German commanders, especially those in the army who had been protesting the idea of the LwFDs from the beginning. Though the LwFDs were younger, they still were outfitted with older recruits to bring them up to strength. The size of the divisions and their assigned equipment still tended to be on par with other static units. Most importantly, their designation as static units meant that they would receive little in the way of motorized transport.[51]

The 16th LwFD had six infantry battalions in two regiments. Its artillery regiment actually appears to be stronger than those of many other LwFDs, with one battalion of twelve German 105-mm pieces and a second battalion containing eight French 155-mm guns and a battery of four fully motorized French 75-mm pieces. The division's Flak battalion added eight 88-mm Flak-36 pieces and twenty-four 20-mm Flak-38 guns, while the antitank battalion was armed with eighteen 75-mm and sixteen 50-mm guns. The division also had several company-sized support units, namely the engineers, signal troops, and various administrative branches.[52]

The 17th LwFD was organized almost identically to the 16th, with six infantry and three artillery battalions, along with companies of various support units. The antitank battalion was smaller than that of the 16th, with only twelve 75-mm pieces and four assault guns. The 18th LwFD was in a similar position to the 17th, with nearly identical organization and almost the same equipment, though instead of German 105-mm guns, one artillery battalion contained twelve Russian 76-mm pieces.[53] The three divisions saw almost no action in 1943 through early 1944, mainly conducting training exercises and building obstacles to hamper possible Allied invasion efforts against France.[54]

When the army took the units over in November 1943, several major changes took place to the Luftwaffe divisions in France. All three lost their Flak battalions, but all of them also lost a significant number of troops to the Luftwaffe. The 16th FD (L) in particular lost two thousand men to the Luftwaffe. The 17th got two *Ost* battalions to help replace the personnel the Luftwaffe kept, but the three divisions were ultimately left at varying strength levels. Approaching the Allied landings in Normandy in June 1944, the 17th and 18th FD (L)s each had more than nine thousand men, but the 16th was down to just under seven thousand. In addition, unlike several of the field divisions in the East, the western units did not receive replacements for their lost Flak units, leaving their artillery components one battalion lighter than they should have been.[55] This left the three still-inexperienced and already poorly equipped *Bodenstandig* divisions in even worse shape to face the invasion of Western Europe that would be coming soon. Morale was also visibly a concern; the commander of the 18th FD

(L) had to send multiple messages to his officers to make sure they actually took care of their men, as "how the men would face the enemy was directly impacted by their superiors."⁵⁶

The 11th FD (L) in the Greece

Another unit that saw mixed results from the army reforms was the 11th LwFD, stationed in Greece for most of the war. The division was formed in October 1942 and was a little stronger than the average field division. The unit contained six infantry battalions in two regiments along with full-strength antitank and Flak battalions. The division's artillery originally was underequipped, but in summer 1943 the artillery would be dramatically strengthened to twelve German 75-mm pieces and twenty French 75-mm guns. Unlike the divisions in France, which were largely stuck with horse-drawn transport, the 11th was actually fairly well-equipped with motorized units.⁵⁷

The 11th LwFD was initially deployed to Crete in January 1943 to join the garrison there; however, over the course of March and April the division moved to mainland Greece to help deal with the increased partisan activity in the country. The division spent most of 1943 battling these partisan units, achieving some fairly good successes. The 11th participated in two other notable actions in the year, one of which was the execution of Operation *Achse* (Axis), beginning on 8 September 1943. Following the surrender of Italy, Germany forcibly and brutally disarmed the Italian army, inflicting over 30,000 casualties and taking over 800,000 prisoners in doing so. The 11th took part in disarming several Italian units in their Balkan garrisons.⁵⁸

As a further result of the Italian surrender, the British were able to occupy several small islands in the Aegean Sea. The German garrison in the Balkans was ordered to try and take those back, and elements of the 11th were tagged to support the attack on the island of Leros. The assault took place over a four-day period in mid-November 1943. The Germans were successful, driving the British off of the island and inflicting one thousand casualties. The Germans suffered only about four hundred casualties of their own, and by its own account, the regiment from the 11th LwFD performed well in the engagement: "The troops, though under heavy fire . . . drove the enemy from their positions during the army's storming of the island."[59]

At the time of the army takeover of the LwFDs on 1 November 1943, the 11th still mustered about ten thousand men. Several changes were implemented to the unit: the Luftwaffe retained the Flak battalion, along with 1,100 men. To compensate, the division received 1,250 replacements from the army, but they were all older recruits of ultimately limited use. In addition, the division's bicycle and signal companies were expanded to battalion size. The division's artillery component also changed, replacing the usual German and French pieces for more obsolete captured Yugoslavian and Russian guns.[60] This might have been a problem for a division serving in the major theaters, but the 11th FD (L) remained in the Balkans for the rest of the war battling partisans, and the Germans found the equipment changes acceptable in this circumstance.

The 19th and 20th FD (L)s in Italy

The other two divisions in the Mediterranean theater were stationed in Italy, and both ultimately suffered due to the army absorption. The 19th LwFD had started losing men to the army even before the unit was completed. As part of the wholesale German effort to reequip divisions that had been destroyed at Stalingrad, from 24–28 February 1943 the 19th lost over 1,600 recruits and 4 batteries of artillery pieces to the 24th Panzer Division and 44th Infantry Division. In mid-April, the division was deployed to France for some additional training that lasted until late May. On 6 June 1943 the 19th LwFD received 450 reinforcements from the 65th Infantry Division, but these were men that the army division had considered unfit for combat. Another 930 men from the 65th would also be transferred into fortress garrisons.[61] Upon being absorbed by the army on 1 November 1943, the 19th lost its Flak battalion but gained some artillery replacements. The entire divisional artillery complement consisted of captured enemy pieces: twenty-four Russian 76-mm guns, twelve Russian 122-mm howitzers, and four Polish 105-mm howitzers.

In January 1944 the division's antitank unit also lost its assault guns due to German needs in the East. As of May 1944 the 19th was listed under the German Fifteenth Army's reserves and had even been reclassified as the 19th *Luftwaffen-Sturm-Division*. Though it had been reclassified as a "storm division," it lacked any specialized units or manpower to justify the change. As of 1 June the division listed a complement of about 9,400 men, but it would soon lose another full artillery battalion. Soon after, the division would be sent to Italy.[62]

Meanwhile, the 20th LwFD was formed with almost identical strength to the 19th and was deployed to Denmark in July 1943. The unit spent most of 1943 in training but suffered dramatic changes when the army took over the LwFDs in November. The 20th lost its Flak battalion and also lost a full third of its manpower, being reduced to just four battalions in size. Hitler ordered the 20th to be turned into a more mobile unit; the army responded by equipping all six infantry companies with bicycles and motorizing the artillery and antitank complements. The division, along with the 19th, was sent to Italy in early June 1944.[63] While it might have been more mobile, the 20th FD (L) on paper certainly looked weaker, especially in manpower.

The army reforms undertaken after 1 November 1943 changed the Luftwaffe field divisions for the remainder of the war. On paper, the results were mixed. Some divisions, such as the 11th, 12th, and 21st, came out ahead, with greater strength in terms of manpower, artillery, or both. Other units, such as the 1st, 13th, 16th, 19th, and 20th, emerged in worse shape, ultimately losing manpower, artillery strength, or both. Many of the remainder did not seem to have changed much at all. Though all of the remaining FD (L)s received army officers, additional troops, and other reinforcements, it would not be clear that such changes would affect the field divisions' performance from the previous year. The remaining Luftwaffe personnel in the field divisions were still the same men whom General Meindl had largely and frankly described as feeling "neither like fliers or soldiers" and acting as "sacrificial pawns" in the aftermath of their first year of deployment, and there is no evidence that these troops felt any better about their chances of success in the wake of the army's reformation of their units.[64]

Several of the divisions' commanders, as well as some of those officers' superiors, described their own opinions of these formations in memoirs and official documents. The army takeover does not appear to have changed their opinions of the field divisions.[65] The full impact of the army's changes is best examined in the major combat operations involving the FD (L)s from 1944 to 1945.

CHAPTER FIVE

LUFTWAFFE FIELD DIVISIONS IN THE WEST, 1944–45

Keeping Things in Context

Following the army's takeover of the Luftwaffe field divisions in November 1943, the formations remained under army control for the rest of the war and continued to serve on every front of the European theater. This chapter will cover the actual combat operations fought by those units for the remainder of the war in the Western theaters: France, Italy, and also the Balkans.

Because World War II was a global conflict, events in one theater often impacted the others. For instance, among the reasons that Hitler called off Operation Citadel, the offensive at Kursk on the Eastern Front that began on 5 July 1943, was because of Operation Husky, the Allied invasion of Sicily, beginning just five days later. As the Germans failed to penetrate at Prokhorovka, just south of Kursk, on 12 July, the Soviets launched a counteroffensive code-named Operation Kutuzov north of Kursk the same day. Meanwhile in Sicily, Field Marshal Albert Kesselring managed to see the Allied advance for himself and reported that the Axis could not hold the island, convincing Hitler of the need for additional resources to be deployed to the Mediterranean. With Operation Citadel not going anywhere and German strength needed elsewhere, Hitler called off the drive on Kursk on 12 July.[1] There are clear operational and strategic links between the Western and Eastern fronts of the European Theater, and thus it is critical for historians and others who study the war to keep a global view of the conflict to help understand the various decisions being made by all relevant parties.

The Western and Mediterranean FD (L)s

The impact of the army takeover in 1943 did not seem to matter much to the field divisions on the Western and Mediterranean fronts. With few exceptions, the units in question would see their first action in summer 1944. Despite the reorganization efforts of November 1943, the general lack of combat experience along with the fact that these units were put up against some of the best units the Allied armies had to offer led to disastrous results for the Luftwaffe divisions.

The FD (L)s assigned to the Western Front were generally considered of poorer quality than even those field divisions on the Eastern Front. The 16th, 17th, and 18th FD (L) stationed in France were all labeled specifically as *Bodenstandig* divisions, static units that mostly lacked a mobile component. There were many static formations assigned to the west prior to the Allied invasion of Normandy in June 1944; fifteen static units were sent to France over the course of just 1943 to free up better-quality units for the Eastern Front. By early 1944 the German army counted sixty divisions in total in France, but nearly half were second- or third-rate: old men, young boys, recovering wounded, survivors of the Eastern Front rotated westward, and a large number of foreign *Hiwis* of, at best, dubious fighting quality.[2]

In Italy, the 19th and 20th FD (L)s were technically the last two field divisions ever put together.[3] In both cases, the units suffered from an incomplete building process that was further interrupted by the army takeover in November 1943. Neither division was technically static, with both the 19th and 20th being classified as *Luftwaffe-Sturm-Divisionen* ("storm divisions") but lacking any extra training or equipment to justify the designation. The 20th FD (L) was marginally more mobile than a static unit, with all of its infantry equipped with bicycles and its artillery component motorized, though it also had lost a third of its strength to the Luftwaffe during the army takeover.[4]

The other two divisions stationed in the west were the 14th FD (L), part of the twelve-division garrison in Norway, and the 11th FD (L) stationed in the Balkans battling partisans. The 14th, though it never saw action, is a good representation of the manpower the Germans largely wasted on defending Norway. Thanks to a combination of Hitler's desire to defend every inch of European coastline in anticipation of the Allied invasion as well as Allied deception operations that continued to suggest Norway was a target, the Germans maintained a very large force in the area. In mid-1944 the German garrison in Norway numbered 372,000 men, and the 14th on paper was one of the stronger Luftwaffe field divisions with over 13,000 men under arms. The unit was the only FD (L) to maintain an anti-aircraft battalion after the army takeover in 1943, with one artillery battalion reequipped with three batteries of 88-mm Flak guns. The division even had a five-company battalion of reserves.[5] Though the Norway garrison did see some of its personnel pulled to reinforce the crumbling front lines in late 1944, the 14th FD (L) remained on station in the country for the rest of the war and ultimately survived. However, due to the paucity of action, any judgment of its combat ability is pure speculation.

Meanwhile, the 11th FD (L) only barely saw action against a regular Allied army, mainly facing partisan groups for the duration of its deployment in the Balkans. However, out of all the Luftwaffe divisions stationed in the west, the 11th perhaps had the best overall record, surviving to the end of the war and conducting its operations with a good degree of skill. On paper, the unit was lacking, having only with captured Russian and Yugoslavian artillery pieces, but in general the unit was equipped well enough to deal with its partisan opponents.[6]

The German Mess in France, 1944

The German situation in France in 1944 led to one of the worst fiascos in German military history after the Allies invaded Normandy on 6 June. The German high command was already convoluted at the start of the war; the formation of OKW, back in 1938, theoretically put a strategic planning group atop the three separate branch commands (OKH, OKL, and *Oberkommando der Marine*), but it was not utilized as such by Hitler during the war itself. Rather, Hitler intended OKW to supplant the role of the army officer corps, especially the general staff, which he viewed as decadent, conservative, and too aristocratic for his new Reich. The Luftwaffe and navy understood their role in the drama between Hitler and the army, and their commanders often sided with OKW over OKH, leaving the army in the lurch. As OKW was not designed to efficiently run the war, it ended up not doing that at all. Most German operations were not jointly conducted, with the army taking center stage, the navy unable to provide much assistance to a continental war, and the Luftwaffe's role gradually diminishing as the war dragged on.[7]

By 1942 a division of responsibilities left OKH in charge of the Eastern Front, with OKW running the rest of the war. In early 1942 Hitler added yet another level to this already complex structure by creating a new army high command, *Oberbefehlshaber-West* (OB-West), giving the command to Field Marshal Gerd von Rundstedt, the commander of the main German thrusts against Poland and France in 1939–40 as well as the original commander of Army Group South in 1941. This put Rundstedt in charge of all German forces in Western Europe. Since then, however, OB-West had basically served as a manpower reserve for the Eastern Front, with no fewer than thirty-eight divisions sent eastward between January and October 1943. Fresh divisions were sent east, burned-out ones sent west, and in general the constant to and fro of manpower made operational planning impossible in the west.[8]

In a report made to Hitler in October 1943, Rundstedt laid out a very discouraging picture. He had a two-thousand-mile front to cover, which was weakly occupied and "hopelessly incomplete." Construction efforts to build defenses along the coast, the well-known Atlantic Wall, were certainly strong in a few certain areas, such as the Pas-de-Calais, but in most cases it was barely a picket line. Divisional front lines were so large that they bordered on the absurd; the 18th FD (L), for example, had to cover eighty miles by itself. Moreover, many of Rundstedt's men were of second-rate quality or worse. This created a thin line of defenders with almost no operational depth. Artillery in nearly all his units was a mix of captured foreign pieces, and the Western Front in general lacked airpower, fuel, and any means to launch a mobile counterattack should they meet an enemy assault.[9]

Hitler appeared to listen to the report, issuing Führer Directive No. 51 on 3 November 1943 that ordered an immediate strengthening of forces in the west. Though the order was seemingly sensible, the Germans and Hitler completely bungled its implementation. The directive had forbidden any further redeployment of western units eastward, but the military situation in early 1944 forced Hitler's hand. The Red Army launched a series of offensives in January 1944 that required the Germans to send reinforcements to the east, and at the end of the same month the Western Allies had landed at Anzio in Italy, prompting the move of several more units, including two panzer divisions. To bolster France, Hitler chose instead to set up yet another military command. Army Group B was moved into area of northern France, under the command of Field Marshal Erwin Rommel. Rommel's arrival was redundant, and it created a command rivalry in France between himself and Rundstedt. Rommel's command took Rundstedt's two strongest units, the Seventh and Fifteenth Armies, as well as control over the Normandy coastline. Even though Rundstedt remained in overall command, he now constantly had to fight against Rommel's takeover of his manpower. Rundstedt finally won over Hitler to create a new Army Group G in southern France and confirm him as being in overall command, but this situation was not fully resolved until 10 May 1944, barely a month prior to the Allied invasion.[10]

The net result of all the German confusion was an army that on paper was manifestly incapable of properly defending France. The sixty divisions in France on average each held a sixty-mile front line, nearly four times the recommended space that a World War II infantry division could effectively cover.[11] Even in the most heavily defended sector around Calais, the "well-off" German Fifteenth Army's divisions were still holding twenty-mile frontages; in the weaker areas such as Brittany, the average division covered more than one hundred miles. Superior quality over quantity was a traditional German strength that could overcome this problem, but this was not the case in France. By 1944 the average German infantry division counted just six infantry battalions rather than the nine of the early-war *Heer*. Ironically, this also made the average German regular infantry division the same strength and size as a typically "understrength" Luftwaffe field division of the previous year, a status most of the FD (L)s had, at best, retained in 1944.

Much of OB-West's manpower was recuperating from their ordeal on the Eastern Front. Many of those troops were overage, suffering from stomach ailments, and recovering from severe frostbite cases. More striking was the notable presence of around forty-five *Ost* battalions in France, consisting of foreign conscripts and POWs who "volunteered" to fight for the German army instead of sitting out the war in a prison camp. These units were never trusted and often were deployed with German units on either side of them to keep an eye on them.[12] Finally, fully half of the German divisions in France were static divisions, composed of the poor manpower described above, given fewer heavy weapons and little to no means of transport, and assigned the dual mission of resisting the Allies for as long as possible, and then dying in place. These static units also included three of the Luftwaffe field divisions. The German army defending France in 1944 was a far cry from the one that had conquered the country so easily in May 1940.[13]

The complex command structure continued to haunt the Germans when the invasion came in June 1944. Rundstedt did not command the naval or air units assigned to France's defense, and though they were heavily outnumbered by their Allied counterparts, the fact that the army had no control over its combined arms made things even worse for the Germans. This arrangement was convoluted at best: coastal artillery remained under navy control as long as they were pointed out to sea, but as soon as fighting shifted to land, the army took over. Those coastal batteries had to be constructed to army specifications so that they could be pointed inland, a design the navy was unfamiliar with. Rundstedt could make recommendations to, but not compel anything from, the Luftwaffe and Kriegsmarine forces in France.[14]

The Germans in France were outnumbered, their forces were of poor quality, and their command structure made no sense. Their fortifications, while impressive visually, were incomplete and sparsely manned. Even many Germans secretly doubted the usefulness of the Atlantic Wall, which proved to be a waste of resources and manpower.[15] Success in France was contingent on the ten panzer divisions assigned to the region being able to properly spearhead mobile counterattacks against the invasion, wherever it landed. This led into the major operational problem of fighting inland: Allied air superiority. Fighting an enemy with control of the air would seriously hinder the way the German army wanted to fight. Nonstop bombing forced all movement to take place at night, a disadvantage great enough that Rommel actually wanted to put the panzers near the coast to help smash the Allied landings. Rundstedt disagreed, wanting to employ the more traditional method of organizing an operational reserve force that could respond to any landings. He also argued that putting the panzers on the coast would expose them to Allied naval fire, which would be just as devastating as being struck from the air. A compromise was reached; naturally, it was an imperfect decision. Both Army Groups B and G received three panzer divisions to deploy where needed, while the remaining four divisions were organized into a reserve group known as *Panzergruppe West*. This new formation did not answer to either Rommel's or Rundstedt's command but was instead placed under the direct authority of Hitler himself.[16] This only further fractured the German command structure, making it even more complicated on the eve of the invasion.

The FD (L)s in France Head toward the Front

The situation in France was mirrored by the status of the three Luftwaffe divisions posted in the region. The 16th FD (L) possessed 9,800 men and just 28 artillery pieces and 32 antitank weapons. One of the unit's artillery battalions was also reequipped with Russian 76.2-mm and 122-mm pieces, replacing several batteries of French 155-mm guns left behind for coastal defense purposes.[17] The commander of the 16th, General Karl Sievers, did not have much confidence in the fighting morale and discipline of his men, and on 14 June 1944, when it was clear that the division would be deployed to action, he issued a lengthy order to his officers reminding them how to properly maintain discipline as well as punishing infractions.[18] Meanwhile, the 17th and 18th each had around 9,500 men and, according to Rommel himself, possessed "unimpressive" fighting abilities. The 18th at least had a decent number of antitank weapons and German-made artillery pieces, but all three of these units were still static formations and thus ill-equipped to do more than simply attempt to hold the line.[19]

The commander of the 18th FD (L), General Joachim von Tresckow, was likewise not impressed with his own unit; neither was anyone else.[20] From 17 to 19 April 1944 the 18th was one of six divisions inspected personally by Field Marshal Rommel, whose comments were not encouraging; in particular, he found a severe lack of junior officers and NCOs. At least some efforts were made to improve the division, including a transfer of new antitank weapons, but it remained short of officers.[21] The 17th FD (L), meanwhile, had spent most of 1943 and early 1944 helping to construct defenses along the Atlantic Wall. The division built numerous pillboxes and bunkers and emplaced nearly a quarter of a million anti-glider stakes and other obstacles, enough so that the men chose the design of an anti-invasion obstacle imposed on a divisional shield for their unit insignia.[22] The unit had also received a third infantry regiment in early 1944, bringing its divisional strength in line with its peers.

None of the FD (L)s in France saw action when the Allies launched their invasion of Normandy on 6 June 1944. The landings were all ultimately successful, and at the cost of a fraction of the expected casualties. The Allies' euphoria immediately following the success quickly turned to bitter disappointment as the battle for Normandy itself turned into a slog that lasted another six weeks. The Germans, for all their pre-invasion problems, whipped together what units they could and sent them into the combat zone, forming a cohesive defense line and then contesting the Allies for every inch of ground.[23] The major difficulty for the Germans moving northward was Allied air supremacy. The two German armored divisions nearest the beaches, the 12th Panzer and Panzer Lehr Divisions, were fifty and ninety miles away, respectively. Both units were very well-equipped; in the case of Panzer Lehr, it possessed a full strength of 14,699 men, 1,000 trucks, 700 armored vehicles, and nearly 200 tanks, including 99 panzer Mark IVs, 89 Mark V Panthers, and even 8 Mark VI Tigers.[24] The drive north took two days for Panzer Lehr, dodging aerial attacks the entire way, and at one point divisional commander General Fritz Bayerlein even lost track of his own unit. Once the division reached its positions in Normandy on 8 June 1944, the unit had lost 85 armored vehicles, 5 tanks, and 123 trucks, a sizeable toll for a division that had yet to fire a shot after only a two-day advance to the front.[25]

The movement of the three Luftwaffe divisions was likewise hampered. The 16th FD (L) took nearly three weeks to reach the front thanks to disrupted rail transport; the bulk of the unit did not arrive in Normandy until 1 July 1944. The 17th and 18th did not reach combat until mid-August.[26] Initial combat was deadly; the 16th immediately deployed two battalions forward to relieve the Panzer Lehr division. However, at the same time the Luftwaffe units were relieving the Panzer Lehr, the position was hit by a British assault. The German defenders were in disarray, and the two battalions from the 16th suffered 75 percent casualties, nearly 500 men in total. The battalions were so demoralized that Rommel had them attached to the 21st Panzer Division to hopefully restore some fighting spirit. A suggestion was made that the men of the 16th could fully replenish the strength of the 21st Panzer, and this idea would later be partly implemented.[27]

Caen, Goodwood, and the 16th FD (L)

The stalemate (*Stellungskrieg*) that developed in Normandy was a direct result of deployments and geography. The British and Canadian forces on the eastern edge of the front had the open plains of the Calvados region in front of them, culminating in the city of Caen—an original, though overly ambitious, goal of the original D-day landings. This offered the Allies the best opportunity to break through the German lines but also attracted the strongest part of the German defenses. Seven panzer divisions, including four heavy battalions containing Tiger I tanks, guarded the Caen sector. While only two panzer divisions faced the Americans in the west, Normandy's terrain aided them greatly. The region facing the Americans was an array of ancient small farms, separated by the *bocage*, giant hedgerows ten feet high. This blocky setup made each farm a tiny defense line, making every engagement a small-scale encounter and severely limiting American resources. Ironically, the Allies faced a backward scenario: the British, the army that could not afford heavy losses at this point, were facing a front line that would be impossible to attack without taking those casualties, while the Americans were tied down in a place that limited their large supply of resources and kept them pinned down for weeks.[28]

The British, led by Field Marshal Bernard Montgomery, launched multiple thrusts at Caen over the month of June that were parried each time by the Germans. On 13 June the British 7th Armored Division was sent to try and outflank Caen's defenses. The unit was ambushed by a Tiger tank company at Villers-Bocage and lost twenty-four tanks, nine halftracks, and a smattering of smaller vehicles in just five minutes. The next attempt, Operation Epsom on 25 June, was also halted. Finally, on 8 July Operation Charnwood allowed Montgomery to take the northern half of Caen following a massive carpet-bombing that heavily disrupted the German line. Despite the gains, enough Germans survived and regrouped that the British were again stalled.[29] The crux of this futile effort by Montgomery was the disastrous Operation Goodwood, launched on 18 July 1944. Involving Montgomery's entire 21st Army Group and opening with another massive carpet-bombing campaign, the operation still failed to break through the line. The involvement of the 16th FD (L) merits some additional examination, though.

Caen was considered the foundation of the German defense of Normandy, and the Germans expected another British assault toward the city, given that half of it was already in Allied hands. The Germans constructed four separate defense lines in a position ten miles in depth. The 16th FD (L) was stationed just east of Caen, with heavy artillery and Flak support as well. Since it first deployed, the division had been steadily taking losses; during Operation Charnwood on 7 July German lines were pummeled by more than 460 British bombers, dealing losses to the 16th right before they were hit by the British 3rd Armored Division. The division was steadily driven backward over the next two days. Finally, the arrival of reinforcements in the form of a company of assault guns as well as a grenadier regiment from the 21st Panzer Division helped to stabilize the line. The rest of the 21st Panzer and elements of the 1st SS Panzer Division "*Leibstandarte Adolf Hitler*" were placed behind the lines of the 16th and its neighbor, the 272nd Infantry Division. It is also apparent from both pre- and post-operational intelligence reports that the British recognized the 16th as a low-value unit. The commander of the 16th, General Kurt Sievers, believed that his unit would be at the center of the next Allied offensive.[30]

Rommel attempted to bolster the position of the 16th with a defense in depth. There were multiple belts of defenses east of the Orne River and

Caen itself, with the 272nd Infantry and 16th FD (L) forming the first line. Heavy flak and artillery support was behind the line to help reinforce the position, and Rommel managed to get 2,400 men to replenish the ranks of the 16th. This was welcomed at the front line after the heavy losses suffered in early July. The forward-most elements of the German line amounted to a small infantry screen, with the main line of resistance two hundred yards behind them. Behind the infantry lay the antitank and reserves followed by the artillery, Flak, and finally the panzers of the 1st SS and 21st Panzer Divisions.[31]

This resistance amounted to almost nothing when the Allied bombardment began on 18 July 1944. The German positions around Caen were carpeted with 100,000 artillery shells and 7,800 tons of aerial bombs dropped from 2,200 bombers. The 21st Panzer Division's remaining tanks were buried where they sat. The 16th FD (L) was bombed almost into nothingness. All of its battalion and regimental commanders were out of action, either killed or wounded. After the bombardment and resulting British advance, the 16th fell apart almost immediately.[32] The division was effectively destroyed during the fighting; OKW listed the division as simply "lost" from 23–25 July.[33] The division was formally dissolved in early August, with the few remnants sent to both the 21st Panzer Division and the new 16th *Volksgrenadier* Division.[34]

The 16th FD (L) was a static division, lacking motor transport and armed with inferior equipment. The division had seen no action prior to the 6 June 1944 landings, but once it was deployed to combat on 1 July, it was destroyed in less than a month. The division was always a second-rate formation, even after the army takeover of 1 November 1943. The 16th was also put up against some of the best units the Allies had to offer and in mid-July faced some of the most withering bombardments of the entire war. It was a clear example of the poor quality of both static divisions as well as the average Luftwaffe field division.

The 17th and 18th FD (L)s Enter the Fray

Despite the destruction of the 16th FD (L), Operation Goodwood was a failure. However, just two weeks later, the Americans finally scored a breakout victory with the great success of Operation Cobra in August 1944. As the Allies began their drive out of Normandy in northern France, they launched an additional invasion of southern France, code-named Operation Dragoon, on 15 August 1944. Facing the U.S. Seventh Army in the landing area was the German Nineteenth Army, a force with an on-paper strength of three corps, but thanks to troops being pulled north to aid in the Normandy defense, the entire army now only contained seven divisions. Two of those units pulled northward were the 17th and 18th FD (L)s, both of which were sent to the Dunkirk-Calais region. When Dragoon hit the beach, the rest of Nineteenth Army and Army Group G consisted mainly of *Ost* battalions and reserve-quality troops. The army group retreated just two days after the landings on 15 August.[35]

The Luftwaffe divisions possessed a grand total of just seventy-one artillery pieces when the invasion came, and neither unit was called to the front line until mid-August. The 17th FD (L) finally reached the front line on 19 August. It immediately was placed under LXXXI Corps, just west of Paris, and made responsible for holding the corps' left flank. Its commander, General Hans Höcker, noted that while his division was composed of "good troops," they still fell apart quickly in combat.[36] Just two days later on 21 August Allied divisions punched through the 17th and the neighboring 344th Infantry Division. Within a week of fighting, the division was so badly mauled that the decision was made to disband the unit. The order formally came down on 22 September 1944, with the division's remnants mostly placed under the 167th *Volksgrenadier* Division.[37] General Höcker himself was actually transferred to command the same unit. Despite its origin as a unit of thrown-together recruits and Luftwaffe remnants, Höcker offered a simple yet telling analysis of his new unit: "nicht schlect" (not bad). Though a not insignificant percentage of his new command was the leftovers of his last one, Höcker's opinion is heavily based on the fact that this was an army division, following army standards, rather than a former Luftwaffe formation.[38] This is further evidence that German army officers assigned to the Luftwaffe field divisions continued to hold on to the mental stigma of the Luftwaffe divisions' disastrous first year of action. It certainly appears that at least some of these officers continued to retain a degree of their disdain for their own units even as they were actively ordered to retrain the units to fall more under army standards. Such an arrangement cannot have been helpful in preparing the Luftwaffe divisions for further action in 1944.

The 18th FD (L) was not even ordered to the front line until 14 August, when it was sent to reinforce the routing German Seventh Army coming out of Normandy. The division took eight days to move on foot from Calais to the town of Mantes, on the Seine just west of Paris. The unit was told to launch a counterattack to try and slow down the advance of the American Third Army under Gen. George S. Patton. The 18th committed one regiment and its fusilier battalion, but this failed to slow the incoming American units and resulted in heavy German casualties. The 18th launched a second regiment into the fray on 27 August to allow the first group of attackers to retreat; ultimately, the battalions that saw combat lost half their strength.[39]

The German command situation had changed dramatically since 6 June, with Rundstedt replaced by Field Marshal Günther von Kluge. His command did not last long; he committed suicide on 19 August in the wake of the Normandy breakout, the encirclement of the Falaise pocket on 19 August, and his implication in the failed 20 July 1944 plot to assassinate Hitler. Field Marshal Walter Model replaced Kluge and was thus responsible for stitching the shredded elements of OB-West back together. Model might best be described as "Hitler's fireman," always the commander put in place when everything fell apart. On the Eastern Front, he had defended the Rzhev salient, saving the overwhelmed 2nd LwFD in the process. He had also propped up Army Group South following the dismissal of Erich von Manstein, as well as perhaps his crowning achievement, leading Army Group Center following the catastrophic Soviet summer 1944 offensive and launching a perfectly timed counterattack in front of Warsaw just weeks before being moved to the Western Front. However, in the West, Model was working with basically nothing; three of his remaining panzer divisions could call on just ten tanks between them at this point. To make matters worse, the Allies launched a full offensive on 26 August that involved all four of their field armies.[40]

Retreating from Mantes, the 18th fell back toward Rouen. The unit was unable to withdraw as a cohesive division, so General Tresckow split the formation into two combat groups. The 18th also took over a regiment from the nearly destroyed 17th FD (L) that was retreating in the same direction. While much of the retreat went well, on 30 August an American armored division caught one of the three groups and scattered most it. The unit was nearly wiped out; what was not destroyed by the American armor was hit by follow-up air attacks by Allied fighter-bombers (in German, *Jäger-bomber* or *Jabos*).[41]

By 1 September the unit began moving toward Cambrai but was quickly surrounded the following day along the Amiens-Cambrai-Mons road by the U.S. First Army. The 18th was not alone; it and five other German divisions were now trapped in the so-called Mons pocket. By 4 September 24,000 Germans surrendered. Tresckow was able to lead a few hundred men out of the pocket, breaking his tiny force into several groups of forty men each. He was wounded on the trek, but his tiny unit managed to reach German lines in Belgium on 18 September, completing a two-week journey of over 150 miles. The 18th was effectively destroyed between Mantes and Mons. Tresckow was awarded the Knight's Cross and was made a corps commander in the fall of 1944, but the few remnants of his Luftwaffe field division were assigned to the 18th *Volksgrenadier* Division.[42]

The 17th and 18th FD (L)s were both commissioned as static divisions, third-rate units that were not designed for any action beyond holding a position against an enemy. They performed as such; even with the reforms of the army takeover, both divisions were destroyed in under a month of combat, with the 17th ground to powder in just one week and the 18th only lasting two. Their fates, along with the rapid demise of the 16th FD (L), show the near-futility of deploying static units en masse in France and forcing them to go up against elite Allied units that were much better equipped and trained and were mobile.

The 19th and 20th FD (L)s Hold the Line in Italy

The 19th and 20th FD (L)s were deployed to action in early June 1944. Both units were attached initially to Fourteenth Army, although by this time the front line was in doubt. Though the Allies had invaded Italy in early 1943, the Germans were able to hold up the Allied advance quite easily since the terrain heavily favored the defender, and the Germans had several separate defense lines set up across the narrow width of the Italian boot. The strongest, the Gustav line, ran just south of Rome. The German Tenth Army had held firm against the Allies since the winter of 1943. The unit cohesion within the German army was still quite strong despite the host of manpower and personnel issues growing within the force. Tenth and Fourteenth Armies were both examples of this. Tenth Army along the Gustav line contained three divisions that had been mostly destroyed in Stalingrad in February 1943, and much of the German manpower in Italy contained reserve-quality units as well as ethnic Germans from occupied territories whose ability could be questionable. Much of Tenth Army was understrength as well. The Germans and the Allies both had a new obstacle to overcome: the mountainous terrain. Neither side was very experienced in mountain warfare, but the Germans were not holding a line so much as a series of fortified points.[43]

To try and break the stalemate, the Allies began 1944 with the launch of Operation Shingle and an amphibious assault on the beaches of Anzio, a position behind the Gustav line. If the Allies broke through here, they could collapse the entire German defensive position. The Germans managed to quickly react, and Anzio became instead its own pocket, trapped by a new Fourteenth Army, quickly scraped together under General Eberhard von Mackensen.[44] The Germans stopped the Allies cold but could not dislodge them from the beach. Still, at the time, the Germans were holding firm and had reason to be pleased.[45]

The Allied solution for the Anzio and Gustav line problems was Operation Diadem, planned between February and April and launched on 11 May 1944. The offensive finally shattered the Gustav line, broke the Anzio beachhead, and captured Rome itself on 4 June.[46] Still, the fighting continued, and it was right around this time when the 19th and 20th FD (L)s reached the front to reinforce Fourteenth Army. Neither of the two units was in exceptional shape. The entire divisional artillery complement of the 19th FD (L) consisted of captured enemy pieces: twenty-four Russian 76-mm guns, twelve Russian 122-mm howitzers, and four Polish 105-mm howitzers. As of 1 June the division listed a complement of about 9,400 men.[47]

Meanwhile, the 20th FD (L) mustered just four infantry battalions in size. As part of the reclassification to *Sturm-Division*, Hitler had ordered the 20th to be turned into a more mobile unit. The best the army could do was to equip six of the ten infantry companies with bicycles and to motorize the artillery and antitank complements. The division, along with the 19th, was sent to Italy in early June 1944.[48] While it might have been more mobile, the 20th FD (L) on paper certainly still looked weak, especially in manpower.

The two Luftwaffe divisions were assigned to the XIV *Panzerkorps*, under the command of General Fridolin von Senger und Etterlein, which was under Fourteenth Army's control. Senger und Etterlein did not have a very high opinion of these two units, noting that they had been "constituted from redundant air force personnel and had retained this appellation although they had been incorporated into the army. Lacking fighting experience, they were not battle worthy."[49]

Field Marshal Albert Kesselring was in overall command of the German defense of Italy, and following the fall of Rome, he had moved his forces about ninety miles north to a new defensive position centered on Lake Trasimeno. The 20th FD (L) reached the town of Grosetto on 12 June and immediately faced an American onslaught. The division was steadily driven back, suffering heavy casualties, and the rest of Fourteenth Army retreated as well.[50] Following the retreat from the Lake Trasimeno line, the Germans next fell back to a position along the Arno River, centered between the cities of Pisa and Florence. The two Luftwaffe units were stationed on Fourteenth Army's right flank near the town of Piombino. The two units faced American divisions approaching from the south. The U.S. 36th Infantry ("Texas") Division began its advance on 21 June 1944, moving up Highway One toward Piombino, eventually meeting the 19th FD (L). The 19th was unable to put up much resistance; within three days it began falling back, conducting a fairly strong series of rearguard actions. Down the line to the east, the 20th FD (L) teamed up with several other units to resist the advance of U.S. and French forces around Siena, but it too soon had to retreat. The two Luftwaffe divisions rallied around Piombino, at least temporarily holding the line as of late June 1944.[51]

On 25 June the U.S. 36th Division was withdrawn from the area to prepare for the upcoming Operation Dragoon and the invasion of southern France. Its replacement was the 34th Infantry Division. Combined with the U.S. 1st Armored Division, the two American units launched their next attack on 3 July, the brunt of which was pointed directly at the 19th FD (L). Though the Luftwaffe units were getting some reinforcements in the form of the 65th Infantry and 26th Panzer Divisions, they were too slow in arriving. The 19th FD (L) was immediately forced to fall back to the village of Rosignano-Solvay, which it fiercely defended for the following week.[52]

The Americans were constantly hit by German artillery and mortar fire over the next several days as the two sides battled for Rosignano-Solvay. The 19th acquitted itself fairly well in combat, launching several bloody counterthrusts against the Americans that collapsed with heavy casualties. Finally on 10 July, the 19th FD (L) was forced to retreat from Rosignano-Solvay. The 20th FD (L), which had been fighting on the 19th's left flank, fell back as well, along with the 65th and 26th Panzer Divisions. The right flank of Fourteenth Army was battered, so much so that the Germans could not mount any sort of defense of the important port city of Livorno just to the north. The 19th FD (L) laid down booby traps, mines, and other surprises to try and slow the American advance, and the Germans destroyed the port facilities in Livorno. The Germans were able to stabilize their line just to the north of Livorno by 19 July 1944.[53]

Despite the stabilization of the front, the 19th FD (L) had taken severe losses. The division had gone into Italy with more than nine thousand men, but after six weeks in Italy the formation had fought itself out. Before July was over, OKW decided to disband the 19th FD (L). The unit officially was out of service by 15 August 1944, its remnants mostly added to the 20th FD (L). Additional parts of the unit were moved north to Denmark to form the core of the newly forming 19th *Volksgrenadier* Division.[54] The 19th FD (L) originally had been formed as a static division, but after its incorporation into the army and move to Italy, it had generally acquitted itself quite well. This is an indication that the army takeover of the division had possibly improved the effectiveness of the 19th in combat, although since the unit had not seen action prior to its service in Italy, this is obviously difficult to fully prove.

The 20th FD (L) had fared a little better than the 19th in the Allied assault beginning on 21 June 1944. The division was stationed around the town of Siena and was paired with the German I *Fallschirmjägerkorps*. The

20th's neighbors included several other elite formations, including the 26th Panzer, 29th *Panzergrenadier*, 4th *Fallschirmjäger*, and 356th Grenadier divisions. The army and Luftwaffe troops were able to hold up the assault of two French-African colonial divisions from General Alphonse Juin's French Expeditionary Corps from 22 to 26 June, limiting the French to only a two-mile advance. Despite the Germans holding against the French, the U.S. 1st Armored Division was able to outflank the German position, enabling the French to break through and forcing another German retreat. The 20th FD (L) took heavy losses in these actions and was ordered relieved following the fighting; however, even as late as 30 June, the unit was still on the line. The remnants of the unit were paired with elements of the 3rd *Panzergrenadier* Division under an ad hoc *Kampfgruppe* Crisolli, named for General Wilhelm Crisolli, the commander of the 20th FD (L).[55] The fact that the Luftwaffe division commander was named to command the *Kampfgruppe* is a statement of the trust placed in General Crisolli. Though the division had not seen action before June 1944 and was not trusted by the average German army officer, the 20th was regarded highly enough after the last three weeks of fighting that its commanding officer was put in charge of what was technically a better-quality unit.

Kampfgruppe Crisoli took part in defending alongside the 19th FD (L) around Piombino during the Allied assault of 3 July 1944. Following the retreat north, the Germans took up position along what became known as the Gothic line, just north of Livorno. This line would become the final German defensive position in Italy; the Germans would hold these positions until April 1945. The 20th FD (L) suffered severe losses but gained some needed replacements in the form of the remnants of the now-dissolved 19th FD (L). *Kampfgruppe* Crisolli was moved behind the line as a reserve unit and spent the next several months battling Italian partisans behind the line. This area was a virtual no-man's land, where German patrols and vehicles were subject to constant partisan attacks. This spread to the *Kampfgruppe* as well when on 12 September 1944 the partisans assassinated General Crisolli himself. Crisolli's operations officer, Colonel Kaspar Völcker, took charge of the unit.[56]

A few days later, the 20th FD (L) was deployed to the Adriatic coast, going into action against the British Eighth Army. The unit was not deployed as a single unit, however; two regiments were attached to the 26th Panzer Division west of Ravenna, while the rest of the unit was divided between the 29th and 90th *Panzergrenadier* divisions south of Bologna. The division suffered heavy losses through October and November, and by 8 December 1944 the decision was made to disband the unit. The elements of the units were scattered across several army formations, in particular the 26th Panzer Division but also a few smaller units.[57] The 20th FD (L) can be described as an average, at best, Luftwaffe field division. The army tried hard to improve the unit's quality; this is evident from its redesignation as a *Sturm-Division*, the increased mobility of the unit, and the infusion of army officers and personnel after November 1943. Given the division's performance against good-quality Allied units, the Luftwaffe formation performed reasonably well in the meantime.

However, the performance of almost every German unit in Italy was at least reasonable. The Allies spent half of the war trying to punch through one German defensive line after another, advancing an inch at a time over some of the best terrain a defending tactician could dream of. The Allies had double the Germans' strength but could not achieve a strategic breakthrough along the lines of the breakout from Normandy. Every battle was essentially a frontal assault, with the Allies advancing headlong at each German defense line. The Germans only needed to allocate eleven divisions to the Italian theater to delay the Allies all the way until the very last week of the war, and two of those units were the 19th and 20th FD (L)s. Their overall commander, Field Marshal Kesselring, was a Luftwaffe officer with considerable command experience, but he was tasked with fighting arguably the easiest part of the European War: defending the narrow, mountainous Italian boot from an opponent grinding its way up. Historians likely give Kesselring far more credit than he deserves, and likewise the divisions under his command are probably toted too highly for their actual worth.[58]

The Fighting Retreat of the 11th FD (L) from the Balkans

The last of the western Luftwaffe field divisions and the only one that served in combat in the western theater of Europe that survived the war was the 11th FD (L), serving in the Balkans and primarily fighting partisans in Greece for much of the war.⁵⁹ The division saw action soon after the orders came through for the army to take over the Luftwaffe divisions. Following the surrender of Italy in September 1943, the Italian units in Greece chose to stand down and surrender for the most part. However, the Italian garrisons on the various Greek islands often resisted. The commander of the garrison on Cephalonia was shot dead, along with four thousand of his men, for refusing a German demand to surrender. The British went as far as to reinforce the Italians on several occupied several islands in the Aegean Sea, including Stampalia, Levita, Calino, and Leros. Fearing that the British move might further shift Turkey into the Allied camp, the Germans organized an assault to retake the islands. The 11th FD (L) was the backbone of that force. A single company from III./Luftwaffe-Jäger-Regiment 21 quickly retook Stampalia via an aerial landing, while on 12 November 1943 three additional battalions from the 11th were deployed to Leros along with a paratrooper battalion. The battle for Leros lasted just four days, but the British were driven off the island at a cost of 1,000 casualties, plus 3,200 soldiers taken prisoner by the Germans. The Germans suffered 400 casualties of their own, though 145 of those were from a single battalion, the II./Luftwaffe-Jäger-Regiment 22. That battalion had begun the operation with only 395 men. The German garrison on Leros remained until the end of the war, but the pocket of men left on the island were of essentially no use to the German war effort.⁶⁰

The capture of Leros proved the most significant operation conducted by the 11th FD (L) during the war, though they remained in place fighting partisans for much of the rest of the conflict. Between March and August 1944, the division launched numerous anti-partisan operations, all focused in central Greece, with middling results. The anti-partisan campaign was very brutal, often resulting in atrocities and reprisals for any actions committed by the Greek resistance movement. The 11th FD (L) took part in some of these atrocities, especially following the withdrawal of its neighboring unit, the 4th SS Police Division, farther north. This extended the area of responsibility of the 11th from Attica to also include Thessaly, which was infested by guerrillas. The division quickly began losing control of the area, and within days even keeping the railroads open was becoming difficult.⁶¹

By September 1944 the Germans began their retreat from the Balkans as the Red Army began closing in from the east. On 8 September the Soviets had begun their drive toward Budapest, and all of the German forces in the Balkans now risked being cut off by the Red Army's advance. The Germans hurriedly retreated; in the case of the 11th FD (L), the move was apparently urgent enough that General Gerhard Henke, the divisional commander, even struck a deal with the guerrillas of the Greek People's Liberation Army to give the communist-wing partisan group certain heavy weapons and equipment in exchange for unmolested passage through their territory.[62] The guerrillas took the deal to prepare for the upcoming Greek civil war; as with other resistance movements across Europe, the various groups were not wholly united. The other two main Greek guerrilla groups, the National Republican Greek League and National and Social Liberation, were both anti-communist. These three groups had been fighting each other as well as the Germans since mid-1942; now with the Germans retreating from the Balkans, the way was clearing for a full-scale civil war to resume post–World War II.[63]

The 11th FD (L) rapidly retreated northward along the route of Athens-Thebes-Lamia-Larissa-Salonika-Skopje. On the way, it encountered unexpected resistance moving farther to the northwest from Salonika to Skopje. Bulgaria, up to this point an ally of the Germans, turned on them. With the Red Army invading Bulgaria on 8 September, the Bulgarian government was overthrown and the new state shifted allegiance to the Allies, declaring war on Germany just one day later. Three Bulgarian armies of some 450,000 men advanced into Yugoslavia and northern Greece. Along with the Soviets, they ultimately drove the Germans out of the Balkans and into Austria. The entry of the Bulgarians caused the 11th to pause its retreat to defend Skopje from the Bulgarian First Army from 10 September to 16 November 1944.[64]

After holding off thrusts from combined Bulgarian and Soviet units, the 11th was forced to retreat again. The Red Army had taken Belgrade on 20 October and began an offensive aimed at Budapest on 29 October. The Budapest offensive was more a series of separate thrusts rather than one continuous advance. The first two assaults, taking place from 29 October to 24 November 1944, were launched by the 2nd Ukrainian Front, under the command of Rodion Malinovsky. They gained considerable territory but failed to take Budapest itself. Still, the capture of Belgrade and pressure on Budapest further endangered the escape route of the German forces in the Balkans.⁶⁵

The 11th FD (L) was pulled farther northward out of Greece and into Yugoslavia. In late November 1944 the division was reassigned to the XXXIV Army Corps. The unit continued to move north, launching an occasional delaying or rearguard attack to cover its retreat. The most significant action seen by the unit was an offensive against the partisan forces of Marshal Josip Broz (better known as Marshal Tito) in the Papuk Mountains of Yugoslavia in early February 1945. This operation involved five other divisions and was planned to drive out the partisan threat temporarily to allow the unobstructed retreat of Second Panzer Army from Yugoslavia. In addition, the Germans hoped to capture several supply depots that were in the target area. The operation was launched on 15 February and made some decent gains, capturing some depots and temporarily driving out the partisans.⁶⁶

The 11th was transferred to Osijek on 6 March 1945 to support Operation *Frühlingserwachen* (Spring Awakening), a large German counterattack against Soviet forces in southern Hungary launched that same day. The German Sixth Army, Sixth Panzer Army, and Second Panzer Army moved against the 3rd Ukrainian Front, on the west bank of the Danube River south of Budapest. The German goal was to reach the Danube. The 11th FD (L), along with Army Group E in Yugoslavia, was to protect the flank of Second Panzer Army from the army of Tito's partisan forces to the south. This German offensive would fail, ending in a Soviet counterattack that drove the three armies back to their starting locations and ultimately resulting in the fall of Vienna on 13 April.⁶⁷

During *Frühlingserwachen* the 11th faced down the Yugoslav 16th Partisan Division at Obijek, and while holding fairly well, the unit had to retreat when the German offensive failed. The 11th was nearly trapped by Yugoslavian partisans in mid-April 1945, forcing a quick retreat to the west. Fighting in this area was brutal, and though the division escaped, it had lost a great deal of its strength. The division continued its retreat northward, eventually making it through Zagreb and into Austria in early May.

When the war ended on 8 May 1945, the 11th had reached the region of St. George in southern Austria. There it managed to surrender to British forces advancing from the west.[68]

The 11th FD (L) was one of four Luftwaffe field divisions that survived the war and in general performed well in its duties before, during, and after the army takeover of the formations in November 1943. Despite lackluster equipment, the division spent much of the war fighting partisan units in the Balkans that were similarly ill-equipped. The 11th did well fighting guerrilla formations in Greece and Yugoslavia from 1942 to 1945, though it is notable that the 11th was not assigned to support any major German offensives against Red Army forces. The only "regular" formations the 11th faced were a tiny British garrison on Leros and the Bulgarian First Army briefly in September 1944. While it was successful against the British, the Bulgarians drove the 11th and other German units in the area out of Greece altogether.

Examining the performance of the six Luftwaffe field divisions that saw combat on the Western Front, one thing is abundantly clear: the reforms of the army takeover of November 1943 did not help the performance of these specific divisions in the long run, if they did anything at all. In the case of the three divisions in France, the reforms implemented by the army were largely nullified by those units' lack of combat experience. In addition, the general situation in France also contributed to the field divisions' failure in combat. The 16th, 17th, and 18th FD (L)s were consistently thrown directly into the front line against superior Allied units and, as a result, survived a combined one month in combat. As they were static divisions, they were technically fulfilling their mission: fight first and rely on German reserves to reinforce the line, though those reserves either failed to accomplish that mission or did not exist in the first place. Static divisions were not meant to fight prolonged engagements or make strategic maneuvers, and these divisions prove the point.

The divisions in Italy fared slightly better, though the terrain of northern Italy amplified the abilities of all of the German units stationed there. Though both the 19th and 20th FD (L)s were given "elite" unit classifications, they really did not earn those titles when being run over by Allied divisions in the mountains. Likewise, the 11th FD (L) in the Balkans did very well in its mission against Greek partisans, but the one time it engaged a regular army, it was driven back along with every other German unit in Bulgaria. It is telling that the 11th was always deployed behind the line, even when the Germans were launching counterattacks against the Red Army in their area. The division, like the majority of Luftwaffe field divisions, was not trusted in actual combat. The fact that it survived the war is only really because its retreat was being covered by regular divisions as it moved northward out of the Balkans into Austria. As a whole, the field divisions of the West showed little improvement on the disastrous performance of 1942–43. The next chapter examines whether the divisions in the East fared any better.

CHAPTER SIX

LUFTWAFFE FIELD DIVISIONS IN THE EAST, 1944-45

Eastern Front Strategic Situation, Early 1944

The last chance the German army had to possibly make an impact on the Eastern Front was the offensive against Kursk in July 1943, code-named Operation Citadel.[1] With the failure of that assault, all of the momentum shifted to the Red Army for the remainder of the war. The Soviets systematically launched a series of hammer blows against German Army Groups North, Center, and South beginning in the autumn of 1943.[2] While these strikes did their part in driving the Germans back, it was a second wave of massive offensives launched in 1944 that truly broke the main line of German resistance in the east. These Soviet thrusts methodically battered each German army group in turn and ultimately drove the Germans all the way to Berlin. The surviving Luftwaffe field divisions on the Eastern Front were involved in three of the 1944 operations, two in the north and one in the center. In the north, the Leningrad-Novgorod offensive from 14 January to 1 March 1944 opened the year with the liberation of Leningrad after nearly three years besieged by the Germans, while the Baltic offensive of 14 September to 20 November 1944 sealed Army Group North into the Courland pocket, which mostly isolated the last remaining FD (L) in the east for the rest of the war. Meanwhile, in the center of the front line, the massive Operation Bagration from 22 June to 19 August 1944 that crushed Army Group Center also smashed several Luftwaffe divisions on the northern flank of the army group.

The bulk of the Luftwaffe field divisions had always been utilized on the Eastern Front, and their deployment did not change following the army takeover on 1 November 1943. At that time, seventeen of the field divisions were still active, with ten on the Eastern Front. The campaigns of 1944 largely proved catastrophic for these units. The 3rd FD (L) in the Center and the 5th FD (L) in the South were both smashed in early 1944; by summer 1944, two divisions were left in the Center, and none in the South.[3] The six divisions in the North, meanwhile, were crushed under the Soviet Leningrad-Novgorod offensive of January 1944, leaving just two in existence by summer 1944. Those six divisions assigned to Army Group North—the 1st, 9th, 10th, 12th, 13th, and 21st—had mostly seen limited action to this point in the war; however, a severe lack of antitank weapons and artillery and varying amounts of manpower left several of these units in poor shape to try and contest a major Soviet offensive.

The two FD (L)s stationed with Army Group Center as of June 1944—the 4th and 6th, as part of LIII Corps—were in even worse shape than the units with Army Group North. In early 1944 the two divisions were stationed around Vitebsk, at the border between Army Groups North and Center, covering a front line with far too few men and resources. The 4th FD (L) mustered forty-eight pieces of artillery but only four infantry battalions. It had suffered heavy losses fighting the Soviets in the fall of 1943, and the only reinforcements it had received were shattered remnants of the disbanded 3rd FD (L). Meanwhile, the 6th FD (L) was in even worse condition: constant engagements since October 1943 had bled the division down to just 436 combatants by summer 1944. Vitebsk was one of several spots the Red Army was targeting for its upcoming summer offensive, and these two field divisions, side by side in the German line, were essentially all that stood in the way.

The Red Army Unleashed

The year 1944 belonged to the Red Army. The Soviets had not only defeated the last German offensive at Kursk in July 1943 but also fully rebuilt and recovered their military from the losses suffered in 1941–42. The Soviets had developed their own doctrinal approach to warfare, usually referred to as "deep battle," generally credited to Red Army officers Mikhail Tukhachevsky and Georgii Isserson. Whereas the German army focused on rapid operational movement and swiftly surrounding and eliminating pockets of enemy resistance, the Red Army's deep battle focused on an attack in depth, launching simultaneous and sequential operations at the same target on the line. Overwhelming force would flood the enemy front line, and the Red Army would systematically smash its way through enemy positions. Given that the German army was primarily holding the front line and was down to very little in the way of strategic reserve forces, they found themselves unable to stop the hammer blows of the Soviets as the Red Army began its drive toward Germany itself.[4]

The Soviets launched no fewer than ten major offensives during the year, beginning with the Leningrad-Novgorod offensive in January and ending with operations aimed at Budapest-Belgrade and into Finland in the fall. In autumn 1943 after the end of the Kursk campaign, the Germans could field a total of about 3 million troops in the East (700,000 of them from the minor Axis nations), organized into 177 divisions (including 26 panzer divisions) and armed with 2,300 tanks, 8,000 artillery pieces, and 3,000 aircraft. The Red Army, meanwhile, amounted to 6.4 million men, 5,800 tanks, 10,100 artillery pieces, and 13,000 aircraft. The Soviets had the means and ability to concentrate heavy force at one spot to overrun the assuredly weaker German force. They also utilized deception operations to hide their targets.[5]

Beginning in December 1943 the Soviets launched a massive offensive against Army Group South in an effort to liberate the Ukraine. In a clear indication of things to come, Army Group South's 437,000 soldiers, which included 109,000 Romanian and Hungarian troops, faced down a Soviet force of no less than 2.2 million. Each of the German formations in the army group was already a shadow of its former self. While the group contained four German armies and twenty-five divisions, including fourteen panzer divisions, each of those panzer units had an average of fourteen tanks. Each of the group's eleven infantry divisions had been whittled down to a fighting strength of less than a regiment. In short, the force was insufficient to cover its 540-mile front line.[6]

German morale was not much better. A report made by Colonel Oldwig von Natzmer, the divisional operations officer of *Panzerdivision Grossdeutschland*, indicated that his men were "so apathetic that it is entirely the same to them whether they are shot by their own officers or by the Russians. Whether we can hold our current positions . . . is entirely unclear. The number of men actually in the trenches is so small that one man deployed in a rifle pit can usually not even see his neighbor."[7] Although the *Grossdeutschland* Division was considered an elite unit, one of its battalions had to cover a 1.4-mile front with just 65 men. More regular divisions, and especially a number of the Luftwaffe field divisions, were in much worse shape. Natzmer's conclusion on the situation was succinct: "Commentary superfluous."[8] It was almost a question of when, not if, these units would be shattered by the Soviets. If the German regulars and officers who so often made jokes at the expense of the Luftwaffe divisions felt this terribly about their colleagues' situation, it is not difficult to imagine how much worse the Luftwaffe troops considered their own circumstances.

The Soviets drove Army Group South out of the Ukraine entirely, freeing the Crimea in the process. The army group was battered beyond recognition, ultimately being broken up into two forces: Army Groups North Ukraine and South Ukraine. By May 1944 the southern sector had been driven back all the way to the Balkans. The offensive had a major impact on Germany's allies: Romania began sending out diplomatic feelers to make peace with the Soviet Union, the Germans had to occupy Hungary to prevent its defection, and only Bulgaria's government desperately tried to hang onto the German alliance.[9]

Leningrad-Novgorod Offensive, 14 January–1 March 1944

Early 1944 also saw major action in the northern theater. After three years of stalemate around Leningrad, the Red Army launched a multipronged offensive to finally relieve the city and shatter Army Group North. As this had been a relatively quiet theater in light of the rest of the Eastern Front, the Germans had deployed six of the remaining Luftwaffe field divisions in the area, spread out along the entire front line. The Leningrad front actually consisted of three major positions: to the west of Leningrad itself was the Oranienbaum pocket, an isolated position that had been surrounded back in 1941. The region was heavily fortified and guarded by several Red Army rifle divisions as well as the Soviet Baltic Fleet. Though under siege on land, the pocket remained open to the sea, allowing the Red Army to resupply and reinforce the position by water. In the middle of the line was Leningrad itself, mostly surrounded by German and Finnish forces, though some supplies and reinforcements were able to get through to the city over Lake Ladoga. Finally, to the east lay the main front line between Army Group North and the northernmost Soviet formations trying to relieve Leningrad.[10]

The six FD (L)s around Leningrad were widely spread out along the line. The 9th and 10th FD (L)s were stationed to the west, holding positions side by side along the Oranienbaum pocket between that area and Leningrad itself. The other four Luftwaffe divisions were spread out in positions along the main line east of Leningrad. The 12th FD (L) was toward the northern point of the line, flanked by several other regular army divisions just southwest of Lake Ladoga. Descending along the line was the 13th FD (L), positioned along the Volkhov River just north of Chudovo, the 1st FD (L) just north of Novgorod, and finally the 21st FD (L) to the south between Staraya Russa and the town of Kholm.[11] These positions had remained fairly static for most of 1943, but they were about to be severely tested.

The 9th and 10th FD (L)s at the Oranienbaum Pocket

The Red Army launched the Leningrad-Novgorod offensive on 14 January 1944. The Soviets planned an offensive featuring multiple thrusts at the German positions around Leningrad. The 2nd Shock Army, which had been quietly shipped into the Oranienbaum pocket by the Soviet Baltic Fleet, planned a breakthrough against the western edge of the pocket, aiming toward Leningrad. In its path were two Luftwaffe divisions, the 9th and 10th FD (L)s. At the same time, the Red Army's Leningrad, Volkhov, and

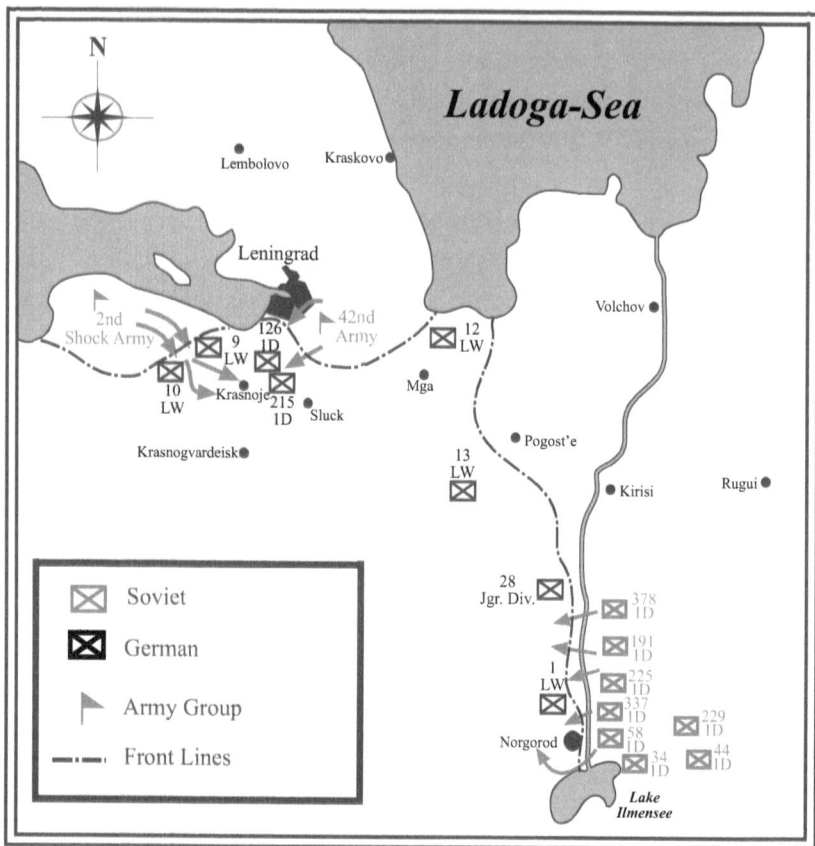

MAP 2. Soviet Northern Offensive, 14–27 June 1944. Disposition of LwFD and Soviet Attacks

2nd Baltic Fronts would launch a series of thrusts against the entire front line of Army Group North, from Kholm all the way north to Leningrad itself.[12]

Army Group North was already at a critical point. As its sector had been quiet essentially since 1941, many of the army group's best units had been transferred to the central and southern sections of the front line where fighting was heavier. Come January 1944, the army group's two armies, the Sixteenth and Eighteenth, fielded a total of about 500,000 men in 44 divisions. That number included only one panzer grenadier division and no true panzer divisions; the entire army group could only count on 146 tanks and

140 aircraft for support, alongside about 2,400 artillery pieces. The Soviet forces facing Army Group North held essentially a two-to-one advantage over their German counterparts in manpower, not to mention a several-fold edge in armor, artillery, and airpower. Along with the 2nd Shock Army in the Oranienbaum pocket, the Red Army's Leningrad and Volkhov Fronts mustered six armies facing Eighteenth Army's positions, while the 2nd Baltic Front farther south fielded five additional armies against the German Sixteenth Army. All told, the Red Army had 822,000 men supported by 550 tanks, 650 aircraft, and 4,600 artillery pieces. More than 35,000 partisans also supported the Soviets by harassing the German rear.[13]

Army Group North had lost several more divisions to Army Group Center, and all it had acquired in return was an additional sixty miles of frontage to defend. The group commander, Field Marshal Georg von Küchler, had planned to pull the army group back nearly 150 miles to consolidate his position and allow some of his units to recover their strength. Hitler instead continually refused to let the army group fall back, keeping it fixed in place and ultimately leaving it more vulnerable to the Soviets. The Red Army planned to concentrate its forces into several thrusts, turning what initially was just a two-to-one edge over the Germans into a nearly eight-to-one superiority at the points of contact. Army Group North defended nearly every village and town along the line, but it lacked the mass and heavy weapons to resist the concentrated Soviet attacks. Furthermore, the Germans had virtually no reserves available and thus no way to react to any Soviet breakthroughs on the line. The one edge the Germans possessed was a defense in relative depth; though the upcoming Soviet offensive would free Leningrad and drive back the entirety of Army Group North, the group would mostly survive the onslaught, unlike other German army groups that would face near-extinction in the other Soviet offensives of 1944.[14]

The six Luftwaffe field divisions assigned to Army Group North were a mixed bag. The 12th and 21st FD (L)s were both notably more effective as combat units than other Luftwaffe divisions. In particular, the 12th was listed as a first-tier unit for Army Group North in terms of combat effectiveness, although this also reflected the poor state of the army group as much as it was a compliment for the Luftwaffe personnel.[15] Despite having over forty divisions at the army group's disposal to cover its more than six-hundred-mile-long front line, "a number of those units were of suspicious value... such as the six Luftwaffe field divisions, mocked by the army soldiers as 'Luftwaffe failed projects.' But most of the army formations also presented a worrying situation. . . . the 16th Army had fourteen infantry battalions with a strength of less than 100 men."[16] Much of the rest of Army Group North's major formations were understrength, and it is a very telling concern that one of those six mocked Luftwaffe "failed projects" ranked in the top seven divisions in the group.

The Germans had no choice but to work with these units in the line; considering that Army Group North was essentially the reserve formation for the entire Eastern Front at this point, there was no support coming for it. This was particularly the case with the 9th and 10th FD (L)s around the Oranienbaum pocket. The III SS Panzer Corps, which actually contained only two infantry divisions, covered the western (left) flank of the pocket. Meanwhile, the two Luftwaffe units sat side by side on the eastern flank of the pocket. The Germans were nervous enough about having two Luftwaffe field divisions adjacent on the line that they placed a single SS engineer battalion from the 11th SS *Nordland* Division between the divisions to shore up the line, but a mere battalion of engineers as reinforcements, SS or no, proved far too little, too late.[17]

The Red Army offensive began on 14 January. The Soviet 2nd Shock Army began its breakout attempt by blasting the German positions with a barrage of 104,000 artillery shells over just 65 minutes.[18] General I. I. Fedyuninsky, 2nd Shock Army's commander, had planned his entire offensive against the positions of the Luftwaffe divisions on the right flank of the Oranienbaum pocket. Fedyuninsky had just three brigades covering nearly twenty-six miles of the pocket utilizing false radio messages and phantom troop movements to hide this fact from the Germans. Meanwhile, he threw his other nine divisions at the point directly between the two Luftwaffe divisions, a frontage just six miles wide south of the town of Korovino.[19]

The Red Army drive out of the Oranienbaum pocket was pointed in that direction to link up with the Leningrad front's own push out of Leningrad itself. The Soviet 42nd Army moved toward the southwestern edge of the city, aiming to cut through the German 126th and 215th Infantry Divisions and link up with the 2nd Shock Army coming out of the Oranienbaum pocket. The two Soviet pushes, traveling east-west and west-east, would only have needed to advance about ten to fifteen miles to link with each other, thus breaking the siege of the Oranienbaum pocket and helping to finally end the siege of Leningrad.

The Leningrad-Novgorod offensive is one of the chief examples some historians use to insinuate that the Allies specifically targeted the FD (L)s in combat operations.[20] Similar examples noted thus far include the 2nd LwFD in the Rzhev salient during Operation Mars in 1942 or the 16th FD (L) being bombed into oblivion in Operation Goodwood in 1944. In the specific case of the breakout from Oranienbaum, the two Luftwaffe divisions not only were weak links in the German line but also fit operational Soviet planning nicely. The Soviets had excellent information about the divisions making up Army Group North, and the two field divisions were a German weak point in the perimeter around Oranienbaum that also offered the Soviets the shortest path to achieve their goals.[21]

The 9th FD (L) took the brunt of a push by five Red Army rifle divisions and one tank division pressing forward between the towns of Korovino and Jlino, driving into the Luftwaffe division's left flank. The heavy assault simply steamrolled the Luftwaffe unit, forcing it to retreat in disarray. The 9th FD (L) eventually met back-to-back with the German 126th Infantry Division, itself pushed back by Soviet forces attacking out of Leningrad. The two units were surrounded by 18 January, suffering heavy losses. The following day, most of the trapped Germans were able to escape the pocket, though the 9th FD (L) had been mauled. Between 14 January and 1 February 1944, the division suffered approximately 3,100 casualties; 315 killed, 1,196 wounded, and a startling 1,548 missing, most of whom were probably captured. In addition, the division commander, Colonel Ernst Michael, was killed in action on 22 January.[22]

The 126th Division likewise took heavy losses; the leading German unit for the breakout was the 424th Grenadier Regiment of the 126th. Of the whole regiment, only 150 men and a few antitank guns survived.[23] Though much of the 9th FD (L) escaped the pocket, it was leaderless and shattered from facing down overwhelming force. The bulk of the 9th's remnants were absorbed into the battered 126th Infantry Division to restore that unit to something resembling optimum strength. The units joined a general German retreat farther west. For all intents and purposes, the 9th FD (L) was broken within just five days of combat, which is both an indictment of the unit's quality as well as a marker for the sheer force thrown at it by the Red Army.

The 10th FD (L) was hit by the same drive that struck the 9th. The opening artillery bombardment hit the division's entire front line, splintering trees, flattening bunkers, and ripping into the Luftwaffe personnel. The Red Army artillery was joined by guns from Soviet warships based off the coast of the Oranienbaum pocket. The bombardment was followed up by a drive by nine Soviet divisions directly between the 9th and 10th FD (L). Three Red Army infantry divisions and elements of the 152nd Tank Division enveloped the 10th FD (L)'s right flank, driving into the unit's position between the towns of Jlino and Zaastrove. Zaastrove fell quickly, though small elements of the Luftwaffe division put up some resistance. These pockets of defenders were really only acting as breakwaters as the Red Army poured in around them.[24]

The situation had reached a critical point by the following day. Thanks to General Fedyuninsky's deception in the Oranienbaum pocket before the offensive began, the III SS Panzer Corps still thought it had major forces in front of it. The only reinforcements that the Germans thought they could spare were a single *Panzergrenadier* battalion, which stiffened the line for just another day. By 17 January the retreat had begun. The 10th FD (L) essentially fell apart, with the bulk of the division breaking and running. Some pockets of the unit managed to maintain cohesion; the 19th *Jäger* Regiment was surrounded but managed to break out and withdraw as a whole. Much of the division mixed in with the III SS Panzer Corps and fell back westward, eventually reaching Narva by 26 January. The remnants of the 10th FD (L) took up positions there and helped kept the Soviets from advancing farther, but the division was disbanded soon afterward in early February 1944. Most of the division was transferred to the 170th Infantry Division.[25]

The 10th FD (L) existed for about thirteen months, seeing very little serious action until January 1944. Despite the army's reforms after the transfer in November 1943, the unit still collapsed after just three days of combat, with losses severe enough that German high command chose to dissolve the division rather than try to rebuild it. Comparing its performance in

January 1944 to that of its immediate neighbor, the 9th FD (L), the latter unit faced down twice the Soviet strength, ended up being surrounded, and managed to survive long enough to break out of the pocket. The 10th, meanwhile, had the advantages of both having a body of SS troops on its flank and an open area to retreat to, yet it failed to maintain its cohesion as the Red Army pressed forward.

The FD (L)s on the Eastern Edge of the Line

As successful as it was, the 2nd Shock Army's offensive out of the Oranienbaum pocket was only one side of the Leningrad-Novgorod offensive. The rest of Army Group North was attacked at several points from Leningrad itself all the way down the line to the south of Novgorod and Lake Ilmen. Four more Luftwaffe divisions were embedded in the line near the points of these offensives: from north to south, the 12th, 13th, 1st, and 21st FD (L)s.

The 12th FD (L) has been noted as one of the best of the Luftwaffe divisions, though it faced among the lightest Soviet forces on 14 January 1944. The unit was classified as a category III formation, capable of mounting a proper defense on its own. Moreover, the division was regarded highly enough that two of its regiments were pulled from the front line to use as reserves for Army Group North, placed as two individual battle groups near the towns of Irboska and Pskov.[26] The rest of the 12th covered its line with seven batteries of artillery and at least a dozen antitank guns, much higher artillery support than the average Luftwaffe division enjoyed. The unit was positioned in the German line between Lake Ladoga and the Volkhov River, alongside four German infantry divisions.[27]

When the Red Army launched the offensive on 14 January 1944, the men of the 12th FD (L) actually held firm against the Soviet assault for nearly six days, finally being forced to make a fighting retreat on 20 January. On 24 January the division experienced a breakthrough in its front line, but divisional commander Colonel Gottfried Weber quickly organized a counterattack that sealed the line temporarily. Despite the success, two days later the division was forced to withdraw toward the town of Chudovo or risk being overrun. For his quick thinking and sound tactical choices, Colonel

Weber received his promotion to general several days later on 1 February 1944.[28] The division continued to perform well and hold its line.

The 12th FD (L) and its command formation, the XXVIII Army Corps, had faced strong Soviet pressure since 14 January, but to the south the Red Army had hit XXXVIII Army Corps much harder. The corps also included one of the reserve regiments of the 12th as well as the 1st and 13th FD (L)s, along with an SS brigade and the 28th *Jäger* Division. By 28 January the corps had been reduced to just 9,100 men in four battle groups: *Kampfgruppe Schuldt*, containing the regiment from the 12th FD (L) plus five battalions of the Latvian SS brigade and survivors of the 13th FD (L); *Kampfgruppe Speth*, with the 1st FD (L) and 28th *Jäger* Division; and *Kampfgruppen Bock* and *Pohl*, each of which amounted to only a regiment in strength. The state of the XXXVIII Corps was only worsened when *Kampfgruppe Schuldt*'s 4,500 men were transferred north to reinforce XXVIII Corps, though the 12th did get one of its regiments back from the move.[29]

The 12th FD (L) fell back to Luga, holding positions there until mid-February. By this time, after a month of heavy fighting, the 12th still mustered over 7,400 men as its fellow Luftwaffe divisions collapsed around them. The entirety of Army Group North continued to fall back until late February, with the 12th FD (L) ending up taking defensive positions around the town of Pskov, on the southern edge of Lake Peipus. The Red Army's Leningrad-Novgorod offensive stopped on 1 March 1944, having finally freed Leningrad and leaving Army Group North battered but at least still intact. The 12th FD (L) would remain at Pskov until 14 August, defending the city alongside the 8th, 126th, and 212th Infantry Divisions and blocking all Red Army assaults on the city.[30]

The 13th FD (L) did not fare as well in January 1944.[31] On 14 January the unit was stationed with XXXVIII Army Corps on the northern edge of Chudovo, covering a fifteen-mile front line with the dubious density of one antitank gun per mile.[32] The unit's commander, General Hellmuth Reymann, was an army officer, but his unit was at a serious disadvantage.[33] However, the main Soviet assault came farther to the south against Novgorod. Though initially lucky for the 13th, the Red Army quickly shattered the entire right flank of XXXVIII Corps and forced a general retreat for all of Army Group North. The Soviets then launched a major push to the north, running headlong into the 13th FD (L) and its neighboring units. General Reymann managed to keep the 13th together and conduct an orderly fighting retreat starting on 29 January, but the move cost the division heavily. By 28 January XXXVIII Corps' surviving formations had coalesced into four *Kampfgruppen*; what once was a corps now only mustered about 9,100 men. The 13th FD (L)'s survivors formed the bulk of *Kampfgruppe Schuldt*, containing elements of three units: a regiment from the 12th FD (L), the remainder of the 13th, and five battalions of a Latvian brigade, mustering a combined total of 4,500 men. Though existing records from the 13th do not designate its true strength on 28 January, a generous estimate would place the division at perhaps three thousand strong, which would indicate that the 13th lost over 60 percent of its strength in the previous two weeks of fighting.[34] By 5 February the division had fallen back to Luga.[35] The division maintained positions around Luga for two weeks until retreating again toward Pskov, reaching a position west of the city by 4 March 1944. The retreat had essentially destroyed the 13th FD (L), however, and the division was disbanded in early April. Many of the survivors were placed in the 12th FD (L) as well as several other units.[36]

As with the 9th and 10th FD (L)s, though it did not collapse and run, the 13th was simply overwhelmed after only a few weeks of fighting in what essentially was its first real battle. While it had not faced the direct assaults of the Red Army and had largely performed fairly well, the army takeover in November 1943 had ultimately weakened the unit, with only a small infusion of army officers and NCOs attempting to replace the personnel lost in the transfer. Considering its weakened state with the near-collapse of the entirety of Army Group North, it is no surprise that the heavy casualties suffered from January to April 1944 were crippling to the division.

Farther south, the 1st FD (L) had as difficult a time with the January 1944 offensive as the 9th and 10th FD (L)s had around the Oranienbaum pocket.[37] The 1st was stationed with XXXVIII Army Corps along the Volkhov River on the northern edge of Novgorod. This area received one of the strongest Soviet attacks on the morning of 14 January. The Soviet formation facing the city was the 59th Army, under General Ivan Korovnikov. He planned a multipronged attack, with one division attacking the city directly to pin down the defenders and two pincers flanking the city on both sides. Four rifle divisions crossed the frozen Lake Ilmen south of the city, while the 225th Division crossed the frozen Volkhov River and crashed headlong into the 1st FD (L) north of Novgorod. The four flanking divisions to the south went around Novgorod, cutting off most possible escape routes and hitting the 1st in the rear.[38] While some historians have posited that the 1st FD (L) was specifically targeted due to its location, it should be noted that this is the exact same plan the Red Army used to outflank and surround Stalingrad back in November 1942.[39]

The division would have had a hard enough time battling this offensive without its almost complete lack of heavy weapons and antitank guns; the division only had fifteen artillery pieces to work with. Without the heavy support, the 1st essentially relied on the natural barrier of the Volkhov River for its main defense, and that river was frozen in January 1944, exposing the division's weaknesses plainly. The unit, along with some other scattered German formations, took up positions in and around Novgorod to defend themselves but failed to notice the Soviet 225th Division moving to cut off the northern road, the last possible escape route from the city. Though the Germans broke out on 19 January, only a small number escaped the pocket. The 1st FD (L), now shattered, managed to join up with the remnants of the 28th *Jäger* Division as part of *Kampfgruppe Speth*, one of the four *Kampfgruppen* that held together the few survivors of XXXVIII Corps. By 2 February the *Kampfgruppe* only mustered 2,200 men, representing about a quarter of the remaining manpower of XXXVIII Corps. The division's records make clear that the 1st FD (L) lost the majority of its approximately 6,400 men in the week of fighting around Novgorod; the division barely mustered a battalion's worth of men by 20 January. The 1st FD (L) was officially dissolved soon after, having essentially been destroyed in the battle for Novgorod.[40]

The sixth Luftwaffe division facing down the Leningrad-Novgorod offensive was the 21st FD (L). The former Division Meindl was positioned with X Corps south of Novgorod and Lake Ilmen, between the towns of Kholm and Staraya Russa. As such, it managed to avoid the initial thrusts of the January 1944 offensive. In late January the division was redeployed farther north with the rest of X Corps when Soviet success around Novgorod temporarily opened a rift between the Eighteenth and

Sixteenth Armies and the situation required German reinforcements to be sent. The corps did well, holding the line until the whole army group began its retreat to the west on 15 February. The 21st FD (L) itself held back an assault by the full strength of the Soviet 1st Shock Army and limited the Red Army to an advance of only a few miles at a time. The Germans capitalized on the Luftwaffe division's success and reinforced the position with two batteries of assault guns, elements of the 30th Infantry Division, and the full strength of the 15th Latvian SS Division. Though the Soviets broke through at Novgorod, they were unable to succeed in trapping and destroying Army Group North's southern flank.[41] By the end of February, following a general pullback by the full army group, the 21st found itself around Pskov. Along with the 12th FD (L), the two units were the only surviving Luftwaffe divisions in the north in the aftermath of the Leningrad-Novgorod offensive.[42]

Preparations for Operation Bagration

With the success of the Leningrad-Novgorod offensive, the Soviets shifted to their next assaults. The liberation of Leningrad was only one of ten major offensives conducted by the Red Army in 1944. As the north was liberated, the Red Army also drove the German Army Group South out of the Ukraine. Starting on 26 March 1944 the Soviets launched another offensive that liberated the Crimea, capturing a large number of German and Romanian troops when Sevastopol fell on 9 May. The Germans had little time for any respite afterward, as the worst of the offensives was yet to come.[43]

Operation Bagration was the Soviet masterstroke of 1944, resulting in the largest victory by the Red Army that year and the near-destruction of Army Group Center in its entirety.[44] The Soviets outplanned, outnumbered, and outmatched the Germans in every aspect of the campaign. The standard historiography offers the narrative of the prebattle planning for Bagration revolving around Soviet *maskirovka* and their deceiving the Germans, masking their true target and causing the Germans to send their strength elsewhere. Though this certainly was the case, explaining the German misjudgment also must include the full picture of the strategic situation.

Following the battering offensives against Army Groups North and South, the Eastern Front began to look like a question mark, with Army Group Center forming the bulge around the city of Minsk. To the south, Army Group South was now divided in two: Army Groups North Ukraine under Field Marshal Walter Model and South Ukraine under General Ferdinand Schörner, and the southern theater offered the Soviets a bulge of their own into German lines, an ideal springboard for a renewed offensive.[45]

The Germans were convinced that the Soviets would renew their southern offensive; once breaking through the German lines, they could either wheel to the left, south toward the Balkans, or to the right, north toward the Baltic, and in either case they stood a chance to encircle multiple entire German armies. Without much in the way of aerial reconnaissance in the wake of a nearly destroyed Luftwaffe, the Germans essentially relied on deduction and educated guesswork to figure out Soviet intentions. Either goal, the Balkans or the Baltic, offered the chance to encircle multiple German army groups. This would affect both Army Groups North and South Ukraine in either case, leaving Army Groups Center and North vulnerable if the Soviets moved toward the Baltic and Army Groups E and F at stake if they moved toward the Balkans. The Germans tried to put themselves into Stalin's shoes in 1944. They knew how badly they had been weakened in the wake of the fighting in 1943 and early 1944. The southern offensive offered a single chance to possibly bag half the German army in the east all at once, perhaps ending the war in one swoop. It was exactly the kind of offensive the Germans themselves might have dreamt up had the situation been reversed.[46]

The German army had essentially no strategic reserves available for the Eastern Front, and their operational reserve of mobile units had steadily decreased as the offensives of 1943 and early 1944 ground down the Wehrmacht. The Germans did not have the strength left in the East to try and launch a reactionary counterattack wherever the Soviets attacked; rather, they had to guess the Soviet target correctly and face down Soviet mass with their own mass, stopping the Soviet offensive at the outset. Thus, the Germans stripped most of the army of its panzers in the east and gave nearly all of them to Army Group North Ukraine. Army Group Center in particular had but one panzer division left after the move, leaving it severely weakened in the path of the coming Soviet offensive.[47]

Confusion reigned in German intelligence operations in the spring of 1944, thanks to Soviet *maskirovka*. Rather than spotting one single Soviet concentration of mass, the Germans saw several. Nearly every German army in the east reported increased Soviet activity opposite its line, often a sign of an upcoming attack. The Germans only had the strength to face one concentrated offensive, not the half-dozen that appeared to be preparing. More problematic was the fact that in summer 1944 the Western Front featured a ground campaign for the first time since 1941 with the expectation of an Allied landing. This drew in more German resources and attention, as well as a lofty but possibly attainable goal for the war itself: the Germans might win the war by halting the Allied landing in the west, driving off the threat of an Anglo-American invasion for several months at least and allowing the transfer of thirty-five to forty-five divisions eastward to renew the offensive against the Red Army, which could result in Stalin suing for peace. While they failed on both counts, the Germans had this goal in the back of their minds as well as they shifted their forces on the map. The entire German operational reserve for the Eastern Front, a force of eighteen panzer and *Panzergrenadier* divisions, was thus deployed south to prepare for the suspected Soviet offensive, which in turn left both northern army groups especially vulnerable. Army Group Center's Third Panzer Army, which happened to be the parent formation of the 4th and 6th FD (L)s, had no tanks left after the move—just seventy-six assault guns.[48]

Examining the Red Army's side of the operation, grandiose operations such as the great Ukrainian pincer the Germans expected clearly were beyond Soviet capabilities. By 1944 the German army was in a state of near-constant decline. Every division appeared more and more emaciated, even the elite panzer and SS units. The German infantry units were even worse off; the switch to a six-battalion standard infantry division left any infantry unit vulnerable against an assault by a Soviet mobile group and with an even weaker defense against the growing strength of the Soviet air force.[49] This is key when examining the effectiveness of the remaining Luftwaffe field divisions as well. David Glantz states it plainly: the average German infantry division with a six-battalion format was "largely helpless" against a Soviet mechanized formation.[50] Regular infantry divisions, though, even at a six-battalion standard, were still stronger and better trained and equipped than the average FD (L), and this only points to how vulnerable the latter units were on the Eastern Front in 1944.

German weaknesses aside, the Red Army had its own issues. 1944 was the pinnacle of the Red Army's development, and while the force certainly recovered from the disasters of 1941–42, limitations remained. The entire Red Army had been redesigned around smaller formations to allow greater command and control over the hastily trained units; this is why the average Soviet unit was smaller than its comparable German enemies. Moreover, most of these formations were understrength; the staggering casualties, the demand to recover a devastated war economy, and the manpower needed to build specialized units left many regular front line units severely weakened, with some rifle divisions down to two thousand men or less.[51] Soviet command and control was only part of the situation, their logistics being another. The Red Army had vast numbers of men and material, but sustaining an operation on the scale of a grand pincer offensive from Ukraine to the Baltic/Balkans was not feasible even for the Red Army of 1944. While the German army might have considered itself a dashing force of maneuver, the Red Army became a sledgehammer focused on deep battle: capable of smashing through anything in its path but requiring a wind-up to strike any further.

Instead of a single grandiose, continuous campaign to trap the majority of the German army, the Soviets turned to what can be described as "consecutive operations," several offensives instead of one, smashing into different areas of the German lines one after the other. The Soviets were planning not just one offensive but four, all launching over the course of summer 1944, hitting virtually the entire front line and all four German army groups in the Soviet Union. The buildup of operational force across nearly their entire front line was clearly visible to the Germans, and every German army that reported the Soviet buildup was telling the truth. However, once those reports reached Army Group Center commander Field Marshal Ernst Busch, there they stayed. Hitler refused to acknowledge Busch's conclusions that an attack was incoming toward Army Group

Center and sneered at the field marshal's suggestion to withdraw back across the Dnepr River, which at least would have removed the front-line divisions from the opening Soviet artillery barrage. In the single case of Operation Bagration, the Soviet deception was more on the grounds of preparing everywhere at once, forcing the Germans to make a guess as to where the offensive would come. In the end, it did not matter; not only did the Germans guess incorrectly about where the summer offensive would strike, but what they truly failed to deduce was that Bagration was only the first of several offensives about to hit their entire line. Ironically, this meant that the German guess that Army Group North Ukraine was the Red Army's target was correct, but it was just one of several targets. The deployment of the German reserve to that area allowed that German force to hold the Soviets to the smallest gains of all their summer 1944 offensives, but that did nothing to help the other German forces to the north. The Germans only had the strength and reserves available to resist one offensive, not several.[52]

The two sides prior to Bagration could not have been much more different. The Soviets had lined up no fewer than four full fronts possessing 15 field armies, a grand total of 161 divisions, 1.25 million troops, 26,000 artillery pieces, 6,000 tanks, and 7,000 aircraft. The Soviets in Belorussia had massed double the tanks that the entire German army had for Operation Barbarossa on 22 June 1941, which just so happened to be the same date in 1944 that Bagration would launch, a dark twist of irony by the Soviet planners. Army Group Center, four armies and technically 850,000 strong, was realistically far weaker than that number when subtracting the wounded, the noncombat personnel, and the more than 100,000 unreliable Russian Hiwis in the German ranks. Further, the entire German Second Army was not targeted by the initial assault. Ultimately, only about 336,000 Germans faced the incoming offensive, or a quarter the strength of the Red Army attack. Thirty-eight German divisions covered a front line of 660 miles, with the laughable armored support of just 118 panzers and even fewer aircraft. One analysis of the German Ninth Army's front line on 22 June 1944 calculated just 143 German soldiers per kilometer of front, or approximately 350 men facing down each individual Soviet division of more than 6,000.

The entire German operational reserve for Army Group Center consisted of just three divisions, one of them being the 20th Panzer Division, which itself was only fifty-six tanks strong. Moreover, two days prior to the offensive, over 140,000 Russian partisans behind German lines launched a series of operations that ultimately shut down Army Group Center's supply traffic for over 24 hours.[53]

The 4th and 6th FD (L)s and Third Panzer Army at Vitebsk

The 4th and 6th FD (L)s with Third Panzer Army around Vitebsk faced just as bad of a situation. LIII Corps under General Friedrich Gollwitzer held Vitebsk itself, the city declared by Hitler as a *fester Platz* (fortress city) to be held at all costs. The two Luftwaffe field divisions were coupled with the 206th and 246th Infantry Divisions in the city, the four divisions holding a front line of about seventy miles. Neither Luftwaffe unit could call on the manpower to hold its line properly; between them, the two divisions could call on perhaps five battalions of soldiers. The IX Corps on the left and VI Corps on the right flanked the LIII Corps, with just one lone infantry division in reserve to support the entire army. The Third Panzer Army faced the heaviest Soviet artillery barrage of the entire war on 22 June: two hours of steady bombardment with more than two hundred artillery pieces lined up per kilometer. The Soviets chose to blast through the flanks around Vitebsk itself, crushing the IX and VI Corps without much resistance and surrounding the entire LIII Corps in Vitebsk. Within days, the city fell, with virtually the entire corps destroyed. The Third Panzer Army had offered all the resistance of a paper bag; it had collapsed entirely by day two of the offensive.[54]

Fighting in Vitebsk continued until 27 June. The city could not be saved, but as Hitler had declared it a *fester Platz*, he still demanded it be held to the last man, even in the face of pleading requests by General Gollwitzer, his superior General Georg-Hans Reinhardt of Third Panzer Army, and even OKW's own chief of staff, General Kurt Zeitzler. Gollwitzer wisely chose to disobey the Führer and on 26 June ordered his corps to try and break out. However, his force was on foot and could not outrun the mobile Soviet forces encircling the city; mechanized Red Army units had already driven miles behind the city. The Germans initially surprised the Soviets with the breakout attempt, but when the escapees broke and made a run for it, it turned into a slaughter. German command and control collapsed, and Gollwitzer lost contact with his entire corps. Of LIII Corps' original strength of 28,000 men, at least 10,000 went into Soviet captivity, including Gollwitzer himself. Soviet commanders reported at least five thousand German corpses in Vitebsk itself, and some German historians have reported a far larger number of those killed.[55]

The 4th and 6th FD (L)s went with the rest of LIII Corps. The corps began the battle arranged four divisions abreast in front of Vitebsk, with the two Luftwaffe units at the center of the line and flanked by the 246th Infantry Division on the left and 206th Infantry on the right. The 197th Infantry Division from VI Corps in turn was on the flank of the 206th, elements of which would also be trapped in Vitebsk with LIII Corps. On 22 June the Soviet artillery opened up on Third Panzer Army's entire front line. Realizing that a direct assault on the city itself might be problematic, the Soviets instead drove into the two German corps flanking Vitebsk, aiming to surround the city. The Soviets were just repeating the same tactics they had used against Novgorod. These flanking efforts meant that the two Luftwaffe divisions in front of the city actually were bypassed by the main thrust of the Soviet offensive. The 6th Guards and 43rd Armies from the Soviet 1st Balkan Front smashed through the German IX Corps on the left, while the 5th and 39th Armies from the 3rd Belorussian Front blasted through the German VI Corps on the right. Neither corps was able to muster much of a response, and by 24 June the Soviets had trapped the entire LIII Corps along with part of the 197th Infantry.[56] The 4th FD (L) was hit very hard by the first bombardment and quickly driven back into the city; the commander of the 6th, General Walter Peschl, very nearly suffered a nervous collapse.[57]

General Gollwitzer's decision to disobey Hitler and direct a breakout attempt from the city came two days later, but it was already too late. The 4th FD (L) never made it out of the city; a LIII Corps report issued on 26 June at 0825 hours remarked that the 4th "was surrounded in Ostrovo."[58] Gollwitzer himself issued a report soon after at 1312 hours: "4. Field Division (Luftwaffe) no longer exists." The division had been destroyed, and its commander, General Robert Pistorius, killed in action.[59] The 6th FD (L) fared no better. During the breakout attempt, the division found itself under attack from multiple sides, General Peschl was killed, and the already understrength unit began falling apart at the seams. No German relief was coming for LIII Corps, and the formation was ultimately overwhelmed and completely smashed by the surrounding Soviet units by 27 June.[60]

As for the 4th and 6th FD (L)s, both units were initially deployed understrength in 1942 and received extensive reforms from the army takeover a year later. The two units were in almost constant combat for much of their service in the east, and each unit benefited from army officers and the influx of some reinforcements over the course of November 1943 through spring of 1944. Despite this, neither division could be described as more than an average unit. The fact that the 6th especially was able to execute something resembling an orderly withdrawal and fighting retreat can be attributed to the fighting abilities of its officers and men. For a pair of units that, combined, barely mustered the fighting strength of one regular German infantry division, the two Luftwaffe formations did all they could have been asked to do in the wake of such a heavy blow inflicted by the Red Army in Operation Bagration.

Putting Things in Context

One other point demands reexamination. Several works within the historiography have suggested that the Allies, and Soviets in particular, deliberately targeted the Luftwaffe field divisions in their operations because they realized that the Luftwaffe personnel were subpar and more easily broken. In certain cases, this may be true. For instance, in the case of the breakthrough involving the 2nd LwFD in the Rzhev salient in November 1942 or the British bombardment of the 16th FD (L) prior to Operation Goodwood, the Luftwaffe units may have been specifically targeted. At Vitebsk, as they had done at Novgorod, the Soviets deliberately went around the city to surround the German defenders in a pocket, despite the fact that the 4th and 6th FD (L)s were the most forward-deployed divisions and easily represented the weakest available German units. As with the placement of the 9th, 10th, and 1st in the path of certain Soviet offensives discussed earlier, the fact that the Red Army broke through those units appears circumstantial given the refusal to directly attack the 4th and 6th FD (L)s around Vitebsk. By 1944 it did not seem to matter any longer to the Soviets which German units were in the front line. Almost every unit that faced an initial Soviet mechanized offensive was run over all the same, and it was almost standard Soviet procedure to envelop cities instead of attacking them directly. It also really did not matter to the Germans; with their reserves spent, every unit had to be in the front line now, whether they were prepared or not.

The state of the German army by summer 1944 was such that the majority of German infantry divisions crumpled in the same fashion as a Luftwaffe unit in the face of any heavy Allied offensive, whether launched by the Red Army or the other main Allied powers. Allied firepower, numerical superiority, and industrial superiority were finally at their full strength, just as the Germans were falling apart. The same German army that had redefined modern armored warfare from 1939 to 1941 was now largely a mass of infantry divisions of indifferent quality, for the most part forced to move on foot or by horse. The growing mass of front-line–deployed police units, ad hoc formations, static units, and *Volksgrenadier* divisions that slowly enveloped the Wehrmacht marked the German army's fall from grace in the summer of 1944.

The German army's deficiencies were heavily exacerbated by errors from the high command. Hitler's dual insistence on a fixed-position defense and an utter unwillingness to allow his forces to retreat left every German on the Eastern Front in a bad position. To hold the two-thousand-mile-long Eastern Front, with all of its twists and turns, every German army group was stretched to its limit. To mount a fixed-position defense against an increasingly armored and mobile Red Army capable of smashing multiple points simultaneously, the Germans had to maintain a mobile reserve to reinforce threatened sectors and keep breakthroughs from leading to the collapse of the front line. With essentially no depth, the entire German line was nigh incapable of holding back the offensives thrown at it by the Red Army.

The Red Army continued with Operation Bagration after the breakthroughs at Vitebsk and elsewhere, proceeding to essentially run over

Army Group Center, nearly destroying it completely. The Germans suffered over 450,000 casualties and the complete loss of three full armies. The Red Army took around 750,000 casualties.[61] In the aftermath, the remnants of Army Group Center were driven backward, and the Soviets took the opportunity to drive a wedge between Army Groups North and Center and to launch additional offensives to the south toward the Balkans and Romania.

The Survivors: The 12th and 21st FD (L)s and the Courland Pocket

Following the Leningrad-Novgorod offensive and Operation Bagration, only two Luftwaffe field divisions remained active on the Eastern Front: the 12th and 21st FD (L)s with the remnants of Army Group North. The two units had held on as the Soviets renewed their push against the northern sector with a series of offensives opening in early April 1944. The 12th FD (L) remained in position south of the city of Pskov alongside the 126th and 215th Infantry Divisions until the end of August; the 21st FD (L) was stationed farther south down the line next to the 19th SS Division. During this time, both divisions stopped all Soviet attempts to break through the line. The 12th in particular managed this defense despite the fact that the Soviets focused the heaviest attacks the unit itself, stationed in the center of the line, at one point throwing six full rifle divisions directly at the lone Luftwaffe formation. Though the 12th took heavy losses in these actions, it was reinforced with the remnants of the disbanded 13th FD (L), leaving it still undermanned but not in a critical position.[62]

Army Group North by July 1944 was in such bad shape that the two Luftwaffe field divisions were among its strongest remaining units. On 24 July the army group issued a report listing the fighting capability of its remaining thirty-two divisions. Only seven divisions were listed as fully combat effective, including the 12th FD (L). The 21st FD (L) and five other divisions were labeled "partially" effective, but the other nineteen divisions in the army group were noted as either exhausted or, in the case of three other units including the 19th and 20th SS Divisions, completely ineffective in combat.[63] The commander of the 12th FD (L), General Gottfried Weber, had even been awarded the Oak Leaves of the

Knight's Cross on 9 July for his excellent command of the Luftwaffe unit over the past several months.⁶⁴ This is a marked turn for discussing the Luftwaffe field divisions. The 12th and 21st FD (L)s were notably better in combat than virtually any of the other Luftwaffe units, and both divisions ended up surviving the war.

On 5 July 1944 the Soviets followed up Operation Bagration by launching two more offensives that cut Army Group North off from the remnants of Army Group Center by 31 July. The Germans counterattacked soon after, launching Operation *Doppelkopf* on 16 August. Army Group Center detached a reconstructed Third Panzer Army to launch a coordinated effort with units from Army Group North to reunite both groups. The 12th FD (L) was among the northern units that launched a counterthrust to try and regain contact with German units to the south. The German attack was further supported by naval bombardment by the German heavy cruiser *Prinz Eugen* off the coast, near the city of Riga.⁶⁵ Even though Third Panzer Army was sending three weakened panzer divisions and what was left of *Panzergrenadier* Division *Grossdeutschland* against two entire Soviet fronts, Operation *Doppelkopf* was a success, temporarily reopening an eighteen-mile-wide pathway between Army Groups North and Center by 27 August, but at a prohibitive cost to Third Panzer Army.⁶⁶

German success was short-lived. By the beginning of September 1944, Army Group North had been driven backward into the Courland area of Latvia, with the bulk of the group positioned around Riga. Germany's ally Finland left the war soon after, signing a ceasefire with the Soviet Union. On 14 September the Red Army launched its massive Baltic offensive to re-isolate and destroy Army Group North. The 2nd and 3rd Baltic Fronts attacked toward Riga, while the Leningrad Front launched a second attack on 17 September against Estonia, trying to clear out Army Group North from the entire region. The 12th FD (L) around Riga fought off no less than thirteen separate Soviet assaults in as many days, but the division, along with the entire army group, soon had to fall back lest it be destroyed.⁶⁷

General Ferdinand Schörner, commander of Army Group North, ordered a general withdrawal from Estonia. By the end of September, the Germans had left Estonia entirely, with the exception of the West Estonian Islands off the coast of Riga. It was not long before the Red Army launched an amphibious assault on the archipelago on 29 September. The 12th FD (L) was among the German forces sent to reinforce those positions, along with the 218th Infantry Division. The few ships of the Germany navy in the area also provided some naval bombardment to support the island defenders.[68] After several weeks of fighting, the 12th and the other German defenders were ordered to evacuate the islands on 23 November. The several escaping German divisions had suffered a combined 7,700 casualties; only around 4,500 men in total escaped the island. By now, the 12th FD (L) was bled white and was barely able to hold its assigned positions.[69]

The Soviet Baltic offensive continued through October, trapping Third Panzer Army at Memel and permanently severing all communications links between Army Groups North and Center. Over 200,000 men and 26 divisions were now trapped in what became known as the Courland pocket. Hitler would ultimately reclassify the trapped Army Group North as Army Group Courland, ordering it to hold out at any cost. Both the 12th and 21st FD (L) remained trapped in this position for much of the remainder of the war. They were not the only Luftwaffe troops in the pocket; more than 32,000 other Luftwaffe personnel were trapped, including a mix of antiaircraft personnel, signal troops, and a few stray fighter and bomber pilots who had long since lost their aircraft.[70]

The Red Army launched no fewer than six major offensives against the Courland position between 15 October 1944 and 4 April 1945.[71] The 12th FD (L) got a workout, facing down the third of these offensives on 21 December 1944. Two entire Soviet tank corps smashed through the positions of the 19th SS Division, but a swift counterattack that included a regiment from the 12th resolved the situation by 31 December. The Luftwaffe regimental commander, a Colonel Kretzschmar, fell during the battle but had demonstrated such excellent leadership that he was posthumously awarded the Oak Leaves and Swords of the Knight's Cross.[72] The 12th FD (L) received some reinforcements by incorporating a Latvian security battalion into its numbers, but even then, it remained quite understrength.[73]

Though surrounded on land, the Courland pocket remained open by sea, and Hitler had slowly pulled out units to reinforce German positions closer to Germany itself. On 4 March 1945 the 12th FD (L) was ordered by Hitler personally to move to Danzig.⁷⁴ By 17 March the entire unit had arrived. Divisional strength had been greatly reduced by this point: the unit mustered just 4,571 men, 443 vehicles, and 1,203 horses.⁷⁵ Still, this was in keeping with the average strength for a regular German infantry division at this point in the war, especially one that had been in combat for so long without respite. For the rest of the month, the division helped hold the Danzig pocket, though the situation quickly proved untenable. The 12th lost much of its strength and by 31 March was only a skeleton of its former self. Most of what remained of the division managed to board an evacuation ship and retreat to Schleswig-Holstein, where it stayed until the war ended on 8 May 1945.⁷⁶

The 21st FD (L)'s combat history following the Leningrad-Novgorod offensive mirrors that of the 12th, though the two divisions did not serve with each other. From April 1944 through the following summer, the 21st was positioned to the south of the city of Pskov, on a front line between the towns of Ostrov and Volki. The unit was still assigned to XXXVIII Corps and flanked by the German 32nd and 83rd Infantry Divisions in the line.⁷⁷ The 21st faced constant Red Army probing attacks over the course of the summer, but in July 1944 the Soviets tried to outflank the Pskov position by driving directly into the defenses of the Luftwaffe unit.

On the evening of 20 July 1944 Soviet divisions managed to crack the front line of the 21st FD (L), driving the division back several miles and inflicting a large number of casualties. The 21st was exhausted after nearly seven months of continuous combat; four days after the Soviet attack, the division was rated as only "partially combat effective" in a report by Army Group North.⁷⁸ By early August the division had been pushed back into Latvia, and on 5 October it played a prominent role in a rear guard action that allowed XXXVIII Corps to fall back to a defensive position inside the Courland pocket, where it would remain for the rest of the war. The division received some welcome reinforcements in the form of a Latvian SS regiment, which bolstered its greatly weakened line companies in the face of continued Red Army pressure.⁷⁹

The second of the six separate Soviet offensives against the Courland pocket came in late October 1944 at the expense of the 21st FD (L). Parts of the Luftwaffe unit actually broke, and the elements that held could not stop the Red Army. Ultimately, the division had to retreat from its positions around city of Autz. Elements of the 21st remained trapped in the city, succumbing when the Soviets took the city several days later. The Red Army upped the pressure even more with a focused attack on 1 November, hurling a mass of rifle and tank divisions at a mere seven-mile stretch of front, including a drive directly at XXXVIII Corps. The Germans were pushed back about two and a half miles but were able to halt the Soviet offensive despite being outnumbered several times over.[80]

The 21st FD (L) was in critical shape after the close of the second Courland offensive. All told, the so-called division mustered just two companies of infantry, along with a regiment of artillery, its command staff, and its sanitation and signal companies.[81] The Luftwaffe troops remained on the flank of the Latvian 19th SS Division, continually building up their defensive positions in expectation of the next Soviet attack. By now, the battle in the Courland was a sideshow for the rest of the Eastern Front. After the failure of the first attempt at breaking the pocket, every remaining Courland offensive was simply to keep the Germans pinned down. Stalin did focus on the pocket more than his generals, proclaiming as late as March 1945 that the Courland needed to be reduced. The Red Army kept a bare minimum of strength, two fronts containing six armies, around the pocket to prevent a German breakout and continually suppress the trapped defenders. Most of the Courland attacks after the first lacked the strength to truly break through the German lines in the pocket.[82]

That said, the Soviets still made the attempt. Another strong push was launched on 22 December 1944, hoping to catch the Germans unawares around Christmas. This included an attack straight into the 21st FD (L). As diminished as the unit was, the fact that it managed to hold at first is remarkable, although the efforts of the neighboring 19th SS Division to prevent a Soviet breakthrough must be acknowledged as well. Between the two divisions, the German forces were able to destroy eighty-seven enemy tanks and inflict disproportionate casualties on the attackers. Despite the success, they ultimately had to fall back. In early January, what remained of the 21st FD (L) retreated to positions in front of the town of Tuckum on the coast of the Gulf of Riga.[83]

Though the Soviets launched three more assaults against the Courland pocket over the next four months, the 21st FD (L) managed to participate and maintain its resolve until the very end. One officer deserves mention: Captain Heinz Schwoppe, who assumed charge of the divisional replacement battalion in December 1944. At the time, the battalion numbered just eighty men, though it would receive sporadic reinforcements as the battle progressed. The unit became the divisional reserve formation, plugging whatever gaps opened in the front line, and became especially involved in heavy fighting around the town of Doblen in March 1945. One village in the battalion's sector fell to the Red Army eleven separate times; each time, Schwoppe's men retook it. Schwoppe himself was wounded on 26 March and was evacuated from the front line. In the field hospital, Sixteenth Army commander General Friedrich-Jobst von Kirchensittenbach awarded Schwoppe the Knight's Cross for the leadership he provided his battalion.[84] Captain Schwoppe's hard fighting in the face of an essentially hopeless situation casts a good light on the rest of his unit. Long since reduced to regiment strength or even less, the 21st FD (L) continued to fight on.

On 8 May 1945 the 21st FD (L) surrendered with the rest of Army Group Courland. The battles of the Courland pocket inflicted approximately 120,000 German and 160,000 Soviet casualties over the period of 9 October 1944 to 8 May 1945. About 189,000 Germans ultimately surrendered in the pocket, including 28 generals and over 5,000 officers. Of the German total, the 21st mustered just five hundred men on the day the war ended.[85]

Evaluating the 12th and 21st FD (L)s

Examining the 12th and 21st FD (L)s over the last nine months of the war yields an interesting picture. The 12th FD (L) was certainly an atypical Luftwaffe field division. It survived some of the harshest fighting of the Eastern Front and performed well every step of the way. Existing historiography frustratingly offers no explanation for why this division did well and so many of its fellow units did not, though some answers can be gleaned from the unit itself. When it was created, the formation was stronger than many of its fellow field divisions and possessed a much stronger battery of artillery support than the average Luftwaffe unit. It largely avoided major action in the first year of deployment, remaining in essentially the same spot for most of 1943, and this likely allowed the unit to train a bit more than the divisions that were simply thrown into action immediately. In the wake of the army takeover of the Luftwaffe divisions, the 12th also was one of the few divisions to come out ahead in terms of its manpower and equipment. All these factors caused the Germans to rate the 12th FD (L) as one of the better units in Army Group North preceding the Leningrad-Novgorod offensive on 14 January 1944. Once it finally faced real combat, the division fought as well as, if not better than, many of its neighboring regular army units. The 12th received reinforcements several times, keeping it at something resembling fighting strength, and it lasted until the last month of the war before finally succumbing to heavy Soviet pressure.

Likewise, the 21st FD (L) remained doggedly resistant to every attempt to destroy it. Unlike the 12th, however, there is a clear reason why this division outperformed so many of the other Luftwaffe field divisions. Having initially begun as Division Meindl, the first real Luftwaffe division, the unit had received its initial training from experienced paratroopers. This was in stark contrast to its successors, which had been trained by largely clueless Luftwaffe personnel, and this difference showed in the 21st's operational successes in the months preceding the creation of the LwFDs in September 1942. The unit also possessed a far greater artillery component than any other Luftwaffe division. In short, this was the one Luftwaffe field division that received proper training and something resembling proper equipment before its deployment. The 21st also came through the army takeover of the LwFDs in good shape, unlike many of the other Luftwaffe units attached to Army Group North. It maintained its position around Staraya Russa from its initial deployment in summer 1942 all the way to the Leningrad-Novgorod offensive in January 1944. Even as it was driven into its final positions in the Courland pocket afterward, the 21st maintained fierce resistance the entire way, ultimately being one of just four Luftwaffe divisions to survive the war.

Most of the Luftwaffe field divisions were assigned to the Eastern Front, and eight of them still existed at the start of the major Soviet offensives beginning in early 1944. Despite the army reforms of November 1943, all but two of these divisions were utterly crushed within days of being hit by a Soviet offensive. The 4th and 6th FD (L)s evaporated in the fall of Vitebsk during Operation Bagration, while the 1st and 10th collapsed in the face of Red Army thrusts in the Leningrad-Novgorod offensive. The 9th and 13th FD (L)s survived their initial encounters, but breaking free of the front line and conducting fighting retreats to the west cost each unit heavily enough that they were ultimately dissolved by German high command and their remnants given to other units. None of these units showed really any improvement after the army took over control of the Luftwaffe divisions in 1943.

The 12th and 21st FD (L)s hold the distinction of being not just two of the four Luftwaffe field divisions to survive the war but also by far the two most combat-effective divisions out of all twenty-one that deployed. Both divisions held on until the end of war, putting up significant resistance the entire way, and even when they were down to skeleton strength they stayed intact. Their success compared to their fellow Luftwaffe divisions can be attributed to several key points: better initial training, better equipment, and better leadership overall. The 21st FD (L) in particular was perhaps the only Luftwaffe field division to receive an effective amount of training and equipment before being deployed, and its status as the largest overall FD (L) in terms of manpower allowed it to succeed where many other divisions failed. Both the 12th and 21st FD (L)s also benefited from better unit leadership and unit cohesion than almost every other Luftwaffe formation. While a large number of other FD (L)s simply collapsed in the face of enemy assaults, both the 12th and 21st had the training and strength to perform well beyond the reputation of the rest of the Luftwaffe field divisions.

CONCLUSION

When examining the circumstances that led to the creation and deployment of the Luftwaffe field divisions in September 1942, it is tempting to accept German Field Marshal Erich von Manstein's description of the situation: "sheer lunacy."[1] The first of the units were deployed with a severe lack of training and equipment, and they were often far smaller in organizational size than regular German infantry divisions. Given their resulting poor combat record, Manstein's opinion seems correct, but it still needs to be put into proper context.

The Luftwaffe field divisions were created for three primary reasons. First, the German manpower crisis in the winter of 1941–42 required an infusion of reinforcements to the Eastern Front. While the army wished for Luftwaffe soldiers to be simply reassigned to formations that were part of the regular *Heer*, the army instead received Luftwaffe ground units as support, thanks to the second impetus for the LwFDs: the internal atmosphere within the German high command and the tension caused by the growing Nazi influence upon the regular German military. Hitler's chief crony Hermann Goering offered a solution to the army's manpower problem: twenty-two divisions' worth of "good National Socialists" that Goering wanted kept under his command whom he promised would be not only loyal to Hitler, but also an effective force in combat. This was yet another example of Hitler undermining the authority of the army and the German general staff and creating a military that only answered to him and his wishes rather than to any traditional chains of command or military doctrines.

The final origin for the LwFDs was that there were plenty of Luftwaffe-controlled units fighting on the ground already even before the winter crisis of 1941–42. By the end of the war, the Luftwaffe fielded between sixty and seventy divisions of troops. By August 1944 the Luftwaffe mustered 2.8 million personnel. Given that it was by that time drastically weakened in the air, this only further shows the enormous size of the Luftwaffe's ground complement, even in the wake of the transfer of troops to the army in 1942.[2] The German paratroop units, Flak divisions, and even the Hermann Goering Parachute Panzer Corps have been nearly universally accepted as effective forces by historians. Even the more improvisational Luftwaffe ground units deployed prior to the LwFDs saw success in combat.[3] Ultimately, these smaller units' success set a precedent for future units to be formed. Luftwaffe personnel were not an example of "scraping the bottom of the barrel"; given proper equipment and training, these men were completely capable of fighting side by side with army units.

The latter point was exactly where the Luftwaffe failed its new field divisions in September 1942. It is clear from records that about 80 percent of the original 200,000 Luftwaffe personnel that joined the LwFDs did so voluntarily, but to say that the organization and training of their new units went poorly is an understatement. Though Goering initially ordered that his new units should be assigned to "quiet" sectors to compensate for their likely weaknesses, this was not done due to a combination of army ignorance of the order, some German intelligence failures, and manpower needs at the various parts of the front line.

This first year of combat proved a disaster for the majority of the divisions. All told, the LwFDs suffered a 45 percent casualty rate between 17 September 1942 and 20 September 1943. Without question, the prevalent opinions of the ineffectiveness of the LwFDs are valid for that first year. When they saw real combat, the divisions were often scattered and cast aside. Morale in these units subsequently suffered because of their deficiencies. Despite Luftwaffe suggestions to reform the divisions, finally on 20 September 1943, Hitler ordered OKH to take control of the LwFDs and integrate them into the regular army by 1 November 1943.

The German army undertook several reforms to the LwFDs, but other issues undercut these reforms. The best that the *Heer* could manage for its lower-priority formations was to transform the majority of the FD (L)s into static divisions, such as what happened to the units in the West.[4] On paper, the results were mixed. Some divisions came out ahead, with greater strength in terms of manpower, artillery, or both. Several other units emerged in worse shape, ultimately losing manpower, artillery strength, or both. Many of the remainder did not seem to have changed much at all. Worse, the remaining Luftwaffe personnel in the field divisions were still the same men whom General Meindl had described as feeling "neither like fliers or soldiers" and acting as "sacrificial pawns" in the aftermath of their first year of deployment; there is no evidence that these troops felt any better about their chances of success in the wake of the army's reformation of their units.[5]

Those negative feelings were justified based on the combat experience of the FD (L)s after the army takeover. The three FD (L)s in France had barely seen action prior to the Allied invasion of Normandy, but each of the 16th, 17th, and 18th FD (L)s was cut to pieces quickly. After weeks of dodging Allied air attacks in a slow march from southern France to the north, the 16th FD (L) collapsed within three weeks of combat, bombed nearly into oblivion in front of Caen during Operation Goodwood. The 17th fell apart after just a week of action, and the 18th only lasted two weeks before being surrounded in the Mons pocket.[6]

The 19th and 20th FD (L)s fared a little better in Italy, thanks predominantly to the defensibility of the terrain. Even with the defensive advantage, the 19th only lasted two months in combat before being disbanded in August 1944.[7] The 20th FD (L), meanwhile, lasted until December, performing better than the 19th FD (L), though it is likely that its neighboring formations and the Italian terrain helped the Luftwaffe troops succeed.

The 11th FD (L) also performed reasonably well, but as with the FD (L)s in Italy, its success can be attributed to its environment. The majority of the division's service in the Balkans involved fighting partisans rather than enemy armies. Even the division's command felt that the 11th could not handle a fight against a major military force, as once the Red Army began encroaching on the Balkans from the east in September 1944, the 11th immediately began a retreat north. This avoidance of full-scale combat almost certainly contributed to the division surviving the war and enabling it to reach Austria and surrender to the British in May 1945.

The remaining Luftwaffe field divisions on the Eastern Front, even with army training, reinforcements, and improved equipment, proved to still be below average at best. Four of the six FD (L)s assigned to Army Group North reflect this condition, although the other two formations, the 12th and 21st FD (L)s, were the best two of the Luftwaffe units. The Red Army's Leningrad-Novgorod offensive shattered Army Group North's positions and drove the Germans hundreds of miles back to the west. The 9th and 10th FD (L)s collapsed within the first week of the offensive, while the 1st and 13th FD (L)s only lasted three weeks in the face of the Soviet drive against Novgorod. A similar fate befell the 4th and 6th FD (L)s assigned to Army Group Center, which were outmaneuvered and destroyed outright when the Red Army retook Vitebsk at the start of Operation Bagration in June 1944.[8]

A total of four Luftwaffe field divisions survived the war out of twenty-one deployed. As for the overall performance of these units in combat, only the 12th and 21st could actually be called effective. Both divisions held on until the end of the war, putting up significant resistance the entire way, and they stayed intact even when they were down to skeleton strength. Their success compared to their fellow Luftwaffe divisions can be attributed to better initial training, better equipment, and better overall leadership. While a large number of other FD (L)s simply collapsed in the face of enemy assaults, both the 12th and 21st had the training and strength to perform well beyond the reputation of the rest of the Luftwaffe field divisions. A few other field divisions, namely the 5th and perhaps the 11th and 20th, held up longer than their fellow Luftwaffe units, but their overall performance can be labeled as acceptable at best.

Aside from these five good or acceptable units, every other Luftwaffe field division deployed in World War II proved subpar. The regular *Heer* never considered these units any better than their original incarnations. Given that nearly all of the remaining divisions collapsed within weeks of seeing real action again, whether in the Soviet offensives of January and June 1944 or the fighting in Normandy, this opinion was justifiable. The only FD (L) that survived World War II at full strength was the 14th, and that was only because it was stationed in Norway and never saw action. Seventeen of the other twenty FD (L)s were destroyed by the war, and the other three survivors were barely battalion-sized when they surrendered in May 1945.

Goering's order of 17 September 1942 specifically called for "volunteers," stating that "he who voluntarily joins this corps must do it with a strong heart and without hesitation. However, he can expect special considerations for courageous service, including promotion and decoration." Goering's order also notified the Luftwaffe personnel office to direct these men to him so that he could personally approve them for the new divisions. While the majority of the recruits for the divisions were in fact volunteers, Goering and the Luftwaffe utterly failed to prepare them properly for the war they were now doomed to fight.

A pair of letters sent to the wife of one fallen Luftwaffe soldier paint two very different pictures of the mindset of the men in the units. The first, from a company commander *Leutnant* Siegel, alerted a Frau Westphal of the death of her husband, *Oberfeldwebel* Wilhelm Westphal. It strikes a rather plain, administrative tone: "With a heavy heart, I as company commander have to convey the painful news to you that your dear husband ... Wilhelm Westphal ... died 23.4.1943 in the tough defensive battles at the Kuban bridgehead."[9] The second letter, from Westphal's fellow *Feldwebel* Schröter, is a little more descriptive but still impersonal: "He was an example for the men, had an indomitable idealism and was an optimist in every respect." Schröter vividly described when Westphal was hit by Russian mortar fire and the injuries he sustained across his right side, leg, and arm, and how Westphal's men kept him comfortable until he succumbed to his injuries.[10] There clearly was at least some form of camaraderie and unit cohesion at work within the field divisions, but the impersonal nature of both letters strikes more a propagandistic tone than one of heartfelt feelings from friends professing grief over a man's death.

The fighting quality of the German army in World War II has remained its most enduring historical image since the end of the war, but that myth has been steadily brought back down to earth in recent decades as historians have properly examined the men of the German military and the declining quality of the armed forces as the war progressed. While examples such as the *Volksgrenadier* divisions, *Volkssturm* units, and *Ost* battalions are better known, the Luftwaffe field divisions now should properly join the historiography as yet another example of the faltering German army's fighting quality. The twenty-one deployed field divisions were a sizable percentage of German strength, especially on the Eastern Front, and reflected a growing number of so-called static divisions counted within the German order of battle: units that could man a front line but that were equipped and trained for little else.

The detrimental effect of the Luftwaffe field divisions on the German strategic situation is further reinforced by the conclusion that the Allies clearly learned the weaknesses of the divisions through not just the experience of fighting the Luftwaffe units but also through intelligence gathering from interrogating German POWs. As the formations' weaknesses became better known, they were often targeted by major Allied offensives in the last years of the war. The U.S. Army had excellent intelligence on its foes, and the resulting technical manual *Handbook on German Military Forces* released by the War Department in 1943 clearly distinguishes the Luftwaffe field divisions—labeled as Air Force field divisions in the manual—as being made up of "surplus personnel," containing a wide variety of equipment, and having suffered heavy losses, with many already disbanded by the fall of 1943. Thanks to manuals such as this and other gathered information, any American soldier in Europe could know who he was fighting and how skilled they might be, and their commanders could plan offensives accordingly.[11] The targeting of the 16th FD (L) during Operation Goodwood in the summer of 1944 and also the Soviet thrust from the Oranienbaum pocket through the 9th and 10th FD (L)s earlier that year prove that Allied armies would at least sometimes target these formations as weak spots in the German line. The poor quality of these units and other less-than-effective German formations was demonstrably more apparent as the war fully turned on the Germans after 1944 and the Allies were consistently able to blast through these weak spots with superior firepower, numbers, and resources, leaving gaping holes in the German line that after 1944 were increasingly difficult for the meager reserves to close.

The failure of the Luftwaffe field divisions is far worse when one understands that the Germans were not the only army in World War II forced to turn military personnel from non-army branches into fighting soldiers on the front line, and in some cases these other units worked out fairly well when compared to the FD (L)s. The U.S. Army instituted the Army Specialized Training Program (ASTP), designed to train junior officers and NCOs in technical skills. However, by 1944 the Army became concerned that several hundred thousand men in the technical program might not be the best use of some of the country's best manpower. In March 1944 the program was drastically reduced, with over 110,000 students transferred to other duties. This included nearly 73,000 transferred to the army ground forces. While many of those who joined the infantry were used to replenish divisions kept stateside as reinforcement pools for the formations sent overseas, tens of thousands joined the war. Despite some early friction with their new comrades and officers, the ASTP troops were properly trained, had the equipment resources of the U.S. Army behind them, and proved their value on the front line.[12]

Not every army that used nonstandard personnel as soldiers had the success of the ASTP. Japan regularly forced naval and air personnel into becoming soldiers due to necessity in certain combat situations, with the February 1945 Battle of Manila being one of the best examples of this. The city was defended by close to 20,000 Japanese troops, but over 12,500 of them were naval personnel under the command of Rear Admiral Sanji Iwabuchi. He was determined to fight to the death to recover personal honor from the earlier loss of his battleship *Kirishima*. His troops were not well trained or well-equipped, but they resisted the Allied advance on Manila for a full month. The natural difficulty of urban combat likely increased the effectiveness of the Japanese resistance in the city, but the sailors became known for both their fierce fighting and the horrific massacre they perpetrated against the Filipino civilian population in Manila as the Allies closed in around them.[13]

If there is a lesson to be learned from the experience of the Luftwaffe field divisions and other irregular military formations, it can only be that if any army has to use such formations, they need the time to properly train and equip the soldiers involved. The volunteers who joined the LwFDs were high-quality recruits trained for war but not for infantry combat, and it cost them dearly as similarly untrained Luftwaffe officers tried to make their air force support personnel into a ground force. Meanwhile, the U.S. Army Specialized Training Program actually trained their own recruits. Plus, these soldiers had already spent nearly a year in college and had higher intelligence and skill than normal recruits as a result, enabling them to adapt to the new training. It also makes sense to mix non-army personnel into existing infantry formations so proper army officers and trained soldiers could help bring the new infantry up to speed and to generate comradery. The United States deployed the ASTP troops into existing army units rather than creating their own formations from scratch without army support, as Goering did with the Luftwaffe field divisions. Even introducing officers and men of the *Heer* into the field divisions in 1943 only resulted in minor upgrades to the units; such a late response could not override the original lack of training and equipment. The ASTP participants largely became excellent soldiers, while the men of the FD (L)s only considered themselves "sacrificial pawns."

It is easy to blame Goering and Hitler for the field divisions' predicament; the units were created as a reflection of Goering's vanity, and Hitler trusted the Reichsmarschall enough to let him create these formations in the face of legitimate army concerns. When Goering was proven very wrong, Hitler ignored most of the suggested reforms for the field divisions and simply handed them over to the army to figure out the mess. Though Hitler and Goering had their part in the creation of this predicament, the role of the army cannot be discounted, either. The army deployed these units where they were needed, not necessarily where it was best for them, which led to many divisions seeing heavy action without being ready for it. Further, the army's 1943 reforms of the divisions had the potential to help, but it is also clear that even with the reforms in place, many army generals, and even some of the FD (L)s' own division commanders, still maintained their low opinions of the field divisions. The stigma of that first year of deployment never went away. Even considering the few units that proved effective despite the odds, perhaps Erich von Manstein did say it best: the saga of the Luftwaffe field divisions appears to have been "sheer lunacy."

NOTES

Introduction

1. See Martin Van Creveld's *Fighting Power* (Westport, CT: Greenwood Press, 1982). See also Jörg Muth, *Command Culture* (Denton: University of North Texas Press, 2011), James S. Corum, *The Roots of Blitzkrieg* (Lawrence: University Press of Kansas, 1992), and Robert M. Citino, *The German Way of War* (Lawrence: University Press of Kansas, 2005). Citino perhaps says it the most plainly: "There are few notions in modern history more secure than that of German military excellence." See *German Way of War*, xii.
2. Joseph Vilsmaier, dir., *Stalingrad* (Senator Films, 1993). Examples of typical Western Allied film portrayals of the German army include Steven Spielberg, dir., *Saving Private Ryan* (DreamWorks, 1998) and Franklin Schaffner, dir., *Patton* (20th Century Fox, 1969); also consider the miniseries by Tom Hanks and Steven Spielberg, dirs., *Band of Brothers* (HBO Enterprises, 2001). In all three of these works, the German army is barely examined beyond a few individual perspectives, appearing simply as faceless opposition to the protagonists.
3. Wolfram Wette, *The Wehrmacht: History, Myth, Reality* (Cambridge, MA: Harvard University Press, 2006), Waitman Wade Beorn, *Marching into Darkness* (Cambridge, MA: Harvard University Press, 2014), Christopher Browning, *Ordinary Men* (New York: Harper Perennial, 1993), and Omer Bartov, *Hitler's Army* (New York: Oxford University Press, 1992).
4. Geoff Megargee, *Inside Hitler's High Command* (Lawrence: University Press of Kansas, 2000). See also Citino, *German Way of War*, as well as his *Death of the Wehrmacht* (Lawrence: University Press of Kansas,

2009) and *The Wehrmacht Retreats* (Lawrence: University Press of Kansas, 2012), and Adam Tooze, *The Wages of Destruction* (New York: Viking, 2006).

5. For modern analysis of the German panzer divisions, see Karl-Heinz Frieser, *The Blitzkrieg Legend* (Annapolis: Naval Institute Press, 2005), R. L. Dinardo, *Germany's Panzer Arm* (Mechanicsburg, PA: Stackpole, 1997), and Dennis Showalter, *Hitler's Panzers* (New York: Berkely Caliber, 2009). For information on the Luftwaffe's performance in the war, see Williamson Murray, *The Luftwaffe* (Baltimore: Nautical & Aviation Publishing Company of America, 1985) and James S. Corum, *The Luftwaffe* (Lawrence: University Press of Kansas, 1997). In addition, for a general overview that includes German weaknesses in these areas, see Richard Overy, *Why the Allies Won* (New York: W. W. Norton, 1995).

6. Many influential secondary works suggest this point, including Van Creveld, *Fighting Power*, Williamson Murray and Allan R. Millett, *A War to Be Won* (Cambridge, MA: Harvard University Press, 2000), Gerhard Weinberg, *A World at Arms* (New York: Cambridge University Press, 1994), and Showalter, *Hitler's Panzers*.

7. For the best existing work detailing the *Volkssturm*, see David Yelton, *Hitler's Volkssturm* (Lawrence: University Press of Kansas, 2002). The *Volksgrenadier* divisions have received far less scholarship; one of the best available sources is Douglas Nash, *Victory Was Beyond Their Grasp: With the 272nd Volksgrenadier Division from the Huertgen Forest to the Heart of the Reich* (Philadelphia: Casemate, 2015). Nash's work only focuses on a single unit in one area of the war; there is currently no work that offers general coverage of the *Volksgrenadier* units as a whole. Likewise, there are almost no available secondary works examining the *Ost* battalions in their entirety, though there is a brief description of these formations of conscripts in Stephen Ambrose, *D-Day* (New York: Simon & Schuster, 1995), 34.

8. Erich von Manstein, *Verlorene Siege* (Bonn: Bernard & Graefe, 2011), 298–99. See also Kevin Ruffner, *Luftwaffe Field Divisions 1941–45* (London: Osprey, 1990), 9–10.

9. Officially, twenty-two LwFDs were mobilized, but the 22nd LwFD was never fully completed, with its personnel ultimately added to the 21st.

10. The five major secondary sources that have been written about the LwFDs include: Egon Denzel, *Die Luftwaffenfelddivisionen 1942–45* (Neckargemünd: Kurt Vorwinckel Verlag, 1976), Werner Stang, "Zur Geschichte der Luftwaffenfelddivisionen der faschistischen Wehrmacht," *Zeitschrift für Militärgeschichte* 8 (1969): 196–207, Werner Haupt, *Die Luftwaffenfelddivisionen 1941–45* (Friedberg: Podzun-Pallas, 1993), Ruffner, *Luftwaffe Field Divisions*, and Antonio Muñoz, *Goering's Grenadiers: The Luftwaffe Field Divisions 1942–1945* (New York: Axis Europa Books, 2002). While these are the main books on the subject, many other secondary works make passing mention of the LwFDs throughout. A few examples include Weinberg, *A World at Arms*, David Glantz and Jonathan House, *When Titans Clashed: How the Red Army Stopped Hitler* (Lawrence: University Press of Kansas, 1995), and F. W. von Mellenthin, *Panzer Battles* (Norman: University of Oklahoma Press, 1956). The information in these blurbs is often sparse—usually just a brief explanation of what the LwFDs were and a lamentation of the foolishness behind their creation.

11. Gerhard Weinberg, "Unexplored Questions about the German Military during World War II," *Journal of Military History* 62, no. 2 (1998): 375–76.

12. The existing historiography on this subject is astonishingly sparse. Most works follow the same format, giving a basic description of the formation of the divisions and their ill-preparedness for combat, followed by a universal condemnation of Hitler, and especially Goering, for their waste of human resources in forming the divisions. A particular weakness of several of these works is their general lack of citations and a dismal bibliography. None of the previous works has explained the creation of the divisions as anything more than a grievous blunder by Goering. In addition, there is universal acceptance of the party line that Goering wanted to maintain control over his loyal National Socialist personnel rather than surrendering them to the army "still steeped in the traditions of the Kaiser." Also, there is little acknowledgment in the earlier works of the background behind the creation or training of the divisions. Some of the existing historiography has other problems beside content or how arguments are supported. For instance,

the article by Werner Stang, though it was among the first sources to describe the LwFDs, was written in East Germany during the Cold War, and the article reads as if it was tailored for a Soviet audience. The constant use of the adjective/pejorative *faschistischen* when discussing the Wehrmacht is a clear indicator of this, and the article essentially brushes aside the divisions as a wholesale mistake, rather than asking any prudent questions regarding the history of the LwFDs. Antonio Muñoz's work is absolutely worthwhile due to its high level of detail, including a large number of maps and specific information on each individual unit. Nonetheless, his book has some issues such as spelling errors (the consistent misspelling of Division Meindl as "Miendl" [*Goering's Grenadiers*, 335]), and, more grievously, unsubstantiated arguments—for instance, without providing any citations or supporting evidence, Muñoz states, "I don't believe that it was a surprise that the Soviets chose to launch their attack against this Air Force infantry division" (16).

13. Manstein, *Verlorene Siege*; Albert Kesselring, *Soldat bis zum den letzten Tag* (Schnellbach: S. Bublies, 2000); and Walter Warlimont, *Im Hauptquartier der deutschen Wehrmacht* (Frankfurt: Bernard & Graefe, 1962).

14. Included in the archival documents found at the Bundesarchiv-Militärarchiv and the U.S. National Archives are an interview with Oberst Hans Höcker, the commander of the 17th LwFD during the Allied campaigns in 1944, and several studies written for the U.S. Army by Eugen Meindl himself. See Hans Höcker, "Nachlass von Hans Höcker," Manuscript N108, Bundesarchiv-Militärarchiv, Freiburg, Germany. See also Eugen Meindl, "II. Fallsch. Korps, 6 Juli bis 24 Juli 1944," Manuscript B-401, NARA, College Park, MD, and Meindl, "2nd Paratroop Corps in Northern France, 20 July–12 September 1944," Manuscript A-923, USAHEC, Carlisle, PA.

Chapter 1. Creation of the Luftwaffe Field Divisions, Part I

1. For more on the Battle of Moscow and winter crisis of 1941–42, see David Stahel's works *Operation Typhoon: Hitler's March on Moscow* (Cambridge: Cambridge University Press, 2013), *The Battle for*

Moscow (Cambridge: Cambridge University Press, 2015), and *Retreat from Moscow* (New York: Farrar, Straus and Giroux, 2019). See also Burkhardt Müller-Hillebrand, *The Organizational Problems of the Army High Command and Their Solutions, 1938–1945* (MS #P-041f, World War II Operational Documents Collection, Combined Arms Research Library [CARL]), 10–17, and Bernhard Kroener, "Die Winterkrise 1941/42. Die Verteilung des Mangels oder Schritte zu einer rationelleren Personalbewirtschaftung," in *Das Deutsche Reich und der Zweite Weltkrieg*, vol. 5, no. 1 (Stuttgart: Deutsche Verlags-Anstalt, 1999), 871–989 (hereafter DDRZW).

2. The internal struggles within the German high command reflect several main issues: Hitler's growing influence over the German military, the influence of Nazism in the German military, Hitler's propensity to favor loyal subordinates, no matter how bungling, over any other options, and Hitler's basic distaste for and distrust of the German general staff and Prussian officer traditions in the German army. As this chapter will explain, this struggle was present in the German military's hierarchy going back to Hitler's rise to power in 1933. While it has a dramatic impact on the war as a whole that has been examined in detail in a number of well-known works such as Ben Shepherd, *Hitler's Soldiers: The German Army in the Third Reich* (New Haven: Yale University Press, 2016), Basil H. Liddell Hart, *The German Generals Talk* (New York: William Morrow, 1948), Helmut Heiber and David Glantz, *Hitler and His Generals* (New York: Enigma Books, 2003), Matthew Cooper, *The German Army* (New York: Bonanza Books, 1984), F. L. Carsten, *The Reichswehr and Politics, 1918–1933* (Oxford: Oxford University Press, 1966), and John W. Wheeler-Bennett, *The Nemesis of Power: The German Army in Politics, 1918–1945* (London: Macmillan, 1964), this situation had huge implications for the Luftwaffe field divisions' origins and history.

3. The evolution of the tactics and doctrine of the Prusso-German army into the creation of the panzer division is best shown in Citino, *German Way of War*, xiii.

4. Citino, xiv.

5. Citino, 63–103, 142–90. For more on the Prussian defeats of Austria and France in the eighteenth century, see Geoff Wawro, *The*

Austro-Prussian War (Cambridge: Cambridge University Press, 1996), and *The Franco-Prussian War* (Cambridge: Cambridge University Press, 2003). For more on the impact of the trench stalemate of World War I on the German army, see Robert M. Citino, *Quest for Decisive Victory* (Lawrence: University Press of Kansas, 2000), 143–80.

6. There are a number of fine works on the military discussions during the interwar period. For the best examples, see Williamson R. Murray and Allan R. Millett, eds., *Military Innovation in the Interwar Period* (Cambridge: Cambridge University Press, 1996), and Harold Winton and David Mets, *The Challenge of Change* (Lincoln: University of Nebraska Press, 2000). For studies focused on the Germans in particular, see also Corum, *Roots of Blitzkrieg*, as well as Citino, *German Way of War*, 191–237.

7. Citino, *Death of the Wehrmacht*, 30. Citino remarks that while the names of battle sites make it appear like a lost chapter from Herodotus, this "lends the entire affair a certain epic aura that it does not at all deserve."

8. Citino, *Death of the Wehrmacht*, 48–49.

9. The historiography of the Eastern Front of World War II contains a monumental array of manuscripts that deliver a far more detailed account of the war between Nazi Germany and the Soviet Union. For the best examples, see the following sources: Glantz and House, *When Titans Clashed*, David Glantz, *Stumbling Colossus* (Lawrence: University Press of Kansas, 1998) and *Colossus Reborn* (Lawrence: University Press of Kansas, 2005), and Robert Citino, *Death of the Wehrmacht*, *Wehrmacht Retreats*, and *Wehrmacht's Last Stand* (Lawrence: University Press of Kansas, 2017).

10. See Glantz and House, *When Titans Clashed*, 49–97, and table, 292. See also Citino, *Death of the Wehrmacht*, 34–43.

11. See the entry of 3 July 1941 in Franz Halder, *Kriegstagebuch 1939–1942*, vol. 3 (Stuttgart: W. Kohlhammer Verlag, 1964), 38–39.

12. Glantz and House, *When Titans Clashed*, 292.

13. For more on the Battle of Moscow, see Stahel, *Operation Typhoon* and *Battle for Moscow*, and Kroener, "Die Winterkrise 1941/42," 871–927.

See also Citino, *Death of the Wehrmacht*, 37–47, and Glantz and House, *When Titans Clashed*, 74–87.

14. Glantz and House, *When Titans Clashed*, 87–97; Citino, *Death of the Wehrmacht*, 46–47.
15. The best modern account of the winter crisis of 1941–42 can be found in Stahel, *Retreat from Moscow*. See also Glantz and House, *When Titans Clashed*, 97. Glantz remarks that the Germans had survived only because the Soviets "had attempted more than they could accomplish."
16. For an excellent analysis of the Soviet counteroffensive, see Ernst Klink, "Die Abwehr der Winteroffensiven der Roten Armee," in *DDRZW*, vol. 4 (Stuttgart: Deutsche Verlags-Anstalt, 1999), 600–51. See also Stahel, *Retreat from Moscow*, 232–86, and Glantz and House, *When Titans Clashed*, 87–97.
17. Soviet losses taken from Glantz and House, *When Titans Clashed*, 292. Glantz and House, 307, also provide a figure of 922,000 permanent (meaning killed or disabled) German losses between June 1941 and September 1942, the month the LwFDs would be commissioned. A figure of 1,036,000 overall German casualties between June 1941 and March 1942 is provided in Ruffner, *Luftwaffe Field Divisions*, 4.
18. For more on the impact of the failure of Operation Barbarossa on the German war effort, see David Stahel, *Operation Barbarossa and Germany's Defeat in the East* (Cambridge: Cambridge University Press, 2009). The failure of Operation Barbarossa to defeat the Soviets was one of the two great mistakes committed by Hitler in 1941—the other being the declaration of war on the United States—and the conflict in the east would tie up as much as three-quarters of the German army for the remainder of the war.
19. For more on the Soviet recovery during Barbarossa, see Alexander Hill, *The Red Army and the Second World War* (Cambridge: Cambridge University Press, 2016), 96–153. See also Glantz and House, *When Titans Clashed*, 67–68. It should be noted that Soviet armies, and formations in general, were much smaller than their German counterparts, but the

numbers still greatly favored the Red Army. A Soviet army was roughly the same size as a German corps.

20. F. L. Carsten provides an excellent account of the Reichswehr prior to Hitler's rise to power and includes extensive analysis of Seeckt's impact. See *Reichswehr and Politics*. See also Corum, *Roots of Blitzkrieg*.

21. Germany was under the heel of the Treaty of Versailles for over a decade, and the strict terms of the Reichswehr's construction did not allow for large-scale training of reserve infantry. It was not until 1937 that the Germans could wholeheartedly begin the process of large-scale training and organization of their reserve military formations. For further information, see Müller-Hillebrand, *Organizational Problems*, 1. The Russians and the other Allies, meanwhile, took the same period of time to continue bolstering their pool of reserves. See Glantz and House, *When Titans Clashed*, 67–68.

22. Müller-Hillebrand, *Organizational Problems*, 10–14. For additional discussion of these issues, see DiNardo, *Germany's Panzer Arm*, 1–40, as well as Adam Tooze's landmark work on the German economy, *Wages of Destruction*.

23. Müller-Hillebrand, *Organizational Problems*, 85–86. See also Cooper, *German Army*, 130–66.

24. For further information on some of these expedients, see Robert M. Citino, *Path to Blitzkrieg* (Mechanicsburg, PA: Stackpole, 2008), 229–30. See also Cooper, *German Army*, 130–38.

25. Müller-Hillebrand, *Organizational Problems*, 1.

26. Müller-Hillebrand, 20–25.

27. Müller-Hillebrand, 2–3.

28. Glantz and House, *When Titans Clashed*, 28.

29. Müller-Hillebrand, *Organizational Problems*, 23–27, 42–49, 54–62. See also Cooper, *German Army*, 164–66.

30. Kroener gives an excellent appraisal of the 1942 manpower crisis in "Die Winterkrise 1941/42," 871–989.

31. Müller-Hillebrand, *Organizational Problems*, 46–47.

32. Müller-Hillebrand, 45–50.

33. Ruffner, *Luftwaffe Field Divisions*, 10.

34. Philip W. Blood, "Securing Hitler's *Lebensraum*: The Luftwaffe and Białowieża Forest, 1942–1944," *Holocaust and Genocide Studies* 24, no. 2 (Fall 2010): 248. See also Corum, *Luftwaffe*, 236–38, 241–43. The Luftwaffe's ten POW camps for captured Allied airmen include Stalag Luft III, portrayed in the famous 1963 United Artists film by John Sturges, *The Great Escape*. For more information, see Alan Burgess, *The Longest Tunnel* (Annapolis: Naval Institute Press, 1990).
35. Ruffner, *Luftwaffe Field Divisions*, 3.
36. Manstein, *Verlorene Siege*, 298. For a full breakdown of the Luftwaffe involvement during Operation Barbarossa, see Horst Boog, "Die Luftwaffe," in *DDRZW*, vol. 4, 652–712.
37. Murray, *Luftwaffe*, 119–23. See also James Corum, *Wolfram von Richthofen: Master of the German Air War* (Lawrence: University Press of Kansas, 2008), 281–83, 290–303.
38. Manstein, *Verlorene Siege*, 298. Manstein's thoughts on the oversized Luftwaffe were also apparently shared by members of Goering's staff. Wolfram von Richtofen suggested to Goering in mid-December 1941 that he make spare Luftwaffe troops available for infantry combat (see David Irving, *Göring: A Biography* [New York: William Morrow, 1989], 338). This may have been a factor that led to the initial creation of the storm battalions just weeks later.
39. Murray, *Luftwaffe*, 90–91.
40. The numbers involved here can be confusing, as the existing secondary works often give differing figures. For the concrete number, see Warlimont, *Hauptquartier*, 276–77. Warlimont himself was the originator of the request and relates that the army initially had wanted 20,000 naval personnel and 100,000 Luftwaffe, but Keitel had cut those numbers in half.
41. Every one of the five works on the LwFDs tells this story in relatively this precise level of detail. For the original description, see Denzel, *Luftwaffenfelddivisionen*, 4. For the most recent example, see Muñoz, *Goering's Grenadiers*, 7–8.
42. Warlimont, *Hauptquartier*, 276.
43. Warlimont, 276–77.

44. Warlimont, 277.
45. There is a vast historiography on the relationship between Hitler and his generals, as well as the struggle within the German army over the acceptance of Nazism. Among others, see Shepherd, *Hitler's Soldiers*, Liddell Hart, *German Generals Talk*, 5–6, 81–89, Heiber and Glantz, *Hitler and His Generals*, Cooper, *German Army*, Carsten, *Reichswehr and Politics*, and Wheeler-Bennett, *Nemesis of Power*.
46. Richard Bessel, *Nazism and War* (New York: Modern Library, 2004), 35–38.
47. Wilhelm Keitel, *The Memoirs of Field-Marshal Keitel*, trans. David Irving (New York: Stein and Day, 1966), 19–23. For further discussion, see Gordon Craig, *The Politics of the Prussian Army* (Oxford: Oxford University Press, 1964), 474–79, as well as Hans Gisevius, *To the Bitter End* (New York: Da Capo Press, 1998), 133–73.
48. For one example of the resistance to Nazism, see Theodor Groppe, *SS vs Wehrmacht 1943–1945*, MS B-397, World War II Operational Documents Collection, CARL. Groppe was an early vocal opponent of the spread of Nazism over the Wehrmacht. He was loud enough that he was forced out of his position, dishonorably discharged, and eventually arrested by the SS for continuing to speak out. He spent much of the war imprisoned in a castle in northeastern Germany with other political prisoners.
49. Warlimont, *Hauptquartier*, 24–28. See also Manstein, *Verlorene Siege*, 75–78.
50. For more details on the meeting of 5 November 1937, see Harold Deutsch, *Hitler and His Generals: The Hidden Crisis* (Minneapolis: University Press of Minnesota, 1974), 59–77.
51. Harold Deutsch provides one of the best accounts of the Blomberg-Fritsch crisis in *Hitler and His Generals*. See also Craig, *Prussian Army*, 488–96; Gisevius, *To the Bitter End*, 219–65.
52. See Keitel, *Memoirs of Keitel*, 35–53; Liddell Hart, *German Generals Talk*, 6–7, 20–30.
53. Keitel, *Memoirs of Keitel*, 47–53. See also Walter Warlimont's disparaging remarks about Keitel in *Hauptquartier*, 29, 276.
54. Liddell Hart, *German Generals Talk*, 32–33.

55. Liddell Hart, 31–44, 55–57; Manstein, *Verlorene Siege*, 74–81, 303–18.
56. Quoted in Megargee, *Hitler's High Command*, xiii.
57. Manstein, *Verlorene Siege*, 67–90. Manstein offers a typically frank appraisal of how OKH was undermined and cast aside by Hitler and OKW.
58. MacGregor Knox, "1 October 1942: Adolf Hitler, Wehrmacht Officer Policy, and Social Revolution," *Historical Journal* 43, no. 3 (September 2000): 813–15.
59. Heiber and Glantz, *Hitler and His Generals*, xxxi.
60. Knox, "1 October 1942," 815.
61. Knox, 804–13.
62. This quote is from a February 1944 conversation between Hitler and Dr. Hans Frank and can be found in Heiber and Glantz, *Hitler and His Generals*, xxix.
63. Knox, "1 October 1942," 801–4, 816–21.
64. Edward Homze, *Arming the Luftwaffe* (Lincoln: University of Nebraska Press, 1976), 49–55. See also Richard Overy, "Hitler and Air Strategy," *Journal of Contemporary History* 15, no. 3 (July 1980): 406–7.
65. Overy, "Hitler and Air Strategy," 407–8.
66. Field Marshal Kesselring gives several examples of this difficulty in command in his memoirs. See *Soldat bis zum letzten Tag*, 224, 275–76.
67. Warlimont, *Hauptquartier*, 276–77. For Manstein's objections, see *Verlorene Siege*, 299.
68. Overy, "Hitler and Air Strategy," 407n7. See also Andreas Nielsen, *The German Air Force General Staff* (New York: Arno, 1959), 185.
69. Nielsen, *German Air Force General Staff*, 187–88.
70. For two of the best examples, see Manstein, *Verlorene Siege*, 299, as well as Warlimont, *Hauptquartier*, 276–77. Warlimont, as mentioned, was at the meeting where the LwFDs were proposed, and his account is cited by Werner Stang's article, the oldest of the secondary literature that actually includes citations. See Stang, "Zur Geschichte der Luftwaffenfelddivisionen," 196. Manstein, though not present at the meeting, relates the same story heard through a third party who was there—possibly Warlimont himself.

71. Liddell Hart, *German Generals Talk*, 88. See also Kesselring, *Soldat bis zum lezten Tag*, 299–300.
72. For the impact of Nazi influence upon the troops of the army, see Shepherd, *Hitler's Soldiers*, 245–301, Bartov, *Hitler's Army*, 106–78, as well as Stephen G. Fritz, *Frontsoldaten* (Lexington: University Press of Kentucky, 1995), 187–218.
73. Ruffner, *Luftwaffe Field Divisions*, 3–4. See also Manstein, *Verlorene Siege*, 311. Manstein bemoans Hitler's penchant for deploying new units instead of replacing losses in existing ones, with the consequence that older units were bled dry while the new suffered heavy losses due to inexperience.
74. Roger Manvell and Heinrich Fraenkel, *Goering: The Rise and Fall of the Notorious Nazi Leader* (New York: Skyhorse, 2011), 230. See also Richard Overy, *Goering: The Iron Man* (London: Routledge, 1984), 164–66. Overy, in particular, notes that Goering possessed "a romantic longing for military distinction."
75. Manvell and Fraenkel, *Goering*, 136.
76. Halder, *Kriegstagebuch 1939–1942*, vol. 1, 318. See also Manvell and Fraenkel, *Goering*, 242–43. For details on the operation against Dunkirk, see Corum, *Wolfram von Richthofen*, 206–8.
77. Corum, *Wolfram von Richthofen*, 254. See also Haupt, *Luftwaffenfelddivisionen*, 8–9. Karl-Heinz Frieser has argued that Halder's complaint was incorrect, and that Hitler's real purpose in holding the Wehrmacht back was not to provide Goering a chance at glory but actually another move by Hitler to assert his overall authority over the German officer corps. See Frieser, *Blitzkrieg Legend*, 305–14.
78. Overy, *Goering*, 170–74; Murray, *Luftwaffe*, 123–25.
79. Murray, *Luftwaffe*, 115–17, 146–50, 154–61; Corum, *Richthofen*, 306–11.
80. Manvell and Fraenkel, *Goering*, 168.
81. *Trial of the Major War Criminals before the International Military Tribunal* (Nuremberg, 1947), vol. 9, 441.
82. Manvell and Fraenkel, *Goering*, 269–70.
83. Manstein, *Verlorene Siege*, 298.
84. Overy, "Hitler and Air Strategy," 417. One major issue here, of course, is the lack of primary sources from Goering or Hitler.

85. Hugh Trevor-Roper, ed., *Final Entries 1945: The Diaries of Joseph Goebbels* (New York: Avon, 1979), 236 (entry of 21 March 1945).
86. Overy, "Hitler and Air Strategy," 418.

Chapter 2. Creation of the Luftwaffe Field Divisions, Part II

1. Manstein in particular notes that the personnel concentrated within the Luftwaffe field divisions were "doubtless . . . first-class soldiers," given the Luftwaffe's ability to choose its recruits. He goes on to say that had they been added to army units as planned, they would have performed well. See Manstein, *Verlorene Siege*, 299.
2. Blood, "Securing Hitler's *Lebensraum*," 248.
3. Excellent books on the activities of German paratroopers in the early days of World War II include Alan Clark, *The Fall of Crete* (London: Blond, 1962), Adam Claasen, *Hitler's Northern War* (Lawrence: University Press of Kansas, 2001), and Ian McDougall Guthrie Stewart, *The Struggle for Crete 20 May–1 June 1941: A Story of Lost Opportunity* (London: Oxford University Press, 1966).
4. Claasen, *Hitler's Northern War*, 101–2.
5. Claasen, 102.
6. Herman Amersfoort and Piet H. Kamphuis, eds., *May 1940: The Battle for the Netherlands* (Leiden: Brill, 2010), 190–97.
7. The background and planning for Operation Mercury can be found in Stewart, *Struggle for Crete*, 1–148.
8. Stewart, 149–60.
9. Stewart, 473–78.
10. Prior to joining the Luftwaffe, Meindl had served in World War I in various artillery units and was among the few officers of the Reichswehr in the interwar period. After World War II began, Meindl would join the Luftwaffe in 1940 and command a regiment on Crete. He later would command the first Luftwaffe field division, train most of the others, and later on in the war was given command of II Parachute Corps in France. Meindl was among the German officers who wrote studies, memoirs, and other documents for the U.S. Army after the war. For more of Meindl's biography, see Franz Thomas,

Die Eichenlaubträger 1940–1945 Band 2: L-Z (Osnabrück, Germany: Biblio-Verlag, 1998), 43–46.
11. Stewart, *Struggle for Crete*, 161–66.
12. Ruffner, *Luftwaffe Field Divisions*, 4–5.
13. In fact, the commanding officer of II Parachute Corps during the fighting in Normandy was General Eugen Meindl, the same man who commanded the first true Luftwaffe field division and would be in charge of training the first wave of LwFDs in autumn 1942. Meindl himself wrote the histories of the II Parachute Corps.
14. For an excellent analysis of German Flak capability during the war, see Edward B. Westermann, *Flak: German Anti-Aircraft Defenses, 1914–1945* (Lawrence: University Press of Kansas, 2005). See 119–20 for data on the debate over army-controlled Flak.
15. U.S. War Department, *German Antiaircraft Artillery* (Call Number MIS 461, World War II Operational Documents Collection, CARL), http://cgsc.contentdm.oclc.org/cdm/singleitem/collection/p4013coll8/id/2922/rec/1, 3–78.
16. "Abschlussmeldung über Flakartillerie im Bereich des Gen.d.Lw. Ob.d.H, 28 February 1942," Manuscript N529/7, BA-MA. See also Westermann, *Flak*, 121.
17. "Abschlussmeldung über Flakartillerie."
18. Westermann, *Flak*, 121.
19. Westermann, 121, 135–36.
20. War Department, *German Antiaircraft Artillery*, 2–9.
21. Westermann, *Flak*, 108.
22. Wolfgang Dierich, *Die Verbände der Luftwaffe 1935–1945: Gliederungen und Kurzchroniken—eine Dokumentation* (Stuttgart: Motorbuch, 1976), 319, 333–43.
23. The Hermann Goering Division, while quite recognizable to World War II historians, actually has not been written about much as a single topic. One extensive work that deals with the unit's history as a whole is Franz Kurowski, *The History of Fallschirm-Panzerkorps Hermann Goering: Soldiers of the Reichsmarshall* (Winnipeg: J. J. Fedorowicz, 1995).

24. Kurowski, *Soldiers of the Reichsmarshall*, 20–139.
25. Kurowski, 150–212.
26. For sources on the unit's service in Sicily, see Hellmut Bergengruen, "Der Kampf der Panzerdivision 'Hermann Goering' auf Sizilien," Manuscript T-2, U.S. Army Historical Education Center (USAHEC), Carlisle, PA. See also Paul Conrath, "Der Kampf um Sizilien," Manuscript C-087, USAHEC.
27. For the Herman Goering Division's role at Salerno, see Wilhelm Schmalz, "Der Kampf der Panzerdivision 'Hermann Goering' bei Salerno vom 9.–17.9.1943," in Siegfried Westphal et al., "Der Feldzug in Italien Apr 1943–Mai 1944," Manuscript T-Ia, USAHEC.
28. For more on Operation Axis, see Elena Agarossi, *A Nation Collapses: The Italian Surrender of September 1943* (Cambridge: Cambridge University Press, 2006). See also Citino, *Wehrmacht Retreats*, 244–49, and Horst Schreiber, "Das Ende des nordafrikanischen Feldzugs und der Krieg in Italien," in *DDRZW*, vol. 6 (Stuttgart: Deutsche Verlags-Anstalt, 1990), 1122.
29. Kurowski, *Soldiers of the Reichsmarshall*, 398–477.
30. Hans von Ahlfen, *Der Kampf um Schlesien* (Stuttgart: Motorbuch Verlag, 1998), 208–9.
31. Ruffner, *Luftwaffe Field Divisions*, 5–6.
32. Blood, "Securing Hitler's *Lebensraum*," 249–51. See also Führer Directive 46 (18 August 1942) cited in U.S. War Department, *Fuehrer Directives and Other Top Level Directives of the German Armed Forces 1942–1945*, Call Number N-16267-B, World War II Operational Documents Collection, CARL, 2013, 58.
33. Blood, "Securing Hitler's *Lebensraum*," 250.
34. Blood, 252–60. Along with the SS and *Einsatzgruppen*, some Luftwaffe units were also detailed for the purpose of rounding up Jews wherever they were found.
35. Blood, 251.
36. Ian Kershaw, *Hitler: A Biography* (New York: W. W. Norton, 2008), 714.
37. Führer Directive 46.
38. Blood, "Securing Hitler's *Lebensraum*," 251–52, 254–58, 266.

39. Blood, 253, 259–60.
40. The war diary for the Luftwaffe *Sicherungsbataillon* (LwSB) is filed under BA-MA RL 31/1, "Kriegstagebuch des Sicherungsbataillon d. Lw (18 July 1942 to 18 March 1943)," while the combat reports and additional documents are under BA-MA RL 31/3, "Anlagen zum Kriegstagebuch des Sicherungsbataillon d. Lw." The first reference to Brauchitsch's involvement is in LwSB, report of 1 August 1942, while the description of the logistics system is in LwSB, report of 6 August 1942.
41. 1st Panzer Division general orders, 18 August–10 September 1942, "Zusammenstellung von Jagdkommandos zur Bandenbekämpfung" (31 August 1942), BA-MA RH 27/1/98.
42. For Herbst's description of his authority, see LwSB, documents 54 and 55.
43. Blood, "Securing Hitler's *Lebensraum*," 256–57.
44. Blood, 257–62.
45. The war diary of the later *Jäger-Sonderkommando d. Luftwaffe* (JSKB) is filed under BA-MA RL 31/4, *Kriegstagebuch des Jäger-Sonderkommando d. Luftwaffe* (6 March 1943 to 3 August 1944), while supporting documents are under BA-MA RL 31/5, *Anlagen zum Kriegstagebuch des Jäger-Sonderkommando d. Luftwaffe*. For the final report of the JSKB, see JSKB, Oberzahlmeister Meier, "Bericht uber den Verlauf der Ereignisse beim Tross des Jägersonderkommando d. LW, 15 July–1 August 1944," 3 August 1944, BA-MA RL 31/5/127. See also Blood, "Securing Hitler's *Lebensraum*," 266.
46. Haupt, *Luftwaffenfelddivisionen*, 10–13. See also Ruffner, *Luftwaffe Field Divisions*, 5–7.
47. Ruffner, *Luftwaffe Field Divisions*, 6.
48. The siege of Kholm has been addressed by a number of secondary works, including a chapter in James Lucas, *Battle Group!* (London: Arms and Armour Press, 1993), 74–86. See also Glantz and House, *When Titans Clashed*, 91–97, as well as Werner Haupt, *Demjansk: Ein Bollwerk im Osten* (Friedburg: Podzun-Pallas Verlag, 1961), 51–55. See also the map in Glantz and House, 88, which clearly shows the Kholm and Demlansk pockets.
49. Lucas, *Battle Group!*, 77.

50. Lucas, 76. See also Glantz and House, *When Titans Clashed*, 97.
51. Lucas, 80–81.
52. Lucas, 77.
53. Muñoz, *Göring's Grenadiers*, 338–43. See also Ruffner, *Luftwaffe Field Divisions*, 7–8.
54. Lucas, *Battle Group!*, 77.
55. Lucas, 77–80.
56. Lucas, 83–85.
57. Muñoz, *Göring's Grenadiers*, 343. Muñoz does not provide a breakdown of the casualties, but it is implied that the III./FR der Lw. 1 suffered heavy losses alongside the other German units in Kholm.
58. Haupt, *Demjansk*, 3–25. See also David Glantz, "The Ghosts of Demiansk: In Memory of the Soldiers of the Soviet 1st Airborne Corps," *Journal of Military History* 56, no. 4 (October 1992): 617–20.
59. Glantz, "Ghosts of Demiansk," 618–19.
60. Few good sources exist that specifically deal with the entire battle of the Demiansk pocket, but readers can find snippets here and there. There is an excellent description of Operation *Brückenschlag* in Werner Haupt, *Army Group North: The Wehrmacht in Russia 1941–1945* (Atglen, PA: Schiffer, 1997), 123–30. For other sources on the fighting within Demiansk itself, see Glantz, "Ghosts of Demiansk," 617–50, as well as Jeff Rutherford, "Life and Death in the Demiansk Pocket: The 123rd Infantry Division in Combat and Occupation," *Central European History* 41, no. 3 (September 2008): 347–80. For both Demiansk and Kholm, see also Ernst Klink, "Die Winterkämpfe im Bereich der Heeresgruppe Nord bis zum Wiedergewinnen einer festen Stellung," in *DDRZW*, vol. 4, 632–42, as well as David Glantz, *The Battle for Leningrad 1941–1944* (Lawrence: University Press of Kansas, 2002), 183–86.
61. Glantz and House, *When Titans Clashed*, 97.
62. Glantz, "Ghosts of Demiansk," 621–22.
63. Kurochkin's orders to 1st Guards Rifle Corps and the 34th Army are quoted in Glantz, "Ghosts of Demiansk," 622.
64. Glantz, "Ghosts of Demiansk," 624–26.
65. Glantz, 626–50.
66. Haupt, *Army Group North*, 126.

67. Ruffner, *Luftwaffe Field Divisions*, 8–9. See also Muñoz, *Göring's Grenadiers*, 343–45.
68. Muñoz, *Göring's Grenadiers*, 343–45.
69. Haupt, *Army Group North*, 126.
70. The OKW dispatch is quoted in Haupt, *Luftwaffenfelddivisionen*, 16–17. See also Muñoz, *Göring's Grenadiers*, 345–46.
71. Ruffner, *Luftwaffe Field Divisions*, 8–9. See also Haupt, *Luftwaffenfelddivisionen*, 17, and Muñoz, *Göring's Grenadiers*, 346–47.
72. Muñoz, *Göring's Grenadiers*, 347.

Chapter 3. The First Year of Combat

1. The main existing secondary works on the LwFDs all acknowledge this point. However, while each of these works addresses the first year of service as obviously disastrous, they merely blame the errors on Hitler and Goering without going any further. There is little discussion of specific details regarding why the LwFDs' training was so mishandled, and also only sparing discussion of the actual performance of the divisions in combat. For specific examples see Ruffner, *Luftwaffe Field Divisions*, 9, and Muñoz, *Goering's Grenadiers*, 8.
2. A comparison of the reported armaments strength of a Luftwaffe field division and a Soviet infantry division is given in Denzel, *Luftwaffenfeldivisionen*, 18–19. The LwFD on paper at least had more manpower—though in reality the average LwFD was often smaller—but the Soviet unit outclassed it in firepower with more automatic weapons, artillery, antitank weapons, and attached vehicles compared to low numbers of each assigned to the German formation.
3. Von Manstein, *Verlorene Siege*, 298–99.
4. Examples of German memoirs that address the LwFDs include von Manstein, *Verlorene Siege*, Kesselring, *Soldat bis zum letzten Tag*, and Warlimont, *Hauptquartier*.
5. Mellenthin, *Panzer Battles*, 175–84. Mellenthin's opinion of the LwFDs mirrors just about every other German memoir that mentions the units. Perhaps the most succinct quote regarding the LwFDs is von Manstein's "sheer lunacy" quip (see Manstein, *Verlorene Siege*, 299),

but almost every German commander who wrote about the units said something similar.

6. Goering's actual order is located under "Der Reichsminister der Luftfahrt und Oberbefehlshaber der Luftwaffe/Luftwaffen-Personalamt," Nr. 64700/42, 17.9.1942, Manuscript NS 19/2730, BA-MA. Goering's order can also be seen in its entirety in Denzel, *Luftwaffenfelddivisionen*, 8. Denzel's work is unique in that he directly copies actual archival documents into the book.
7. Ruffner, *Luftwaffe Field Divisions*, 9.
8. Dierich, *Die Verbände der Luftwaffe*, 675. These deployments stand for where the divisions involved served the most time. Several of the LwFDs would continue to change location, but for the most part this can serve as a standard list. Unlike some of the more trained and equipped units in the German army, such as the panzer divisions, LwFDs tended to stay in the same section of front where they were first deployed.
9. Eugen Meindl, "II. Fallsch. Korps, 6. Juli 44 bis 24. Juli 44," Manuscript B-401, Guide to Foreign Military Studies, NARA, 20.
10. For sources detailing Meindl's combat service in Crete, see Stewart, *Struggle for Crete*. For the fighting around Yukhnov, see Otto Dessloch, "The Winter Battle of Rhzev, Vyasma, and Yukhnov, 1941–42," Manuscript D-137, Guide to Foreign Military Studies, USAHEC, 7–10. For Division Meindl and the fighting around Demiansk, see Klink, "Die Winterkämpfe," 632–42. Meindl also describes his own service in World War II in "II. Fallsch. Korps," 16–20.
11. Meindl, "II. Fallsch. Korps," 21.
12. Ruffner, *Luftwaffe Field Divisions*, 9–10.
13. Meindl, "II. Fallsch. Korps," 21.
14. Ruffner, *Luftwaffe Field Divisions*, 9. Ruffner's book contains no citations to explain where he found this anecdote.
15. Manstein's "sheer lunacy" comment is in *Verlorene Siege*, 298. Manstein further adds that he had "covered all of these aspects in detail" during a prior talk with Hitler (sometime between 20–24 October 1942) and also had sent out a memorandum drafted for Hitler's attention. Hitler had listened to Manstein's arguments "attentively enough, but insisted

that he had already given the matter his fullest consideration and must stick to his decision." Manstein's ego is obviously playing a role here, though it is an interesting observation to note given that Hitler eventually reversed his decision on 20 September 1943 after seeing the poor results of the LwFDs in combat.

16. Goering's order is discussed in Ruffner, *Luftwaffe Field Divisions*, 10.
17. Hitler and Jeschonnek's conversation can be found in Heiber and Glantz, *Hitler and His Generals*, 68–69.
18. Meindl, "II. Fallsch. Korps," 23. See also Glantz and House, *When Titans Clashed*, 132–33.
19. Müller-Hillebrand, *Organizational Problem*, 79–82.
20. Kesselring, *Soldat bis zum letzten Tag*, 224, 275–76.
21. For further examples of Soviet military deception, see David Glantz, *The Role of Intelligence in Soviet Military Strategy in World War II* (Novato, CA: Presidio Press, 1990).
22. Glantz and House, *When Titans Clashed*, 132–33.
23. Glantz and House, 133. See also Muñoz, *Goering's Grenadiers*, 23.
24. Meindl, "II. Fallsch. Korps," 23.
25. Meindl, 24–26. Meindl often remarks in this manuscript about two strategic problems the Germans suffered: a general lack of a strategic reserve and the growing separation between the high command and the front-line officers. This mirrors the larger postwar phenomenon by German officers to blame much of the problems of the war on OKW, and particularly Hitler himself.
26. A comparison of the reported armaments strength of a Luftwaffe field division and a Soviet infantry division is given in Denzel, *Luftwaffenfeldivisionen*, 19–20. The LwFD on paper had more manpower, but the Soviet unit outclassed it in firepower with more automatic weapons, artillery, antitank weapons, and attached vehicles than the low numbers of each assigned to the German formation.
27. Dierich, *Verbände der Luftwaffe*, 676.
28. Ruffner, *Luftwaffe Field Divisions*, 10–11. See also Haupt, *Luftwaffenfelddivisionen*, 20–22, and Denzel, *Luftwaffenfelddivisionen*, 5–7, 16–20.
29. See Denzel, *Luftwaffenfelddivisionen*, 16–20, and Ruffner, *Luftwaffe Field Divisions*, 16–17.

30. See Denzel, *Luftwaffenfelddivisionen*, 19–20. David Glantz also remarks that the Red Army, despite its numerical edge over the Germans, suffered its own share of manpower problems. Key units such as guard formations and armored divisions received top priority for replacements, while the regular rifle divisions were constantly understrength. Divisions numbering between seven thousand and ten thousand men in 1942 were sometimes down to fewer than two thousand by 1945. Such a drop in manpower helps to explain why a weaker Luftwaffe field division could possibly hold against several enemy units at a time. See Glantz and House, *When Titans Clashed*, 156–57.
31. See Haupt, *Luftwaffenfelddivisionen*, 39–49, 62.
32. Ruffner, *Luftwaffe Field Divisions*, 39.
33. There are some details on the 7th LwFD's overall experience at Stalingrad in the unit's "Kriegstagebuch des 7. Lw-Felddivision 27 Sept. 1942–5 Mai 1943," Manuscript RL 34/155, BA-MA, 42. See also Muñoz, *Goering's Grenadiers*, 86–94.
34. "Zur Kriegsgeschichte der 15. Luftwaffenfeld-Division und ihres Luftwaffen-Jäger-Regimentes Nr. 30," Manuscript RL 34/132, BA-MA. See also Ruffner, *Luftwaffe Field Divisions*, 12–13, and Haupt, *Luftwaffenfelddivisionen*, 44–45, 48–49, 62.
35. When contemporary Germans historians discuss the LwFDs, they often cite the 7th and 8th for their troubles. Considering the problems with their training, equipment, and especially how they fell apart in combat, they make perfect punching bags for detractors of the LwFDs. For example, see Manstein, *Verlorene Siege*, 298–99, Mellenthin, *Panzer Battles*, 176, and Ruffner, *Luftwaffe Field Divisions*, 11–13.
36. Muñoz, *Goering's Grenadiers*, 81–83.
37. Muñoz, 84–86, 91–93.
38. Muñoz, 86–88.
39. See Army Group Don, "Kriegstagebuch Abteilung 6, 24 Dez 1942—3 Jan 1943," "Tagesmeldung von 27.12.1942," and "Abteilung Ia von 27 December 1942," Microfilm Roll T-311/270–271, NARA, 523–32.
40. David Glantz and Jonathan House, *Stalingrad* (Lawrence: University Press of Kansas, 2017), 417–21.

41. One of the best descriptions of the battle around Tatsinskaya—though it fails to distinguish specific LwFDs in the engagement—can be found in Horst Scheibert, *Zwischen Don und Donez* (Neckargemünd: Kurt Vorwinckel Verlag, 1961), 50–61. Luftwaffe troops are mentioned several times in the work, but the 8th and 15th LwFDs are rarely specifically labeled as such. See also Army Group Don, "Kriegstagebuch Abteilung 6, 24 Dez 1942—3 Jan 1943," "Tagesmeldung von 29.12.1942," 661–75.
42. See the order to merge the personnel of the 7th and 8th to the 15th in Army Group Don, "Kriegstagebuch 7, 13–20 Jan 1943, Auftrag von 17.1.1943," Microfilm Roll T-311/271, NARA, 335. The order is fairly succinct: in order to "exploit their remaining strength," the LwFD personnel would merge "as soon as the situation allowed for it." See also Muñoz, *Goering's Grenadiers*, 88–90, 95–97.
43. Muñoz, 88–89. This stigmatization of the LwFDs is also quite notable in the official German history in *DDRZW*. Bernhard Kroener's section on the units basically sums up their experience as a crippling disaster, with units thrown to the front line well before they were ready, suffering severe losses. His description does not go beyond the absorption of the divisions into the regular army, casting the divisions aside in much the same manner as many contemporary Germans did in World War II.
44. Manstein's disgust with the LwFDs has been well chronicled at this point, but it is important to note that the 7th, 8th, and 15th were all under his command when they were destroyed. His comments on their performance are in *Verlorene Siege*, 348–53. In particular, he complains that the divisions were thrown into an engagement at the height of an emergency and subsequently decimated in a matter of days.
45. See Manstein, *Verlorene Siege*, 352–53, Mellenthin, *Panzer Battles*, 184, and Scheibert, *Zwischen Don und Donez*, 65–67. See also Citino, *Wehrmacht Retreats*, 63–67.
46. Ruffner, *Luftwaffe Field Divisions*, 12–13. See also Muñoz, *Goering's Grenadiers*, 25–27, and Haupt, *Luftwaffenfelddivisionen*, 44–45.
47. Scheibert, *Zwischen Don und Donez*, 66–67.
48. Muñoz, *Goering's Grenadiers*, 21.
49. Muñoz, 23.
50. Operation Mars has been labeled as "Zhukov's greatest defeat," and one of the best sources on the operation is known by that very name:

David Glantz, *Zhukov's Greatest Defeat: The Red Army's Epic Disaster in Operation Mars, 1942* (Lawrence: University Press of Kansas, 1999). See also Hill, *Red Army and the Second World War*, 347–68. The Soviets were stopped cold in the assault, with no further penetrations of the line beyond the initial strikes. The defeat resulted in nearly 335,000 Soviet casualties—nearly nine times the number suffered by the Germans. See another good description for Operation Mars as a whole in Glantz and House, *When Titans Clashed*, 136–39.

51. Glantz and House, *When Titans Clashed*, 139. Though Mars was known as Zhukov's greatest defeat, it was overshadowed by Soviet successes around Stalingrad farther south at the same time.
52. Glantz and House, 138–39. See also Muñoz, *Goering's Grenadiers*, 23–24.
53. Haupt, *Luftwaffenfelddivsionen*, 39.
54. Muñoz, *Goering's Grenadiers*, 25–27.
55. Haupt, *Luftwaffenfelddivisionen*, 40.
56. General Mahncke's personal war diary was only just published in 2012, and his are only the second memoirs of a Luftwaffe officer translated into English and published since those of Albert Kesselring in 1953. See Alfred Mahncke, *For Kaiser and Hitler*, trans. Jochen Mahncke (London: Tattered Flag, 2012). Mahncke's full unpublished war diary can also be found at the BA-MA in Freiburg, Germany. Mahncke's diary is arrogant and self-aggrandizing, very much in the realm of the postwar German officer's diary: very anti-Hitler, absolving himself of all blame (a photo caption on page 180 of the book shows him "dutifully, but reluctantly," offering the Nazi salute) and suggesting that if he had been listened to, everything would have been different. Erich von Manstein's *Verlorene Siege* is another such memoir. Antonio Muñoz in his work *Goering's Grenadiers* also heavily utilizes Mahncke in his chapter on the 15th Luftwaffe.
57. Mahncke, *For Kaiser and Hitler*, 174.
58. See "Zur Kriegsgeschichte der 15. Luftwaffenfelddivision und ihres Luftwaffen Jäger-Regimentes Nr. 30," 1–2. See also Haupt, *Luftwaffenfelddivisionen*, 62.
59. Mahncke, *For Kaiser and Hitler*, 175; Muñoz, *Goering's Grenadiers*, 223–24.

60. For the 15th LwFD's own records, the division's three-volume Kriegstagebuch is invaluable. See Manuscript RL 34/63–65, BA-MA. Along with the Kriegstagebuch itself, the Freiburg archive has an additional combat history of the one of the regiments of the 15th in Manuscript RL 34/132. See also Army Group Don, "Kriegstagebuch Abteilung 7, 13–20 Jan 1943," "Tagesmeldung von 20 Jan 1943," 6–11. See also David M. Glantz, *From the Don to the Dniepr: Soviet Offensive Operations December 1942—August 1943* (London: Frank Cass, 1991), 385–86.
61. Muñoz, *Goering's Grenadiers*, 227.
62. See "Kriegsgeschichte der 15. Luftwaffenfeldivision und ihres Luftwaffen Jäger-Regimentes Nr. 30," 3–4; Haupt, *Luftwaffenfelddivisionen*, 62.
63. Haupt, 44.
64. Muñoz, *Goering's Grenadiers*, 55–56; Wilhelm Tieke, *Der Kaukasus und das Öl*, trans. Joseph G. Welsh (Winnipeg: J. J. Fedorowicz, 2008), 345.
65. For the end of the 15th, see "Kriegsgeschichte der 15. Luftwaffenfeldivision und ihres Luftwaffen Jäger-Regimentes Nr. 30," 4–7.
66. See Meindl's report in Denzel, *Luftwaffenfelddivisionen*, 9–13. See also Ruffner, *Luftwaffe Field Divisions*, 13–14.
67. See Meindl's report in Denzel, *Luftwaffenfelddivisionen*, 11.
68. Denzel, 10–11.
69. Denzel, 11–12.
70. Denzel, 13.
71. See both Milch's and Ramcke's original reports in Denzel, *Luftwaffenfelddivisionen*, 15. See also Ruffner, *Luftwaffe Field Divisions*, 14–15.
72. See Jeschonnek's original report in Denzel, *Luftwaffenfelddivisionen*, 14.
73. Ruffner, *Luftwaffe Field Divisions*, 15.
74. Ruffner, *Luftwaffe Field Divisions*, 16. For Hitler's faltering confidence in Goering, see Manvell and Fraenkel, *Goering*, 294–326. For the actions at Nevel and Melitopol, see the previous chapter.
75. Haupt, *Luftwaffenfelddivisionen*, 26–27.
76. Haupt, *Luftwaffenfelddivisionen*, 39–42, 44–45, 62. See also Ruffner, *Luftwaffe Field Divisions*, 13–16.
77. See "Tagesbefehl von 24.10.1943," Manuscript RL 34/201, BA-MA, 2. Given the poor record of the 2nd LwFD and the fact that it was

disbanded just weeks after this message was delivered, perhaps it was a false positive, but at least the Luftwaffe commanding officer kept his orders uplifting for what few men he had left.

78. For the best example, see Kroener, "Die Luftwaffenfelddivisionen 1942/43," 833. Kroener's analysis is brief, terse, and also not completely accurate. Kroener's two-page segment in *DDRZW* offers no information that cannot be found in the major secondary works, but his real issue is how seriously hurt he makes the LwFDs out to be. The single paragraph Kroener offers on the integration of the divisions into the army indicates that only a few of the men in the LwFDs survived their initial deployment, which is not correct. Kroener basically cast aside the divisions as irrelevant after they were integrated into the army, which is similar to many German officers in the war as well as historians since.

79. Mellenthin, *Panzer Battles*, 175–84. See also Stang, "Zur Geschichte der Luftwaffenfelddivisionen," 202–7. The comments about the "excellent human material" and "best of equipment" are commonplace among the primary sources. They are also dubious, given the more recent sources that refute that claim. For an analysis of the equipment issued to an LwFD compared to that of a Soviet division, see Denzel, *Luftwaffenfelddivisionen*, 19–20. From his postwar interrogations by the Allies, Goering had notable confidence in his personnel and also states that the Luftwaffe had first pick of the recruitment pool so that the best men would be able to join the branch (see "Interrogation of Reich Marshal Hermann Goering" 1700–1900 Hours, 10 May 1945 Ritter Schule, Augsburg, 3–5).

Chapter 4. Army Takeover of the Luftwaffe Field Divisions, 1943–44

1. The Luftwaffe suggestions for the LwFDs can be found in their original form in Denzel, *Luftwaffenfelddivisionen*, 9–15. Denzel's work has the primary sources for these items directly copied into it. For a concise summary of these ideas, see also Ruffner, *Luftwaffe Field Divisions*, 13–15.

2. For the purpose of clarity: the Luftwaffe field divisions are designated LwFDs prior to November 1943, but following the army takeover they were redesignated FD (L). This book will reflect this change and use the army shorthand for the remainder of the work, though in the longhand these will still be referred to as Luftwaffe field divisions.
3. Haupt, *Luftwaffenfelddivisionen*, 30–32; Ruffner, *Luftwaffe Field Divisions*, 16–18.
4. Ruffner, *Luftwaffe Field Divisions*, 17–18. For an excellent appraisal of the disorganization and logistical failure by OKH to support the LwFDs, see also Müller-Hillebrand, *Organizational Problems*, 73–75.
5. Ruffner, *Luftwaffe Field Divisions*, 18.
6. Muñoz, *Goering's Grenadiers*, 15.
7. Ruffner, *Luftwaffe Field Divisions*, 16–17.
8. Ruffner, 17–18. Ruffner's work has a good summary of the army's changes to the units. Although both Haupt and Muñoz go into greater detail on this, the fact that the two of them divide their book covering chapters for each individual LwFD means that one must read the entire book to get the same information.
9. Ruffner, *Luftwaffe Field Divisions*, 18–20.
10. Muñoz, *Goering's Grenadiers*, 58.
11. The topic of low unit morale in the Luftwaffe field divisions comes across in several sources. General Eugen Meindl's report of 15 May 1943 (in Denzel, *Luftwaffenfelddivisionen*, 9–13) gives a very clear picture of the collapse of unit morale prior to the army reforms. For the morale of the field divisions following the army changes, several sources indicate the situation of individual units. General Joachim von Tresckow, commander of the 18th FD (L), is concerned with morale in his description of his division prior to Operation Overlord; see "18 Air Force Field Division in the Period of 6 June–24 July 44," Manuscript B-419, NARA, 8–14. Likewise, the 1st FD (L) issued a report on 20 December 1943 that indicates not only that the division's morale was low, but also that it continued to deteriorate over the course of a number of probing attacks by the Red Army. See the 1st FD (L)

Kriegstagebuch, "Anlage zum Feindnachrichtensblatt Nr. 5," Microfilm Roll T-315/86/102, NARA, 2-3. There is also a similar report from the 6th FD (L) Kriegstagebuch, "Tagesübersicht von 23.11.1943," Microfilm Roll T-315/366/635, NARA, 1-3.

12. Ruffner, *Luftwaffe Field Divisions*, 20. The *Hiwis* and *Ost* battalions require additional attention from historians, as there are few published secondary works on the subject. However, the existing works that mention these troops do offer good, albeit brief, information on them. For an introductory source on the *Hiwis* and *Ost* battalions, see Nigel Thomas, *Hitler's Russian and Cossack Allies* (London: Osprey Publishing, 2015). For secondary works with notable sections covering these units, see Citino, *Wehrmacht's Last Stand*, 118-27, and Ambrose, *D-Day*, 33-37. See also Walter Dunn, "German Bodenstandig Divisions," in *Scraping the Barrel: The Military Use of Substandard Manpower, 1860-1960*, edited by Sanders Marble (New York: Fordham University Press, 2012), 179-96.

13. Muñoz, *Goering's Grenadiers*, 57-59.

14. Muñoz, 59-62.

15. For more on the Spanish Blue Division, see Gerald Kleinfeld and Lewis Tambs, *Hitler's Spanish Division: The Blue Division in Russia* (Carbondale: Southern Illinois University Press, 1979).

16. The major details of the early deployment of the 1st LwFD can be found in the division's own Kriegstagebuch; the 1st has one of the most complete collections of records available of any Luftwaffe field division. See "Abteilung Ia—Anlagen zum Kriegstagebuch, Bd. 5: Teil 1: 30 Sept 1942-19 Jan 1944," Manuscript RL 34/8, BA-MA. See also Muñoz, *Goering's Grenadiers*, 11-15.

17. See "Bericht von 25.3.1943" in "Abteilung Ia—Anlagen zum Kriegstagebuch, Bd. 5: Teil 1: 30 Sept 1942—19 Jan 1944," 47-48.

18. See "Bericht von 8.4.1943" in "Abteilung Ia—Anlagen zum Kriegstagebuch, Bd. 5: Teil 1: 30 Sept 1942—19 Jan 1944," 40-41.

19. For more on the German officer corps and their average casualties in combat, see Citino, *Death of the Wehrmacht*, 1-13, 303-9.

20. Omer Bartov best explains the impact of the losses suffered by the German officer corps in his landmark work *Hitler's Army*, 29-105. Bartov

details how the German army slowly lost nearly all of its traditional unit integrity over the period of 1942 to 1944. By the late stages of the war, the *Heer* was only held together by a combination of the leadership of a few remaining veterans and the nationalist propaganda of the Nazi Party. This loss of cohesion must have been amplified in many of the Luftwaffe field divisions, given their haphazard assembly process and the demoralizing nature of most of their combat history. Ben Shepherd gives the same opinion in his more recent work *Hitler's Soldiers*, 104–44.

21. See "Bericht über die Abwehrkämpfe der 1. L.W. Feld-Division in der Zeit von 15. als 25. März 1943" in "Abteilung Ia—Anlagen zum Kriegstagebuch, Bd. 5: Teil 1: 30 Sept 1942–19 Jan 1944," 69–75.
22. The various details on the absorption of the 1st LwFD into the army can be found in the division's Kriegstagebuch. See "Abteilung Ia—Anlagen zum Kriegstagebuch, Bd. 1: Teil 1: 5 Jun 1943–20 Jan 1944," Manuscript RL 34/4, BA-MA, 36–51.
23. For more on the weaknesses suffered by the 1st FD (L) immediately prior to the 14 January 1944 offensive, see "Bericht von 9.1.1944" in "Abteilung Ia—Anlagen zum Kriegstagebuch, Bd. 1: Teil 1: 5 Jun 1943—20 Jan 1944," Manuscript RL 34/4, BA-MA, 75–76.
24. Muñoz, *Goering's Grenadiers*, 99–100, 113.
25. The 9th FD (L) had a very quiet deployment compared to the 1st FD (L), with only minor losses in its frontline regiments. For more, see "Kriegstagebuch 1–2 des Jäger-Reg. 17, 15 Januar 1943–31 Oktober 1943," Manuscripts RL 34/117–18, BA-MA. See also Haupt, *Luftwaffenfelddivisionen*, 51–52.
26. Haupt, *Army Group North*, 174.
27. Muñoz, *Goering's Grenadiers*, 115–19.
28. Muñoz, 177–79.
29. The description of Hitler's order that transferred the 13th FD (L) can be seen in the division's "Abteilung Ib—Kriegstagebuch Nr. 2 (Sowjetunion-Nord, 1 Nov 1943–31 Jan 1944)." Manuscript RL 34/60, BA-MA, 1–3. Included in the entry is a fairly detailed account of what was going to change within the division itself. See also Muñoz, *Goering's Grenadiers*, 179–81.

30. Haupt, *Luftwaffenfelddivisionen*, 58. For more discussion of assault guns, see Showalter, *Hitler's Panzers*, 95–97, 294–95.
31. The 12th LwFD saw only light combat action prior to the army takeover of the Luftwaffe divisions. This can be quickly inferred from the casualty figures (*Verlustliste*) listed in a regimental war diary from the unit. See "Kriegstagebuch 1 des Lw. Jäger-Regt. 24, 12. Lw-Felddivision, 18 November 1942–31 August 1943," Manuscript RL 34/126, BA-MA. See also the 12th's divisional "Kriegstagebuch 2, 1.11.1943–31.12.1943," Manuscript RL 34/37, BA-MA.
32. The Army Group North unit classifications can be seen in "Heeresgruppe Nord, Ia./Abt. III–19 Dezember 1943," Microfilm Roll T-311/70, NARA, 511.
33. Muñoz, *Goering's Grenadiers*, 335–46.
34. Muñoz, 351.
35. Georg Jagolski, *21. Luftwaffe Felddivision "Adler" Division: 1942–1945* (self-published, 1987), 202.
36. Jagolski, 172–73. See also Muñoz, *Goering's Grenadiers*, 365–66.
37. Muñoz, *Goering's Grenadiers*, 31.
38. For more on the assault, see "Abteilung Ia—Anlagen zum Kriegstagebuch, Bd. 1–6. 1942–1944," Manuscript RL 34/17/102, BA-MA, 2–6. See also Ruffner, *Luftwaffe Field Divisions*, 12–13.
39. Muñoz, *Goering's Grenadiers*, 31.
40. For more on the 6 October assault, see the 3rd LwFD's "Kriegstagebuch, Eintrag von 6 Oktober 1943," Manuscript RL 34/16, BA-MA, 15–16. See also Muñoz, *Goering's Grenadiers*, 34–35.
41. For more on the Soviet offensive that resulted in the dissolution of the 3rd FD (L), see the division's "Kriegstagebuch, Eintragen von 9 bis 22 Januar 1944," Manuscript RL 34/16, BA-MA, 111–23. See also Muñoz, *Goering's Grenadiers*, 35–37.
42. Muñoz, *Goering's Grenadiers*, 39–41.
43. Muñoz, 67–68.
44. Muñoz, 69–70, 73. For the order to transfer the 6th over to the army, see "Bericht von 1.11.1943," in "Abteilung Ia–Anlagen zum Kriegstagebuch," 584–89.

45. Werner Haupt, *Army Group Center: The Wehrmacht in Russia 1941–1945* (Friedberg: Podzun-Pallas, 1997), 179.
46. For the divisional record of the 24 December 1943 offensive, see "Tagesübersichten vom 24–30.12.1943," in "Abteilung Ia–Anlagen zum Kriegstagebuch," Microfilm Roll T-315/366, NARA, 701–25. Specifically, the report from 30 December also details losses suffered from the offensive, including thirteen artillery pieces.
47. Muñoz, *Goering's Grenadiers*, 75.
48. Muñoz, 73–74.
49. Ruffner, *Luftwaffe Field Divisions*, 22.
50. Muñoz, *Goering's Grenadiers*, 243.
51. Muñoz, 244, 270.
52. The service record of the at least part of the 16th LwFD is nicely summed up in a single document from the 1st Battalion of Jäger-Regiment 31. See "Bericht über die Tätigkeit des Bataillons von der Aufstellungs bis heute, 13.10.1943," in "Anlagen zum Kriegstagebuch des I/J.R. 31 (L)," Manuscript RL 34/134, BA-MA. See also the division's own war diary in "Kriegstagebuch 1 des 16. LwFD," Manuscript RL 34/68, BA-MA. For a secondary source, see Muñoz, *Goering's Grenadiers*, 244.
53. For more on the pre–D-day service of the 17th LwFD, see "Kriegstagebuchen 1–2 des 17. Lw. Felddivision, 1 1 März 1943–31 Januar 1944," Manuscripts RL 34/73–74, BA-MA. See also Muñoz, *Goering's Grenadiers*, 269–70, 283.
54. Muñoz, *Goering's Grenadiers*, 286.
55. Ruffner, *Luftwaffe Field Divisions*, 19–20. See also Muñoz, *Goering's Grenadiers*, 275, 287.
56. "Sonderbefehl den 4 März 1943: Fürsorge fur die Trüppe," Manuscript RL 34/98, BA-MA. See also Joachim von Tresckow's description of his unit in "18 Air Force Field Division," 8–14.
57. The records of the 17th FD (L) contain a large number of reports on the state of their horses, both their total allotment as well as their veterinary personnel. See in particular Manuscript RL 34/74, BA-MA. See also Haupt, *Luftwaffenfelddivisionen*, 56–57, and Muñoz, *Goering's Grenadiers*, 127–29.

58. Haupt, *Luftwaffenfelddivisionen*, 56.
59. Some description and analysis of the battle for Leros can be found in the *Kriegstagebuch* for the 11th FD (L). See "Tätigkeitsbericht für den Monat November 1943" in "Abteilung Ib—Kriegstagebuch mit Anlagen, 1 Nov–31 Dez 1943," 1–2, Manuscript RL 34/33, BA-MA. See also Muñoz, *Goering's Grenadiers*, 132–33.
60. A good breakdown of the 11th's strength is seen a month later in a report from December 1943, offering a comparison to its strength prior to the absorption by the army. See "Anlagen 11 und 12, Geheim von 21.12.43," as well as "Tätigkeitsbericht für den Monat Dezember 1943," Manuscript RL 34/33, BA-MA. See also Muñoz, *Goering's Grenadiers*, 133–35.
61. Muñoz, *Goering's Grenadiers*, 297–99.
62. One of the available documents for the 19th FD (L) details the basic American armor and heavy weapons available to the U.S. Army that would be used in Italy. On paper, the 19th had little answer for an American armored division. See "Feinnachtrichtenblatt Nr. 13/44, 13 Mai 1944," Manuscript RL 34/212, BA-MA. See also Muñoz, *Goering's Grenadiers*, 302–4.
63. Muñoz, *Goering's Grenadiers*, 321–25.
64. See Meindl's report in Denzel, *Luftwaffenfelddivisionen*, 9–13.
65. Such sources include the cited memoirs of Erich von Manstein, Alfred Mahncke, and Walter Walimont as well as official documents written for the U.S. Army by General Eugen Meindl and other LwFD commanders such as Joachim von Tresckow.

Chapter 5. Luftwaffe Field Divisions in the West, 1944–45

1. Citino, *Wehrmacht Retreats*, 200–2.
2. The state of the German defenses of France prior to D-day has been covered in a number of excellent works. For one of the most expansive, see Detlef Vogel, "Die Deutschen in Erwartung einer alliierten Invasion," in *DDRZW*, vol. 7, 451–501. For other examples, see Citino, *Wehrmacht's Last Stand*, 110, Weinberg, *World at Arms*, 664–86, and Megargee, *Hitler's High Command*, 199–202.

3. This is due to the fact that the 21st LwFD was technically just a redesignated Division Meindl, and the 22nd LwFD was decommissioned before being finished.
4. Muñoz, *Goering's Grenadiers*, 303–4, 322–25.
5. 14th LwFD, "Kriegsgliederungen Luftwaffe-Felddivision 14," Microfilm Roll T-207/51–55, NARA. See also Earl Ziemke, *The German Northern Theater of Operations, 1940–1945* (Washington, DC: Department of the Army Pamphlet No. 20-271, 1959).
6. Muñoz, *Goering's Grenadiers*, 133–35.
7. Citino, *Wehrmacht's Last Stand*, 110–11. See also Vogel, "Die Deutschen in Erwartung, 463–86.
8. Citino, *Wehrmacht's Last Stand*, 113–14.
9. Citino, 113–14.
10. Citino, 115–18.
11. Citino, 118.
12. Citino, 120.
13. Hans Speidel, *Invasion 1944: Ein Beitrag zu Rommels und des Reiches Schicksal* (Tubingen: Rainer Wunderlich, 1949), 51–52.
14. Megargee, *Hitler's High Command*, 192–211. See also Citino, *Wehrmacht's Last Stand*, 122.
15. Citino, *Wehrmacht's Last Stand*, 123–25.
16. Citino, 126.
17. Muñoz, *Goering's Grenadiers*, 255.
18. Karl Sievers, "Demerkungen zur Führung von Strafbüchern, 14.6.1944," Manuscript RL 34/72, BA-MA, 2–7.
19. Muñoz, *Goering's Grenadiers*, 276–77, 286–87.
20. von Tresckow, "18 Air Force Field Division in the Period of 6 June–24 July 44." Tresckow's comments touch on every other reason German officers looked down upon the Luftwaffe Field Divisions: poor manpower, lack of training, few trained officers, and lack of mobility.
21. Muñoz, *Goering's Grenadiers*, 287.
22. Muñoz, 274.
23. Citino, *Wehrmacht's Last Stand*, 228.
24. Citino, 229.

25. See Fritz Bayerlein, "An Interview with Fritz Bayerlein: Pz Lehr Division (Jan-July 1944)," Manuscript ETHINT 66, USAHEC. See also Citino, *Wehrmacht's Last Stand*, 231.
26. The 18th FD (L) records include several divisional orders detailing the enemy harassment by air as well as sabotage by French guerrillas. See "Div-befehl für den Marsch Nr. 5, 15.8.1944," Manuscript RL 34/102/22–24, BA-MA, 1–3. See also Muñoz, *Goering's Grenadiers*, 256, 277, 287.
27. Muñoz, *Goering's Grenadiers*, 256–57. See also Hans von Luck, *Panzer Commander* (Westport, CT: Praeger, 1989), 169. Von Luck was the commander of the 21st Panzer Division and mentions in his memoirs the receipt of manpower from the 16th FD (L).
28. Citino, *Wehrmacht's Last Stand*, 243.
29. Citino, 244–45.
30. Muñoz, *Goering's Grenadiers*, 258–60. See also the British after action report for Goodwood, specifically Air Ministry, "Operations of Bomber Command in Close Support, 18th July 1944," Manuscript CAB 106/959, British Archives, 29–32.
31. Muñoz, *Goering's Grenadiers*, 260–62.
32. Muñoz, 262. See also Air Ministry, "Bomber Command," 32. The British report listed that 70 percent of captured German POWs from Goodwood could not be interrogated even twenty-four hours after the bombing attack because they still could not hear.
33. Percy Schramm, ed., *Kriegstagebuch des Oberkommando der Wehrmacht*, vol. 7 (Munich: Bernard & Graefe, 1982), 334.
34. Muñoz, *Goering's Grenadiers*, 263–64.
35. Citino, *Wehrmacht's Last Stand*, 317–19.
36. Höcker, "Einsatz der 17. Lw. an der Invasionsfront vom 24.7.44 bis 31.8.44," in "Nachlass von Hans Hans Höcker."
37. For the full account of the collapse of the 17th FD (L) between 19 August and 22 September 1944, see the divisional "Kriegstagebuch Ia, 17 August–30 September 1944," Microfilm Roll T-315/693, NARA, 171–252. See also the account of the commander of the 17th FD (L), Höcker, in "Einsatz der 17. Lw. an der Invasionsfront vom 24.7.44 bis 31.8.44." See also Muñoz, *Goering's Grenadiers*, 277–79.

38. Höcker's analysis of the 167th Volksgrenadier can be found in Manuscript N108/8, BA-MA.
39. The orders to send the 18th FD (L) can be seen in "Div-Befehl für den Angriff am 23.8.1944"; Muñoz, *Goering's Grenadiers*, 288–89.
40. For more discussion of Model, see Citino, *Wehrmacht's Last Stand*, 325–30.
41. Muñoz, *Goering's Grenadiers*, 289–90.
42. Muñoz, 290–92. The order that dissolved the 18th FD (L) and transferred its troops to the 18th *Volksgrenadier* Division can be seen in "OKH/Abwickl.-u.Betreuungsstab, 21.10.1944," Manuscript RL 34/184, BA-MA, 1–4. See also Ruffner, *Luftwaffe Field Divisions*, 24. For more on the Mons pocket, see Citino, *Wehrmacht's Last Stand*, 330–33.
43. Citino, *Wehrmacht's Last Stand*, 64–80.
44. Citino, 64–80.
45. Citino, 80–95.
46. Citino, 96–106.
47. Muñoz, *Goering's Grenadiers*, 302–4.
48. Muñoz, 321–25.
49. Fridolin von Senger und Etterlin, *Neither Fear nor Hope: The Wartime Memoirs of the German Defender of Cassino* (Novato, CA: Presidio Press, 1989), 259–60.
50. Muñoz, *Goering's Grenadiers*, 325–27.
51. Ruffner, *Luftwaffe Field Divisions*, 35–36.
52. Muñoz, *Goering's Grenadiers*, 308–11; Ruffner, *Luftwaffe Field Divisions*, 36.
53. Muñoz, *Goering's Grenadiers*, 311; Ruffner, *Luftwaffe Field Divisions*, 36.
54. The order to disband the 19th FD (L) can be seen in "Betrage zum 9.8.1944," Microfilm Roll RL 34/212/4, BA-MA. See also Muñoz, *Goering's Grenadiers*, 311–12. Muñoz states definitively that the unit was "not worth raising" and "wholly inadequate," but its combat performance was good, thus indicating that if the Luftwaffe field divisions had been given proper equipment and training, they could have been more successful.
55. Muñoz, *Goering's Grenadiers*, 326–27.
56. Ruffner, *Luftwaffe Field Divisions*, 36.

57. Muñoz, *Goering's Grenadiers*, 328–31.
58. For further discussion on the Italian campaign and overall German performance within it, see Citino, *Wehrmacht Retreats*, 268–74. See also Schreiber, "Das Ende des nordafrikanischen Feldzugs," 1131–132. Historians such as Carlo D'Este in *Fatal Decision: Anzio and the Battle for Rome* (New York: Harper Perennial, 1992), 87–88, have offered glowing opinions of Kesselring in particular, but all of these claims are dubious given the strategic background to the Italian campaign.
59. Muñoz, *Goering's Grenadiers*, 133–35.
60. For a detailed analysis of the assault on Leros, see *German Antiguerrilla Operations in the Balkans (1941–1944)* (Washington, DC: Department of the Army Pamphlet 20-243, 1954), 44–46. For the regimental records of Lw. Jgr. Regiments 21 and 22, see their Kriegstagebuchen, Manuscripts RL 34/119, 34/121, 34/123, and 34/124, BA-MA. See also Muñoz, *Goering's Grenadiers*, 132–33, as well as Ruffner, *Luftwaffe Field Divisions*, 34–35.
61. A lot of archival records are available for the 11th FD (L) in 1943, many of which detail the various progress reports against Greek partisans as well as the general state of the division in that time. See Manuscripts RL 34/33, RL 34/35, and RL 34/122, BA-MA. See also *German Antiguerrilla Operations*, 54–60; Muñoz, *Goering's Grenadiers*, 136.
62. Muñoz, *Goering's Grenadiers*, 137.
63. For more information on the Axis occupation of Greece, the Greek experience in World War II, and the following Greek civil war, see Mark Mazower, *Inside Hitler's Greece: The Experience of Occupation, 1941–1944* (New Haven: Yale University Press, 1995), idem, *After the War Was Over: Reconstructing the Family, Nation, and State in Greece 1943–1960* (Princeton: Princeton University Press, 2000), and Christina Goulter, "The Greek Civil War: A National Army's Counter-insurgency Triumph," *Journal of Military History* 78, no. 3 (July 2014): 1017–55.
64. Muñoz, *Goering's Grenadiers*, 139–40.
65. For more information on the Red Army's Budapest offensive, see Glantz and House, *When Titans Clashed*, 221–26. See also Klaus Schönherr, "Die Rückzugskämpfe in Rumänien und Siebenbürgen im Sommer/Herbst 1944," in *DDRZW*, vol. 8, 731–848.

66. Muñoz, *Goering's Grenadiers*, 141–43. See also Haupt, *Luftwaffenfelddivisionen*, 56.
67. Krisztian Ungvary, "Der ungarische Kriegsschauplatz," in *DDRZW*, vol. 8, 865–925. See also Glantz and House, *When Titans Clashed*, 253–54.
68. Muñoz, *Goering's Grenadiers*, 143–46.

Chapter 6. Luftwaffe Field Divisions in the East, 1944–45

1. For more on Kursk, see David Glantz and Jonathan House, *The Battle of Kursk* (Lawrence: University Press of Kansas, 1999). See also Citino, *Wehrmacht Retreats*, 110–44.
2. For more on the autumn 1943 Red Army offensives, see David Glantz with Mary Elizabeth Glantz, *Battle for Belorussia* (Lawrence: University Press of Kansas, 2016), 3–264. See also Hill, *Red Army and the Second World War*, 502–47, Glantz and House, *When Titans Clashed*, 167–76, and Citino, *Wehrmacht Retreats*, 212–37.
3. See chapter 4 in this book for the loss of the 3rd and 5th FD (L)s.
4. For more on deep battle and its proponents and usage by the Red Army, see G. S. Isserson, *The Evolution of Operational Art*, trans. Bruce Menning, (Fort Leavenworth, KS: Combat Studies Institute Press, 2013). See also Richard Harrison, *The Russian Way of War* (Lawrence: University Press of Kansas, 2001), David Glantz, *Soviet Military Operational Art: In Pursuit of Deep Battle* (London: Frank Cass, 1991), and Mary Habeck, *Storm of Steel* (Ithaca: Cornell University Press, 2003).
5. For the German and Red Army strength in 1944, see Glantz and House, *When Titans Clashed*, 179–86. For more on Soviet deception operations in 1944, see Glantz, *Role of Intelligence in Soviet Military Strategy*, 115–208.
6. The fighting strength of Army Group South is well described in Citino, *Wehrmacht's Last Stand*, 28–29.
7. Natzmer's report is quoted in Karl-Heinz Frieser, "Der Rückzugsoperationen der Heeresgruppe Süd in der Ukraine," in *DDRZW*, vol. 8, 385–86.
8. Frieser, 386.

9. For more on the Red Army's Ukrainian offensive of December 1943–May 1944, see Hill, *Red Army and the Second World War*, 551–65. See also Glantz and House, *When Titans Clashed*, 184–92, as well as Citino, *Wehrmacht's Last Stand*, 29–58. See also Frieser, "Der Rückzugsoperationen," 339–492.
10. See the map of the Leningrad front (map 2).
11. Muñoz, *Goering's Grenadiers*, 151. See also the map of the Leningrad front.
12. Glantz, *Battle for Leningrad*, 333–37.
13. For the situation on the Leningrad front prior to the January 1944 offensive, see Glantz, *Battle for Leningrad*, 327–33. The DDRZW official history gives different numbers but with even greater disparity: barely 400,000 Germans against 1.25 million Soviets supported by 1,580 tanks, 20,183 artillery pieces, and 1,386 aircraft. In either case, the Germans were in trouble. Karl-Heinz Frieser, "Das Ausweichen der Heeresgruppe Nord von Leningrad ins Baltikum," in *DDRZW*, vol. 8, 284–86.
14. Glantz, *Battle for Leningrad*, 330.
15. The Army Group North report that describes the quality of the 12th FD (L) can be found in "Heeresgruppe Nord, Ia/Abt. III-19 Dezember 1943," Microfilm Roll T-311/70, NARA.
16. Frieser, "Das Ausweichen der Heeresgruppe Nord," 284.
17. Muñoz, *Goering's Grenadiers*, 102–3.
18. Haupt, *Luftwaffenfelddivisionen*, 52–53. For a more general description of the operation, see Frieser, "Das Ausweichen der Heeresgruppe Nord," 279–96.
19. Muñoz, *Goering's Grenadiers*, 104–5, 118–19.
20. A major example of the trend arguing that attacking the Luftwaffe divisions led to Soviet success in the Leningrad-Novgorod offensive comes from Muñoz, *Goering's Grenadiers*, 105–6. Muñoz suggests that the "low combat efficiency" of the two FD (L) "had not remained concealed" from Fedyuninsky, and that "it seems that the Soviets had planned their offensive specifically targeting" the Luftwaffe units. His assertions are not backed by citations or any evidence beyond assumptions. However, an additional example can be found in the official

German history of the war, *Das Deutsche Reich und der Zweite Weltkrieg*. From the history's description of Army Group North's situation in early 1944, the six FD (L)s assigned to the army group were specifically mocked as "failed projects," implying that all of these units were weak links for the army group. See Frieser, "Das Ausweichen der Heeresgruppe Nord," 284.

21. For an excellent map showing the distances being discussed, see Glantz, *Battle for Leningrad*, 369.
22. Haupt, *Luftwaffenfelddivisionen*, 53–54.
23. "Heeresgruppe Nord, Ia, 159/44, 17 Januar 1944."
24. The offensive against the 10th FD (L) is described in detail in Haupt, *Luftwaffenfelddivisionen*, 54–55. See also Glantz, *Battle for Leningrad*, 338–45, Haupt, *Army Group North*, 205–7, as well as Muñoz, *Goering's Grenadiers*, 117–19.
25. Muñoz, *Goering's Grenadiers*, 120–21.
26. "Heeresgruppe Nord, Ia/Abt. III–19 Dezember 1943." At this time, Army Group North was almost entirely without reserves, so it is surprising to see a Luftwaffe field division turned to in order to fill the role.
27. Muñoz, *Goering's Grenadiers*, 154.
28. Muñoz, 155.
29. "Armeeoberkommando 18, Ia, 732/44 5 Februar 1944," Microfilm Roll T-311/70, NARA.
30. Muñoz, *Goering's Grenadiers*, 157–59. For additional information, see the map of the Leningrad-Novgorod offensive in Glantz, *Battle for Leningrad*, 369, which traces the path of the German retreat from 14 January to 1 March. The locations of the surviving Luftwaffe divisions can be easily traced from point to point on the map.
31. The 13th FD (L) has one of the most complete sets of archival records available covering the experience of a Luftwaffe field division in the Leningrad-Novgorod offensive. See "Tätigkeitsbericht der Abt. Ic vom 1.11–31.12.43 und 1–31.1.44," Manuscript RL 34-57, BA-MA. See also "Kriegstagebuch Nr. 1 Nachrichten-Abt. 13 (L) 1 Dezember 1943 bis 31 Januar 1944," Manuscript RL 34/169, BA-MA, as well

as "Abteilung Ib—Kriegstagebuch Nr. 2 (Sowjetunion-Nord, 1 Nov 1943–31 Jan 1944)," Manuscript RL 34/60, BA-MA.
32. Muñoz, *Goering's Grenadiers*, 180–81.
33. General Reymann is also noteworthy as being the future last commander of so-called Fortress Berlin in 1945. Along with commanding the 13th FD (L), Reymann would also serve as temporary commander of both the 11th Infantry and 20th SS Divisions during Army Group North's retreat in February 1944.
34. See the entries of 26–28 January 1944 in "Kriegstagebuch Nr. 1 Nachrichten-Abt. 13 (L)." The division is quite frank in its war diary that it had lost a great deal of strength, but it does not give a full count of its current numbers at the time.
35. "Tätigkeitsbericht der Abt. Ic vom 1.11–31.12.43 und 1–31.1.44"; Muñoz, *Goering's Grenadiers*, 181–87.
36. Muñoz, 188–89.
37. The existing archival records for the 1st FD (L) are wonderfully detailed in comparison to most other Luftwaffe field division records, and there is an extensive set of records covering the division's experience in the Leningrad-Novgorod offensive. See "Vorläufige Vernehmung Nr. 284/285," Manuscript RL 34/13, BA-MA, 112–21.
38. David Glantz describes the Soviet battle plans against Novgorod in great detail in *Battle for Leningrad*, 335–37, 345–50.
39. Muñoz, *Goering's Grenadiers*, 16–17. Muñoz, among others, openly states, "I don't believe it was a surprise that the Soviets chose to launch their attack against this division." Whether or not the Soviets targeted the 1st at Novgorod, by January 1944 it was a long-established Red Army tactic to surround a target city and trap German forces inside of it on the Eastern Front.
40. The divisional records of the 1st FD (L) are quite frank in discussing the collapse of the division and how few troops escaped the pocket in Novgorod. Some of its battalions numbered only fifty to seventy men after the division escaped the city. See "Vorläufige Vernehmung Nr. 284/285," 130–32.
41. Glantz, *Battle for Leningrad*, 387–88.

42. Muñoz, *Goering's Grenadiers*, 355–56.
43. The best sources to find the descriptions of these Soviet offensives include Karl-Heinz Frieser, "Die Rückzugsoperationen der Heeresgruppe Sud in der Ukraine," in *DDRZW*, vol. 8, 339–492. See also Glantz and House, *When Titans Clashed*, 179–94.
44. For more on Bagration, see Hill, *Red Army and Second World War*, 570–635, as well as Citino, *Wehrmacht's Last Stand*, 160–215, and Glantz and House, *When Titans Clashed*, 195–215. Citino offers an excellent depiction of the German side of the conflict, while Hill provides an excellent recent Soviet perspective on the operation. Glantz and House provide what remains among the best Soviet perspectives of the Eastern Front. Combined, the two give an excellent combined description of the operation as a whole from each side. As for a German-language source, few can match Karl-Heinz Frieser, "Der Zusammenbruch der Heeresgruppe Mitte im Sommer 1944," in *DDRZW*, vol. 8, 526–603.
45. For more on the German pre-Bagration strategic planning in the east in 1944, see Glantz, *Intelligence in Soviet Military Strategy*, 117–41. See also Citino, *Wehrmacht's Last Stand*, 160–65.
46. Citino, *Wehrmacht's Last Stand*, 160–65; Glantz and House, *When Titans Clashed*, 195.
47. Haupt, *Army Group Center*, 182–92; Citino, *Wehrmacht's Last Stand*, 165–67.
48. Citino, *Wehrmacht's Last Stand*, 165–71.
49. Glantz and House, *When Titans Clashed*, 176.
50. Glantz and House, 176.
51. Glantz and House, 177–80.
52. Glantz, *Intelligence in Soviet Military Strategy*, 117–41. See also Haupt, *Army Group Center*, 187–92, as well as Citino, *Wehrmacht's Last Stand*, 165–69.
53. Karl-Heinz Frieser, "Die Asymmetrie der Krafte," in *DDRZW*, vol. 8, 526–39. See also Citino, *Wehrmacht's Last Stand*, 170–72, 176, as well as Glantz and House, *When Titans Clashed*, 201–4.
54. Karl-Heinz Frieser, "Das Desaster der 3. Panzerarmee bei Vitebsk," in *DDRZW*, vol. 8, 539–43. See also Haupt, *Army Group Center*, 193–97, as well as Citino, *Wehrmacht's Last Stand*, 177.

55. Citino, *Wehrmacht's Last Stand*, 177–81. Karl-Heinz Frieser reports in the *DDRZW* that the Germans lost almost every man that was not captured, bringing the total of dead to between 15,000 and 18,000. See "Das Desaster der 3. Panzerarmee," 542.
56. Frieser, "Das Desaster der 3. Panzerarmee," 539–40.
57. Muñoz, *Goering's Grenadiers*, 42–43. See also Paul Adair, *Hitler's Greatest Defeat* (London: Arms and Armour, 1994), 95–98.
58. Peter von der Groeben, "The Collapse of German Army Group Center," Manuscript T-31, Guide to Foreign Military Studies, USAHEC, 27. See also Gerd Niepold, *Battle for White Russia* (London: Brassey's, 1987), 98. Niepold was the divisional Ia (operations officer) for 12th Panzer Division, and his work is an excellent study on Bagration from the German perspective.
59. Adair, *Hitler's Greatest Defeat*, 98; Haupt, *Luftwaffenfelddivisionen*, 43.
60. Groeben, "Collapse of Army Group Center," 27; Muñoz, *Goering's Grenadiers*, 76–78.
61. For the remainder of Bagration, see Frieser, "Der Zusammenbruch," 543–603. See also Citino, *Wehrmacht's Last Stand*, 182–201, as well as Glantz and House, *When Titans Clashed*, 206–15.
62. Haupt, *Luftwaffenfelddivisionen*, 58. See also Muñoz, *Goering's Grenadiers*, 162–66.
63. Karl-Heinz Frieser, "Die desolate Ausgangslage im Sommer 1944," in *DDRZW*, vol. 8, 623–26. See also Haupt, *Army Group North*, 240.
64. Muñoz, *Goering's Grenadiers*, 165.
65. Karl-Heinz Frieser, "Die Rückzugskämpfe bis Kurland," in *DDRZW*, vol. 8, 626–35. See also Glantz and House, *When Titans Clashed*, 226.
66. Frieser, "Die Rückzugskämpfe," 633–35. See also Glantz and House, *When Titans Clashed*, 227.
67. Muñoz, *Goering's Grenadiers*, 166. See also Haupt, *Army Group North*, 249.
68. Frieser, "Die Rückzugskämpfe," 640–42. See also Muñoz, *Goering's Grenadiers*, 166–67.
69. Muñoz, *Goering's Grenadiers*, 167.
70. Karl-Heinz Frieser, "Die endgültige Abtrennung der Heeresgruppe Nord in Kurland," in *DDRZW*, vol. 8, 642–44.

71. For the combat history of the Courland pocket, see Karl-Heinz Frieser, "Die Kurlandschlachten," in *DDRZW*, vol. 8, 657–78.
72. Haupt, *Army Group North*, 340–45.
73. Muñoz, *Goering's Grenadiers*, 169.
74. "Fernschrieben 4. März 1945," Microfilm T-78/645, NARA.
75. "Vortragsnotiz 9. März 1945," Microfilm T-78/645, NARA.
76. Muñoz, *Goering's Grenadiers*, 170–72.
77. Muñoz, 357.
78. Haupt, *Army Group North*, 240.
79. Muñoz, *Goering's Grenadiers*, 358–59; Haupt, *Luftwaffenfelddivisionen*, 89–91.
80. Muñoz, 359.
81. Haupt, *Luftwaffenfelddivisionen*, 90–91.
82. Glantz and House, *When Titans Clashed*, 228, 239. See also Howard Grier, *Hitler, Dönitz, and the Baltic Sea* (Annapolis: Naval Institute Press, 2007), 81–88. Grier notes that the Soviet view of the Courland position was not much more than self-sustaining prisoners, though the fact that the Red Army continued attacking the position shows that they wanted to try and destroy the last pocket of German forces in the east.
83. Muñoz, *Goering's Grenadiers*, 360.
84. Ruffner, *Luftwaffe Field Divisions*, 38. It should be noted that Ruffner does not include any citations in his book, and the original source for Schwoppe's service has not yet been found.
85. For the surrender of Courland, see Karl-Heinz Frieser, "Die Kämpfe bis Mai 1945," in *DDRZW*, vol. 8, 661–64. For the individual surrender of the 21st FD (L), see Ruffner, *Luftwaffe Field Divisions*, 38.

Conclusion

1. Manstein, *Vorlorene Siege*, 298–99.
2. Blood, "Securing Hitler's *Lebensraum*," 248.
3. The OKW dispatch is quoted in Haupt, *Luftwaffenfelddivisionen*, 16–17. See also Muñoz, *Göring's Grenadiers*, 345–46.
4. For more on these conclusions, see Muñoz, *Goering's Grenadiers*, 8–9.
5. See Meindl's report in Denzel, *Luftwaffenfelddivisionen*, 9–13.

6. Muñoz, *Goering's Grenadiers*, 289–91.
7. "Betrage zum 9.8.1944." See also Muñoz, *Goering's Grenadiers*, 311–12.
8. Frieser, "Das Desaster der 3. Panzerarmee bei Vitebsk," 539–43. See also Haupt, *Army Group Center*, 193–97, as well as Citino, *Wehrmacht's Last Stand*, 177.
9. *Leutnant* Siegel, "E.O. den 3.5.1943," in author's collection. Both this letter and the following "Bericht über den Tod von Obfw. Westphal" were found in the back of this author's copy of Haupt, *Luftwaffenfelddivisionen*. It is clear that the book's previous owner may have been a member of *Obfw*. Westphal's family trying to trace the circumstances of his death. Based on markings within the book, Wilhelm Westphal served in III Battalion, Lw.-Jäger-Regiment 9, 5th LwFD. The Kuban bridgehead was a German defensive position on the Taman Peninsula between the Sea of Azov and the Black Sea that lasted from January through October 1943 after the German army was pushed out of the Caucasus, and Westphal was killed on 23 April 1943 in the midst of this defensive action.
10. *Feldwebel* Schröter, "Bericht über den Tod von Obfw. Westphal," in author's collection.
11. U.S. War Department, *Handbook on German Military Forces 1943*, 221–23.
12. For more information on the Army Specialized Training Program and its personnel in action, see Louis Keefer, *Scholars in Foxholes: The Story of the Army Specialized Training Program* (Jefferson, NC: McFarland, 1988).
13. For more on the Battle of Manila, see James Scott, *Rampage: MacArthur, Yamashita, and the Battle of Manila* (New York: W. W. Norton, 2018). See also Miguel Miranda, *Battle of Manila: Nadir of Japanese Barbarism* (South Yorkshire, UK: Pen and Sword Military, 2019).

BIBLIOGRAPHY

Note: The following archival abbreviations are used throughout this bibliography.

BA: British Archives, London
BA-MA: Bundesarchiv-Militäirarchiv, Freiburg, Germany
CARL: Combined Arms Research Library, Fort Leavenworth, KS
NARA: National Archives and Records Administration, College Park, MD
USAHEC: U.S. Army Heritage and Education Center, Carlisle, PA

Archival Sources

"Abschlussmeldung über Flakartillerie im Bereich des Gen.d.Lw.Ob.d.H, 28 February 1942." Manuscript N529/7, BA-MA.
Air Ministry. "Operations of Bomber Command in Close Support, 18th July 1944." Manuscript CAB 106/959, BA.
"Anlagen zum Kriegstagebuch des I/J.R. 31 (L)." Manuscript RL 34/134, BA-MA.
"Anlagen zum Kriesgtagebuch des Jäger-Sonderkommando d. Luftwaffe." Manuscript RL 31/5, BA-MA.
"Anlagen zum Kriegstagebuch des Sicherungsbataillon d. Lw." Manuscript RL 31/3, BA-MA.
"Armeeoberkommando 18, Ia, 732/44 5 Februar 1944." Microfilm Roll T-311/70, NARA.
Army Air Forces Evaluation Board in the European Theater of Operations. "The Effectiveness of Third Phase Tactical Air Operations in the

European Theater." N13263–2, World War II Operational Documents Collection, CARL.
Army Group Don. "Kriegstagebuch Abteilung 6, 24 Dez 1942–3 Jan 1943." Microfilm Roll T-311/270, NARA.
———. "Kriegstagebuch 7, 13–20 Jan 1943." Microfilm Roll T-311/271, NARA.
Bayerlein, Fritz. "An Interview with Fritz Bayerlein: Pz Lehr Division (Jan–July 1944)." Manuscript ETHINT 66, USAHEC.
Bergengruen, Hellmut. "Der Kampf der Panzerdivsion 'Hermann Goering' auf Sizilien." Manuscript T-2, USAHEC.
Conrath, Paul. "Der Kampf um Sizilien." Manuscript C-087, USAHEC.
Department of the Army Pamphlet 20-201, *Military Improvisations during the Russian Campaign*. World War II Operational Documents Collection, CARL, http://cgsc.cdmhost.com/cdm/singleitem/collection/p4013coll8/id/1927/rec/1.
Dessloch, Otto. "The Winter Battle of Rhzev, Vyasma, and Yukhnov, 1941–42." Manuscript D-137, Guide to Foreign Military Studies, USAHEC.
"Feinnachtrichtenblatt Nr. 13/44, 13 Mai 1944." Manuscript RL 34/212, BA-MA.
"Fernschrieben 4. März 1945." Microfilm T-78/645, NARA.
Goering, Hermann. "Der Reichsminister der Luftfahrt und Oberbefehlshaber der Luftwaffe/Luftwaffen-Personalamt." Nr. 64700/42, 17.9.1942. Manuscript NS 19/2730, BA-MA.
Groeben, Peter von der. "The Collapse of German Army Group Center." Manuscript T-31, Guide to Foreign Military Studies, USAHEC.
Groppe, Theodor. *SS vs Wehrmacht, 1943–1945*. Manuscript B-397, World War II Operational Documents Collection, CARL.
"Heeresgruppe Nord, Ia./Abt. III–19 Dezember 1943." Microfilm Roll T-311/70, Guide to Foreign Military Studies, NARA.
Höcker, Hans. "Nachlass von Hans Höcker." Manuscript N108, BA-MA.
Jeschonnek, Hans. "Besprechungsnotiz am 26.6.43." In Denzel, *Die Luftwaffenfelddivisionen*, 14.
Kleinrath, I. A. "An den Staatssekretär der Luftfahrt u. Generalinspekteur der Luftwaffe (GFM Milch), H.Q. den 19.9.1943, 6. Abteilung (II) Nr. 16567/43." In Denzel, *Die Luftwaffenfelddivisionen*, 15.

"Kriegstagebuch des Jäger-Sonderkommando d. Luftwaffe (6 March 1943 to 3 August 1944)." Manuscript RL 31/4, BA-MA.

"Kriegstagebuch des Sicherungsbataillon d. Lw (18 July 1942 to 18 March 1943)." Manuscript RL 31/1, BA-MA.

Lw-Felddivision. "Abteilung Ia—Anlagen zum Kriegstagebuch, Bd. 5: Teil 1: 30 Sept 1942–19 Jan 1944." Manuscript RL 34/8, BA-MA.

———. "Abteilung Ia—Anlagen zum Kriegstagebuch, Bd. 1: Teil 1: 5 Jun 1943–20 Jan 1944." Manuscript RL 34/4, BA-MA.

———. "Abteilung Ia—Anlagen zum Kriegstagebuch, Bd. 2–11. 1942–1944." Manuscripts RL 34/5–14, BA-MA.

———. "Anlage zum Feindnachrichtensblatt Nr. 5." Microfilm Roll T-315/86/102, Guide to Foreign Military Studies, NARA.

———. "Vorläufige Vernehmung Nr. 284/285." Manuscript RL 34/13, BA-MA.

Lw-Felddivision. "Einheiten der Luftwaffen-Felddivisionen." Manuscript RL 34/116, BA-MA.

———. "Tagesbefehl von 24.10.1943." Manuscript RL 34/201, BA-MA.

Lw-Felddivision. "Abteilung Ia—Anlagen zum Kriegstagebuch, Bd. 1–6. 1942–1944." Manuscripts RL 34/17–22, BA-MA.

———. "Abteilung Ib—Beträge zum Kriegstagebuch, 20 Dez 1942." Manuscript RL 34/25, BA-MA.

———. "Abteilung Ib—Tätigkeitsberichte der Unterabteilungen, 1 Nov 1943–21 Jan 1944." Manuscript RL 34/24, BA-MA.

———. "Kriegstagebuch des 3. Lw-Felddivision (30 Sept. 1943–31 Jan. 1944)." Manuscript RL 34/16, BA-MA.

———. "Lebenslauf und Pressberichte über Generalleutnant Wever." Manuscript RL 34/26, BA-MA.

Lw-Felddivision. "Abteilung Ia—Kriegstagebuch, 1 Nov–31 Dez 1943." Manuscript RL 34/27, BA-MA.

———. "Abteilung Ia—Anlagen zum Kriegstagebuch." Microfilm Roll T-315/366, Guide to Foreign Military Studies, NARA.

———. "Abteilung Ia—Anlagen zum Kriegstagebuch, Bd. 1–2." Manuscripts RL 34/28–29, BA-MA.

———. "Abteilung Ib—Kriegstagebuch mit Anlagenbände, 23 Nov–31 Dez 1943." Manuscript RL 34/30, BA-MA.

———. "Tagesübersicht von 23.11.1943." Microfilm Roll T-315/366/635, Guide to Foreign Military Studies, NARA, 1–3.
Lw-Felddivision. "Kriegstagebuch des 7. Lw-Felddivision (27 Sept 1942–5 Mai 1943)." Manuscript RL 34/155, BA-MA.
Lw-Felddivision. "Kriegstagebuchen 1–2 des Jäger-Reg. 17, 9. Lw-Felddivision. 15 Januar 1943–31 Oktober 1943." Manuscripts RL 34/117–18, BA-MA.
Lw-Felddivision. "Abteilung Ia—Kriegstagebuch, 1 Nov–31 Dez 1943." Manuscript RL 34/31, BA-MA.
———. "Abteilung Ib—Kriegstagebuch mit Anlagen, 1 Nov–31 Dez 1943." Manuscripts RL 34/32–35, BA-MA.
———. "Kriegstagebuch 1–3 des Jäger-Reg. 21, 11. Lw-Felddivision." Manuscripts RL 34/119–21, BA-MA.
———. "Kriegstagebuch 1–2 des Jäger-Reg. 22, 11. Lw-Felddivision." Manuscripts RL 34/123–24, BA-MA.
Lw-Felddivision. "Abteilung Ib—Kriegstagebuch, 2, 1.11.1943–31.12.1943." Manuscript RL 34/37, BA-MA.
———. "Abteilung IVb—Anlagenband zum Kriegstagebuch, 1 Nov–31 Dez 1943." Manuscript RL 34/39, BA-MA.
———. "Abteilung IVc—Anlagenband zum Kriegstagebuch, 1 Nov–31 Dez 1943." Manuscript RL 34/40, BA-MA.
———. "Kriegstagebuch 1 des Lw. Jäger-Reg. 24, 12. Lw-Felddivision, 18 November 1942–31 August 1943." Manuscripts RL 34/126–32, BA-MA.
Lw-Felddivision. "Abteilung Ia—Anlagen zum Kriegstagebuch, Bd. 1–12, 1942–1944." Manuscripts RL 34/44–55, BA-MA.
———. "Abteilung Ib—Anlagen zum Kriegstagebuch, Bd. 1–2, 1942–1944." Manuscripts RL 34/61–62, BA-MA.
———. "Abteilung Ib—Kriegstagebuch Nr. 2 (Sowjetunion-Nord, 1 Nov 1943–31 Jan 1944)." Manuscript RL 34/60, BA-MA.
———. "Abteilung Ic—Tätigkeitsbericht, 1.11–31.12.43 und 1–31.1.44." Manuscript RL 34/57, BA-MA.
———. "Abteilung IIa—Tätigkeitsbericht, 1 Dez 1943–17 Feb 1944." Manuscript RL 34/58, BA-MA.
———. "Abteilung IIb—Tätigkeitsbericht, 1–30 Nov 1943." Manuscript RL 34/59, BA-MA.

———. "Kriegstagebuch des 13. Lw-Felddivision Nr. 1 Nachrichten-Abt. 13 (L) 1 Dezember 1943 bis 31 Januar 1944." Manuscript RL 34/169, BA-MA.

Lw-Felddivision. "Kriegsgliederungen Luftwaffe-Felddivision 14." Microfilm Roll T-207/51–55, Guide to Foreign Military Studies, NARA.

Lw-Felddivision. "Kriegstagebuch des 15. Lw-Felddivision." 3 vol. Manuscripts RL 34/63–65, BA-MA.

———. "Zur Kriegsgeschichte der 15. Luftwaffenfeld-Division und ihres Luftwaffen-Jäger-Regimentes Nr. 30." Manuscript RL 34/132, BA-MA.

Lw-Felddivision. "Kriegstagebuch 1 des 16. LwFD." Manuscript RL 34/68, BA-MA.

Lw-Felddivision. "Einheiten der 17. Lw-Felddivision." Manuscript RL 34/88, BA-MA.

———. "Kriegstagebuch des 17. Lw-Felddivision Ia, 17 August–30 September 1944." Microfilm Roll T-315/693, NARA.

———. "Kriegstagebuchen 1–2 des 17. Lw. Felddivision, 11 März 1943–31 Januar 1944." Manuscripts RL 34/73–74, BA-MA.

Lw-Felddivision. "Div-Befehl für den Angriff am 23.8.1944." Microfilm Roll RL 34/102/97–99, BA-MA.

———. "Div-befehl für den Marsch Nr. 5, 15.8.1944." Manuscript RL 34/102/22–24, BA-MA.

———. "OKH/Abwickl.-u.Betreuungsstab, 21.10.1944." Manuscript RL 34/184, BA-MA.

Lw-Felddivision. "Betrage zum 9.8.1944." Microfilm Roll RL 34/212/4, BA-MA.

Lw-Felddivision. "Abteilung Ia—Anlagen zum Kriegstagebuch Nr. 3, Bd. 1–3." Manuscripts RL 34/109–11, BA-MA.

———. "Abteilung Ia—Kriegstagebuch Nr. 3 (Sowjetunion-Nord, 1 Nov–31 Dez 1943)." Manuscript RL 34/108, BA-MA.

———. "Anlage zum Kriegstagebuch Nr. 3, 1 Nov–31 Dec 1944." Microfilm Roll T-315/770/80–621, Guide to Foreign Military Studies, NARA.

———. "Kriegstagebuch Nr. 3, 1 Nov–31 Dez 1944." Microfilm Roll T-315/770/1, Guide to Foreign Military Studies, NARA.

Lw-Feldivision, Feld-Regiment der Lw. 1. "Einsatzberichte, Meldungen, Befehle (Sowjetunion-Nord, 1942–1943), Beide 1–4." Manuscripts RL 34/217–20, BA-MA.

Lw-Feldkorps. "Luftwaffen-Bataillon Jäger-Personallisten, Sep–Oct 1944." Manuscript RL 34/177, BA-MA.

Meindl, Eugen. "II. Fallsch. Korps, 6 Juli bis 24 Juli 1944." Manuscript B-401, Guide to Foreign Military Studies, NARA.

———. "II FS Corps, Part III: Rhineland (15 Sep 44 to 21 Mar 45)." Manuscript B-093, Guide to Foreign Military Studies, USAHEC.

———. "2nd Paratroop Corps in Northern France, 20 July–12 September 1944," Manuscript A-923, Guide to Foreign Military Studies, USAHEC.

———. "II Parachute Corps in Northern France (26 July to 5 August 1944)." Manuscript A-969, Guide to Foreign Military Studies, USAHEC.

———. "II Paratroop Corps (10 Mar–5 May 1945)." Manuscript B-674, Guide to Foreign Military Studies, USAHEC.

———. "Denkschrift über Rück-und Ausblick für die L.W. Feld-Divisionen, 15.5.1943." In Denzel, *Die Luftwaffenfelddivisionen*, 9–13.

Military Operational Research Unit. "Battle Study: Operation 'Goodwood.'" Manuscript WO 291-965, BA.

Müller-Hillebrand, Burkhardt. *The Organizational Problems of the Army High Command and Their Solutions: 1938–1945*. MS #P-041f, World War II Operational Documents Collection, CARL.

Oberzahlmeister Meier. "Bericht uber den Verlauf der Ereignisse beim Tross des Jägersonderkommando d. LW, 15 July–1 August 1944," 3 August 1944. Manuscript RL 31/5/127, BA-MA.

Reinhard, Hans. "LXXXVIII Inf. Corps (6 June–21 Dec. 1944): Report of the Commander." N17500.58, World War II Operational Documents Collection, CARL, http://cgsc.cdmhost.com/cdm/singleitem/collection/p4013coll8/id/2343/rec/1.

"The Rise and Fall of the Luftwaffe/The End of Hermann." Call Number N10007, World War II Operational Documents Collection, CARL, http://cgsc.cdmhost.com/cdm/compoundobject/collection/p4013coll8/id/834/rec/4.

Schmalz, Wilhelm. "Der Kampf der Panzerdivision 'Hermann Goering' bei Salerno vom 9.–17.9.1943." In Siegfried Westphal et al., "Der Feldzug in Italien Apr 1943–Mai 1944." Manuscript T-Ia, USAHEC.

Schramm, Percy, ed. *Kriegstagebuch des Oberkommando der Wehrmacht*, vol. 7. Munich: Bernard & Graefe, 1982.

Sievers, Karl. "Demerkungen zur Führung von Strafbüchern, 14.6.1944." Manuscript RL 34/72, BA-MA.
"Sonderbefehl den 4 März 1943: Fürsorge fur die Trüppe." Manuscript RL 34/98, BA-MA.
Tresckow, Joachim von. "18 Air Force Field Division in the Period of 6 June–24 July 44." Manuscript B-419, Guide to Foreign Military Studies, NARA.
U.S. War Department. *Fuehrer Directives and Other Top-Level Directives of the German Armed Forces, 1942–1945*. Call Number N-16267-B, World War II Operational Documents Collection, CARL.
———. *German Antiaircraft Artillery*. Special Series No. 10. Call Number MIS 461, World War II Operational Documents Collection, CARL, http://cgsc.contentdm.oclc.org/cdm/singleitem/collection/p4013coll8/id/2922/rec/1.
"Vortragsnotiz 9. März 1945." Microfilm T-78/645, NARA.
"Zusammenstellung von Jagdkommandos zur Bandenbekämpfung" (31 August 1942). Manuscript RH 27/1/98, BA-MA.

Primary Sources

Halder, Franz. *Kriegstagebuch 1939–1942*. 3 vol. Stuttgart: W. Kohlhammer Verlag, 1962–64.
"Interrogation of Reich Marshal Hermann Goering." 1700–1900 Hours, 10 May 1945. Ritter Schule, Augsburg. Author's collection.
Isserson, G. S. *The Evolution of Operational Art*. Translated by Bruce Menning. Fort Leavenworth, KS: Combat Studies Institute Press, 2013.
Keitel, Wilhelm. *The Memoirs of Field-Marshal Keitel*. Translated by David Irving. New York: Stein and Day, 1966.
Kesselring, Albert. *Soldat bis zum letzten Tag*. Schnellbach: S. Bublies, 2000.
Luck, Hans von. *Panzer Commander*. Westport, CT: Praeger, 1989.
Mahncke, Alfred. *For Kaiser and Hitler*. Translated by Jochen Mahncke. London: Tattered Flag, 2012.
Manstein, Erich von. *Verlorene Siege*. Bonn: Bernard & Graefe, 2011.
Mellenthin, F. W. von. *German Generals of World War II as I Saw Them*. Norman: University of Oklahoma Press, 1977.

———. *Panzer Battles*. Norman: University of Oklahoma Press, 1956.
Schröter, *Feldwebel*. "Bericht über den Tod von Oberfeldwebel Westphal, 3 May 1943." Author's collection.
Senger und Etterlin, Fridolin von. *Neither Fear nor Hope: The Wartime Memoirs of the German Defender of Cassino*. Novato, CA: Presidio Press, 1989.
Siegel, *Leutnant*. "E.O. den 3.5.1943." Author's collection.
Speidel, Hans. *Invasion 1944: Ein Beitrag zu Rommels und des Reiches Schicksal*. Tubingen: Rainer Wunderlich, 1949.
Tieke, Wilhelm. *Der Kaukasus und das Öl*. Translated by Joseph G. Welsh. Winnipeg: J. J. Fedorowicz, 2008.
Warlimont, Walter. *Im Hauptquartier der deutschen Wehrmacht*. Frankfurt: Bernard & Graefe, 1962.
U.S. Department of the Army. *German Antiguerrilla Operations in the Balkans (1941–1944)*. Department of the Army Pamphlet 20–243, Washington, DC, 1954.
U.S. War Department. *Handbook on German Military Forces*. Baton Rouge: Louisiana State University Press, 1990.
Ziemke, Earl. *The German Northern Theater of Operations, 1940–1945*. Department of the Army Pamphlet 20–271, Washington, DC, 1959.

Secondary Sources

Adair, Paul. *Hitler's Greatest Defeat*. London: Arms and Armour, 1994.
Agarossi, Elena. *A Nation Collapses: The Italian Surrender of September 1943*. Cambridge: Cambridge University Press, 2006.
Ahlfen, Hans von. *Der Kampf um Schlesien*. Stuttgart: Motorbuch Verlag, 1998.
Ambrose, Stephen. *D-Day*. New York: Simon & Schuster, 1995.
Amersfoort, Herman, and Piet H. Kamphuis, eds. *May 1940: The Battle for the Netherlands*. Leiden: Brill, 2010.
Bartov, Omer. *Hitler's Army*. New York: Oxford University Press, 1992.
Beorn, Waitman Wade. *Marching into Darkness*. Cambridge, MA: Harvard University Press, 2014.
Bessel, Richard. *Nazism and War*. New York: Modern Library, 2004.

Blood, Philip W. "Securing Hitler's *Lebensraum*: The Luftwaffe and the Białowieza Forest, 1942–1944." *Holocaust and Genocide Studies* 24, no. 2 (Fall 2010): 247–72.
Boog, Horst. "Die Luftwaffe." In *Das Deutsche Reich und der Zweite Weltkrieg*, vol. 4. Stuttgart: Deutsche Verlags-Anstalt, 2001.
Browning, Christopher. *Ordinary Men*. New York: Harper Perennial, 1993.
Burgess, Alan. *The Longest Tunnel*. Annapolis: Naval Institute Press, 1990.
Carsten, F. L. *The Reichswehr and Politics, 1918–1933*. Oxford: Oxford University Press, 1966.
Citino, Robert M. *Death of the Wehrmacht*. Lawrence: University Press of Kansas, 2009.
———. *The German Way of War*. Lawrence: University Press of Kansas, 2005.
———. *Path to Blitzkrieg*. Mechanicsburg, PA: Stackpole, 2008.
———. *Quest for Decisive Victory*. Lawrence: University Press of Kansas, 2000.
———. *The Wehrmacht's Last Stand*. Lawrence: University Press of Kansas, 2017.
———. *The Wehrmacht Retreats*. Lawrence: University Press of Kansas, 2012.
Claasen, Adam. *Hitler's Northern War*. Lawrence: University Press of Kansas, 2001.
Clark, Alan. *The Fall of Crete*. London: Blond, 1962.
Cooper, Matthew. *The German Army*. New York: Bonanza, 1984.
Corum, James S. *The Luftwaffe*. Lawrence: University Press of Kansas, 1997.
———. *The Roots of Blitzkrieg*. Lawrence: University Press of Kansas, 1992.
———. *Wolfram von Richthofen: Master of the German Air War*. Lawrence: University Press of Kansas, 2008.
Craig, Gordon. *The Politics of the Prussian Army*. Oxford: Oxford University Press, 1964.
Das Deutsche Reich und der Zweite Weltkrieg. 9 vol. Stuttgart: Deutsche Verlags-Anstalt, 1990–2008.
Denzel, Egon. *Die Luftwaffenfelddivisionen 1942–45*. Neckargemünd: Kurt Vorwinckel Verlag, 1976.
D'Este, Carlo. *Fatal Decision: Anzio and the Battle for Rome*. New York: Harper Perennial, 1992.

Deutsch, Harold. *Hitler and His Generals: The Hidden Crisis.* Minneapolis: University Press of Minnesota, 1974.

Dierich, Wolfgang. *Die Verbände der Luftwaffe 1935–1945: Gliederungen und Kurzchroniken—eine Dokumentation.* Stuttgart: Motorbuch, 1976.

DiNardo, R. L. *Germany's Panzer Arm.* Mechanicsburg, PA: Stackpole, 1997.

Dunn, Walter. "German Bodenstandig Divisions." In *Scraping the Barrel: The Military Use of Substandard Manpower, 1860–1960*, ed. by Sanders Marble, 179–96. New York: Fordham University Press, 2012.

Frieser, Karl-Heinz. *The Blitzkrieg Legend.* Annapolis: Naval Institute Press, 2005.

——. "Das Ausweichen der Heeresgruppe Nord von Leningrad ins Baltikum." In *Das Deutsche Reich und der Zweite Weltkrieg*, vol. 8. Munich: Deutsche Verlags-Anstalt, 1990.

——. "Das Desaster der 3. Panzerarmee bei Vitebsk." In *Das Deutsche Reich und der Zweite Weltkrieg*, vol. 8.

——. "Die Asymmetrie der Krafte." In *Das Deutsche Reich und der Zweite Weltkrieg*, vol. 8.

——. "Die desolate Ausgangslage im Sommer 1944." In *Das Deutsche Reich und der Zweite Weltkrieg*, vol. 8.

——. "Die endgültige Abtrennung der Heeresgruppe Nord in Kurland." In *Das Deutsche Reich und der Zweite Weltkrieg*, vol. 8.

——. "Die Kämpfe bis Mai 1945." In *Das Deutsche Reich und der Zweite Weltkrieg*, vol. 8.

——. "Die Kurlandschlachten." In *Das Deutsche Reich und der Zweite Weltkrieg*, vol. 8.

——. "Der Rückzugsoperationen der Heeresgruppe Süd in der Ukraine." In *Das Deutsche Reich und der Zweite Weltkrieg*, vol. 8.

——. "Die Rückzugskämpfe der Heeresgruppe Nord bis Kurland." In *Das Deutsche Reich und der Zweite Weltkrieg*, vol. 8.

——. "Der Zusammenbruch der Heeresgruppe Mitte im Sommer 1944." In *Das Deutsche Reich und der Zweite Weltkrieg*, vol. 8.

Fritz, Stephen G. *Frontsoldaten.* Lexington: University Press of Kentucky, 1995.

Gisevius, Hans. *To the Bitter End.* New York: Da Capo Press, 1998.

Glantz, David. *The Battle for Leningrad 1941–1944*. Lawrence: University Press of Kansas, 2002.

———. *Colossus Reborn*. Lawrence: University Press of Kansas, 2005.

———. *From the Don to the Dniepr: Soviet Offensive Operations December 1942–August 1943*. London: Frank Cass, 1991.

———. "The Ghosts of Demiansk: In Memory of the Soldiers of the Soviet 1st Airborne Corps." *Journal of Military History* 56, no. 4 (October 1992): 617–50.

———. *The Role of Intelligence in Soviet Military Strategy in World War II*. Novato, CA: Presidio Press, 1990.

———. *Soviet Military Deception in the Second World War*. London: Routledge, 1989.

———. *Soviet Military Operational Art: In Pursuit of Deep Battle*. London: Frank Cass, 1991.

———. *Stumbling Colossus*. Lawrence: University Press of Kansas, 1998.

———. *Zhukov's Greatest Defeat: The Red Army's Epic Disaster in Operation Mars, 1942*. Lawrence: University Press of Kansas, 1999.

Glantz, David, with Mary Elizabeth Glantz. *Battle for Belorussia*. Lawrence: University Press of Kansas, 2016.

Glantz, David, and Jonathan House. *The Battle of Kursk*. Lawrence: University Press of Kansas, 1999.

———. *Stalingrad*. Lawrence: University Press of Kansas, 2017.

———. *When Titans Clashed: How the Red Army Stopped Hitler*. Lawrence: University Press of Kansas, 1995.

Goulter, Christina. "The Greek Civil War: A National Army's Counterinsurgency Triumph." *Journal of Military History* 78, no. 3 (July 2014): 1017–55.

Grier, Howard. *Hitler, Dönitz, and the Baltic Sea*. Annapolis: Naval Institute Press, 2007.

Habeck, Mary. *Storm of Steel*. Ithaca: Cornell University Press, 2003.

Harrison, Richard. *The Russian Way of War*. Lawrence: University Press of Kansas, 2001.

Haupt, Werner. *Army Group Center: The Wehrmacht in Russia 1941–1945*. Friedberg: Podzun-Pallas, 1997.

———. *Army Group North: The Wehrmacht in Russia 1941–1945*. Atglen, PA: Schiffer, 1997.
———. *Demjansk: Ein Bollwerk im Osten*. Friedburg: Podzun-Pallas Verlag, 1961.
———. *Die Luftwaffenfelddivisionen 1941–45*. Friedberg: Podzun-Pallas, 1993.
Heiber, Helmut, and David Glantz. *Hitler and His Generals*. New York: Enigma Books, 2003.
Hill, Alexander. *The Red Army and the Second World War*. Cambridge: Cambridge University Press, 2016.
Homze, Edward. *Arming the Luftwaffe*. Lincoln: University of Nebraska Press, 1976.
Jagolski, Georg. *21. Luftwaffe Felddivision "Adler" Division: 1942–1945*. Self-published, 1987.
Keefer, Louis E. *Scholars in Foxholes: The Story of the Army Specialized Training Program*. Jefferson, NC: McFarland, 1988.
Kershaw, Ian. *Hitler: A Biography*. New York: W. W. Norton, 2008.
Kleinfeld, Gerald, and Lewis Tambs. *Hitler's Spanish Division: The Blue Division in Russia*. Carbondale: Southern Illinois University Press, 1979.
Klink, Ernst. "Die Abwehr der Winteroffensiven der Roten Armee." In *Das Deutsche Reich und der Zweite Weltkrieg*, vol. 4.
———. "Die Winterkämpfe im Bereich der Heeresgruppe Nord bis zum Wiedergewinnen einer festen Stellung." In *Das Deutsche Reich und der Zweite Weltkrieg*, vol. 4.
Knox, MacGregor. "1 October 1942: Adolf Hitler, Wehrmacht Officer Policy, and Social Revolution." *Historical Journal* 43, no. 3 (September 2000): 801–25.
Kroener, Bernhard R. "Die Luftwaffenfelddivisionen 1942/43." In *Das Deutsche Reich und der Zweite Weltkrieg*, vol. 5, no. 2. Stuttgart: Deutsche Verlags-Anstalt, 1999.
———. "Die Winterkrise 1941/42. Die Verteilung des Mangels oder Schritte zu einer rationelleren Personalbewirtschaftung." In *Das Deutsche Reich und der Zweite Weltkrieg*, vol. 5, no. 1. Stuttgart: Deutsche Verlags-Anstalt, 1999.

Kurowski, Franz. *The History of Fallschirm-Panzerkorps Hermann Goering: Soldiers of the Reichsmarshall.* Winnipeg: J. J. Fedorowicz, 1995.
Liddell Hart, Basil H. *The German Generals Talk.* New York: Willam Morrow, 1948.
Lucas, James. *Battle Group!* London: Arms and Armour Press, 1993.
Manvell, Roger, and Heinrich Fraenkel. *Goering: The Rise and Fall of the Notorious Nazi Leader.* New York: Skyhorse, 2011.
Maule, Henry. *Normandy Breakout.* New York: Quadrangle, 1977.
Mazower, Mark. *After the War Was Over: Reconstructing the Family, Nation, and State in Greece 1943–1960.* Princeton: Princeton University Press, 2000.
———. *Inside Hitler's Greece: The Experience of Occupation, 1941–1944.* New Haven: Yale University Press, 1995.
Megargee, Geoff. *Inside Hitler's High Command.* Lawrence: University Press of Kansas, 2000.
Miranda, Miguel. *Battle of Manila: Nadir of Japanese Barbarism.* South Yorkshire, UK: Pen and Sword Military, 2019.
Muñoz, Antonio. *Goering's Grenadiers: The Luftwaffe Field Divisions 1942–1945.* New York: Axis Europa Books, 2002.
Murray, Williamson R. *The Luftwaffe.* Baltimore: Nautical & Aviation Publishing Company of America, 1985.
Murray, Williamson R., and Allan R. Millett. *A War to Be Won: Fighting the Second World War.* Cambridge, MA: Harvard University Press, 2000.
Murray, Williamson R., and Allan R. Millett, eds. *Military Innovation in the Interwar Period.* Cambridge: Cambridge University Press, 1996.
Muth, Jörg. *Command Culture.* Denton: University of North Texas Press, 2011.
Nash, Douglas. *Victory Was Beyond Their Grasp: With the 272nd Volksgrenadier Division from the Huertgen Forest to the Heart of the Reich.* Philadelphia: Casemate, 2015.
Nielsen, Andreas. *The German Air Force General Staff.* New York: Arno, 1959.
Niepold, Gerd. *Battle for White Russia.* London: Brassey's, 1987.
Overy, Richard. *Goering: The Iron Man.* London: Routledge, 1984.

———. "Hitler and Air Strategy." *Journal of Contemporary History* 15, no. 3 (July 1980): 405–21.

———. *Why the Allies Won*. New York: W. W. Norton, 1995.

Ruffner, Kevin. *Luftwaffe Field Divisions 1941–45*. London: Osprey, 1990.

Rutherford, Jeff. "Life and Death in the Demiansk Pocket: The 123rd Infantry Division in Combat and Occupation." *Central European History* 41, no. 3 (September 2008): 347–80.

Scheibert, Horst. *Zwischen Don und Donez*. Neckargemünd: Kurt Vorwinckel Verlag, 1961.

Schönherr, Klaus. "Die Rückzugskämpfe in Rumänien und Siebenbürgen im Sommer/Herbst 1944." In *Das Deutsche Reich und der Zweite Weltkrieg*, vol. 8.

Schreiber, Horst. "Das Ende des nordafrikanischen Feldzugs und der Krieg in Italien." In *Das Deutsche Reich und der Zweite Weltkrieg*, vol. 6. Stuttgart: Deutsche Verlags-Anstalt, 1990.

Scott, James. *Rampage: MacArthur, Yamashita, and the Battle of Manila*. New York: W. W. Norton, 2018.

Shepherd, Ben. *Hitler's Soldiers: The German Army in the Third Reich*. New Haven: Yale University Press, 2016.

Showalter, Dennis. *Hitler's Panzers*. New York: Berkely Caliber, 2009.

Stahel, David. *The Battle for Moscow*. Cambridge: Cambridge University Press, 2015.

———. *Operation Barbarossa and Germany's Defeat in the East*. Cambridge: Cambridge University Press, 2009.

———. *Operation Typhoon: Hitler's March on Moscow*. Cambridge: Cambridge University Press, 2015.

———. *Retreat from Moscow*. New York: Farrar, Straus and Giroux, 2019.

Stang, Werner. "Zur Geschichte der Luftwaffenfelddivisionen der faschistischen Wehrmacht." *Zeitschrift für Militärgeschichte* 8 (1969): 196–207.

Stewart, Ian McDougall Guthrie. *The Struggle for Crete 20 May–1 June 1941: A Story of Lost Opportunity*. London: Oxford University Press, 1966.

Stone, Bill. "Review: Antonio J. Muñoz. *Goering's Grenadiers: The Luftwaffe Field Divisions 1942–1945*." Stone & Stone Books, http://stonebooks.com/archives/020414.shtml#a.

Thomas, Franz. *Die Eichenlaubträger 1940–1945 Band 2: L-Z*. Osnabrück: Biblio-Verlag, 1998.
Thomas, Nigel. *Hitler's Russian and Cossack Allies*. London: Osprey Publishing, 2015.
Tooze, Adam. *The Wages of Destruction*. New York: Viking, 2006.
Trevor-Roper, Hugh, trans. *Final Entries 1945: The Diaries of Joseph Goebbels*. New York: Avon, 1979.
Trial of the Major War Criminals before the International Military Tribunal. 22 vol. Nuremberg, 1946–49.
Ungvary, Krisztian. "Der ungarische Kriegsschauplatz." In *Das Deutsche Reich und der Zweite Weltkrieg*, vol. 8.
Van Creveld, Martin. *Fighting Power*. Westport, CT: Greenwood Press, 1982.
Vogel, Detlef. "Die Deutschen in Erwartung einer alliierten Invasion." In *Das Deutsche Reich und der Zweite Weltkrieg*, vol. 7. Stuttgart: Deutsche Verlags-Anstalt, 1990.
Wawro, Geoff. *The Austro-Prussian War*. Cambridge: Cambridge University Press, 1996.
———. *The Franco-Prussian War*. Cambridge: Cambridge University Press, 2003.
Weinberg, Gerhard. "Unexplored Questions about the German Military during World War II." *Journal of Military History* 62, no. 2 (1998): 375–76.
———. *A World at Arms*. New York: Cambridge University Press, 1994.
Westermann, Edward. *Flak: German Anti-Aircraft Defenses, 1914–1945*. Lawrence: University Press of Kansas, 2001.
Wette, Wolfram. *The Wehrmacht: History, Myth, Reality*. Cambridge, MA: Harvard University Press, 2006.
Wheeler-Bennett, John W. *The Nemesis of Power: The German Army in Politics, 1918–1945*. London: MacMillan, 1964.
Winton, Harold, and David Mets. *The Challenge of Change*. Lincoln: University of Nebraska Press, 2000.
Yelton, David. *Hitler's Volkssturm*. Lawrence: University Press of Kansas, 2002.

INDEX

Achse, Operation. *See* Axis
Afrikakorps, 8, 34
Air Divisions. *See Flieger* Divisions
air force: Allied, 16; Soviet Union, 10, 17, 26, 133
air force, Germany, 13, 16, 23–24, 26, 28, 39; antiaircraft units, 33–34; *Flieger* Divisions, 30–33, 66; *Fliegerkorps*, 52; *Luftflotten*, 17, 52, 65; personnel, 3, 108, 153, 155. *See also* antiaircraft units; *Fallschirmjägers*; Luftwaffe field divisions
Airborne Corps, Red Army, 45–46
Alarmeinheiten (emergency units), 37–41, 83
Ambrose, Stephen, 158n7
antiaircraft (Flak) units, 16, 22, 28, 30, 47–48, 52, 76; battalions, 34–35, 55, 67, 74–75, 79–86, 88–91, 95; formations, 29, 33–35
armed forces high command. *See* Oberkommando der Wehrmacht
Armeeabteilung Hollidt, 59, 60
armies: Bulgaria, 115; Italy, 89, 112; Romania, 56, 60–61, 67, 119, 131
armored divisions: British, 102; U.S., 109, 110
armored vehicles, 9, 11, 14, 34, 42, 100
Army, British, 101, 138; 8th, 110; 21st Group, 102; Armored Divisions, 102
Army, Germany: Second, 135; Sixth, 26, 45, 50, 59, 61, 66–67, 77, 87, 114; Seventh, 97, 105; Ninth, 62–63, 135; Tenth, 107; Fourteenth, 106–9; Fifteenth, 91, 97; Sixteenth, 122, 123, 124, 131, 145; Seventeenth, 59, 67; Eighteenth, 122, 123, 130–31; Nineteenth, 104; *Heer*, 73, 97, 148, 150–52, 155, 183n20; LwFDs and take over by, 73–74; manpower, 119–20, 193n13;

Spanish Blue Division, 78, 80; surrenders, 31, 36, 87, 106, 115, 145, 151–52. *See also* Army Corps; Army Groups; infantry battalions; infantry divisions
Army, Soviet Union. *See* Red Army
Army, U.S.: 1st Armored Division, 109, 110; First, 106; Third, 105; Seventh, 36, 104; 34th Infantry Division, 108–9; 36th Infantry Division, 108; armor and heavy weapons, 187n62; ASTP, 154–55; in France, 101, 103–4, 108–9; intelligence, 153; Meindl and, 169n10, 187n65
Army Corps: II, 41, 44–45, 47; IX, 136, 137; LIII, 64, 118, 136–38; LVII, 65–66; V, 66, 67; VI, 136–37; X, 130; XXIX, 66–67; XXVIII, 128; XXXIV, 114; XXXVIII, 128–30, 143–44; XXXXIII, 63
Army Group Center, 62–64, 105, 117; Third Panzer Army, 133; 6th LwFD and, 74; Army Group North and, 123, 140, 141–42; collapse of, 118, 131, 140, 141; FD (L)s and, 83–87, 118, 133, 151; II LwFK with, 52; Operation Bagration and, 134–36; Operation Barbarossa and, 10, 11; panzer divisions with, 132–33, 136
Army Group North, 41, 44, 59, 64, 117, 125, 173n60, 185n32; 7th *Flieger* Division and, 33; Army Group Center and, 123, 140, 141–42; as Army Group Courland, 118, 142, 145; FD (L)s on Eastern Front with, 74–75, 77–83, 118, 121, 123–24, 127–31, 138, 140–47, 151, 193n15, 193n20, 194n26, 195n33; III LwFK with, 52; Leningrad and, 10, 11; LwFDs and, 74–75; manpower, 122–23; Ukraine, 120, 132, 135

217

Army Group North (Haupt), 173n60
Army Group South, 10, 52, 96, 105, 117, 119, 192n6; FD (L)s and, 118; Ukraine, 120, 131, 132
Army Groups: A, 52, 76; B, 52, 97, 99; Courland, 118, 142, 145; Don, 60; E, 132; F, 132; G, 97, 99, 104; Vistula, 37
army high command. *See Oberbefehlshaber-West*; *Oberkommando des Heeres*
Army Specialized Training Program (ASTP), U.S. Army, 154–55
assassinations, 20, 38–39, 105, 110
ASTP. *See* Army Specialized Training Program
Auftragstaktik ("mission tactics"), 8–9
Austria, 9, 20, 36, 113–16, 151
Axis (*Achse*), Operation, 36, 89

Bagration, Operation, 5, 118, 131–36, 139–41, 147, 151, 196n44, 197n58
the Balkans, 8, 15, 89, 120, 137; FD (L)s in, 95, 111–16, 150–51; LwFDs in, 3; partisans in, 90, 95, 115, 151
the Baltics, 117–18, 121–22, 132, 134, 141–42
Band of Brothers (film), 157n2
Bandenbekämpfung (combating banditry), 37–41
Barbarossa, Operation, 10–12, 15–16, 20, 26, 33–36, 135, 163nn18–19
Bartov, Omer, 183n20
Basic Order Number 3, 54, 62
Battle for Leningrad (Glantz), 194n30
Battle for White Russia (Niepold), 197n58
Battle Group! (Lucas), 172n48
Battle Groups. *See Kampfgruppen*
Bayerlein, Fritz, 100
Beck, Ludwig, 20
Belgium, 8, 31, 106
Belorussia, 135, 137
Bewegungskrieg ("the war of operational movement"), 8, 9, 15
Białowieża Forest, 38, 39
bicycles, 58, 94; infantry divisions with, 90, 91, 108; police battalions, 38
blitzkriegs, 10, 12, 15, 29–30
Blomberg, Werner von, 19–20, 26, 166n51
Bock, *Kampfgruppen*, 128
Bodenstandig units. *See* static units

Brauchitsch, Bernd von, 39, 172n40
Brauchitsch, Walther von, 20
Bridge-Laying. *See Brückenschlag*
Brockdorff-Ahlefeldt, Walter von, 44
Brückenschlag (Bridge-Laying), Operation, 45, 47–48, 173n60
Bulgaria, 113, 115–16, 120
Bundesarchiv-Militäriarchiv, Freiburg, 160n14
Busch, Ernst, 134–35

Caen, France, 101–3, 150
Canada, 101
Carsten, F. L., 161n2, 163n20, 164n20, 166n45
Case Yellow (*Fall Gelb*) offensive, 31
casualties: FD (L)s, 78, 84, 88, 101, 110, 125; Germany, 10, 12, 89–90, 101, 112, 137, 142, 163n17, 197n55; Italy, 89; LwFDs, 6, 50, 59, 61, 64, 68, 71, 76–77, 149, 185n31; Red Army, 12, 78–79, 140, 178n50; replacements for, 2
category III formation, 12th FD (L) as, 82, 127
Cavalry Corps, Romanian, 67
Challenge of Change, The (Winton and Mets), 162n6
Charnwood, Operation, 102
children, deportation of, 38
Chudovo, 80, 121, 127
Citadel, Operation, 70, 93–94, 117
Citino, Robert M., 157n1, 161n3, 162n7, 162n9, 192n6, 196n44, 197n55
Claasen, Adam, 169n3
Clark, Alan, 169n3
Cobra, Operation, 104
Colossus Reborn (Glantz), 162n9
combating banditry. *See Bandenbekämpfung*
conscription, 13, 55, 98, 158n7
Cooper, Matthew, 161n2
Courland pocket, 118, 140–46, 198n82
Crisolli, *Kampfgruppen*, 110
Crisolli, Wilhelm, 110
Czechoslovakia, 20, 36, 39

D-day, 100–101, 158n7, 187n2
D-Day (Ambrose), 158n7
DDRZW. *See Deutsche Reich und der Zweite Weltkrieg, Das*

Index   219

Death of the Wehrmacht (Citino), 162n7, 162n9
Demiansk pocket, 26, 41, 44–48, 82, 172n48, 173n60
Denmark, 8, 10, 31, 91, 109
Denzel, Egon, 159n10, 174n2, 175n6, 176n26, 177n30, 181n1
deployments: FD (L)s, 78, 184n25, 190n39; LwFDs, 3, 17, 25, 41, 50–57, 60–61, 68, 81, 83–85, 87, 89–90, 175n8, 177n33, 183n16
deportation, Jews, 38–39
D'Este, Carlo, 191n58
Deutsche Reich und der Zweite Weltkrieg, Das (DDRZW), 178n43, 181n78, 193n13, 193n20, 197n55
Diadem, Operation, 107
Dierich, Wolfgang, 175n8
Directives, Führer: No. 46, 38, 39; No. 51, 97
Division Meindl, 5, 52–53, 85, 130; 21st LwFD as, 74, 82, 146, 188n3; Demiansk pocket and, 44–48
Dnieper-Carpathian offensive, 77
Dombås, 31
Doppelkopf, Operation, 141
Dragoon, Operation, 104, 108–9

East battalions. *See Ost* battalions
Eastern Front, 34–35, 41, 52, 134, 139, 196n44; air operations, 16, 26, 39; FD (L)s with Army Group North on, 74–75, 77–83, 118, 121, 123–24, 127–31, 138, 140–47, 151, 193n15, 193n20, 194n26, 195n33; historiography, 162n9; LwFDs and, 3, 5, 7, 33, 54, 58–60, 62, 67, 74, 85–87, 105, 117–18, 148, 151, 153, 195n39; OB-West and, 96, 98; OKH and, 21, 96; Operation Citadel, 70, 93–94, 117; panzer units on, 15, 36–37, 132–33
economy, 2, 19, 38, 134, 164n22
Einsatzgruppen, 171n34
emergency units. *See Alarmeinheiten*
Epsom, Operation, 102
Estonia, 141

Fall Gelb offensive. *See* Case Yellow offensive
Fall of Crete, The (Clark), 169n3
Fallreep (Gangway), Operation, 47

Fallschirmjägers (paratroopers), 29, 37, 68; 1st Division, 30, 35, 109; 2nd Division, 69; 4th Division, 110; early war and, 30–33
Fallschirm-Panzerkorp. *See* Parachute Panzer
Fatal Decision (D'Este), 191n58
FD (L). *See* Felddivision (*Luftwaffe*)
Fedyuninsky, I. I., 124, 126, 193n20
Felddivision (*Luftwaffe*) (FD [L]): 1st, 78–81, 118, 121, 127–30, 138, 147, 151, 182n11, 184n25, 195n37, 195nn39–40; 3rd, 83–86, 118; Third Panzer Army at Vitebsk with, 83–85, 136–39; 4th, 83–85, 118, 133, 136–39, 147, 151; 5th, 118, 151; 6th, 83–87, 118, 133, 136–39, 147, 151, 182n11; 9th, 79–80, 118, 121–27, 129, 138, 147, 151, 153, 184n25; 10th, 79–80, 118, 121–27, 129, 138, 147, 151, 153; 11th, 75, 89–90, 95, 111–16, 150–51, 187nn59–60, 191n61; 12th, 81–83, 118, 121, 123, 127–29, 131, 140–47, 151, 193n15; 13th, 80–81, 118, 121, 127–29, 140, 147, 151, 184n29, 194n31, 195nn33–34; 14th, 95, 152; 16th, 76, 88, 94, 99, 101–3, 106, 115, 125, 138, 150, 153, 189n27; 17th, 76, 88, 94, 99–101, 103–6, 115, 150, 186n57; 18th, 88–89, 94, 96, 99–101, 103–6, 115, 150, 182n11, 189n26, 190n39, 190n42; 19th, 90–92, 94, 106–11, 115, 150, 187n62, 190n54; 20th, 91–92, 94–95, 106–11, 115, 150–51; 21st, 81–83, 118, 121, 123, 127, 130–31, 140–47, 151; of Army Group Center, 83–87, 118, 133, 151; with Army Group North, Eastern Front, 74–75, 77–83, 118, 121, 123–24, 127–31, 138, 140–47, 151, 193n15, 193n20, 194n26, 195n33; artillery, 75; ASTP and, 154–55; in the Balkans, 95, 111–16, 150–51; with bicycles, 94; British bombardment of, 138; casualties, 78, 84, 88, 101, 110, 125; as category III formation, 82, 127; collapse of, 147, 150–51, 195n40; Courland pocket and, 140–45; critics, 193n20; deployment, 78, 184n25, 190n39; destruction of, 103, 106, 137–38, 147, 150–52; disbanding of, 129, 140; dissolution of, 86, 103, 109–10, 118, 130, 147, 150, 190n42, 190n54; on eastern edge of line, 127–31; evaluation of,

Felddivision (*Luftwaffe*) (FD [L]) (*continued*) 145–47; in France, 87–89, 94, 96, 98–106, 125, 150, 153; in Greece, 89–90, 187n59, 191n61; with infantry battalions, 79, 107, 118; in Italy, 90–92, 94, 106–11, 150–51, 187n62; *Kampfgruppen* and, 110, 128, 129, 130; Leningrad-Novgorod offensive and, 125, 127–28, 130–31, 143, 147, 151, 193n20, 194n31, 195n37; LwFDs redesignated as, 73, 75, 182n2; manpower, 73, 75–76, 79, 83, 86, 88, 91, 95, 99–100, 108, 118, 128–30, 144, 145, 189n27; on Mediterranean Front, 90, 94–95; morale, 74, 76, 88–89, 99, 101, 182n11; in Norway, 95, 152; OKW and, 103, 109; Operation Bagration and, 131–36; Oranienbaum pocket and, 79, 121–27, 129, 153; records, 186n57, 187n59, 187n62, 189n26, 191n61, 194n31, 195n37, 195n40; reports, 193n15; standout formations, 81–83; static units, 76, 88, 94, 99, 103, 106, 109, 115, 121, 150; storm divisions, 94; surrender of, 115, 145, 151–52; targeting of, 125, 130, 153, 193n20; training, 134; weapons, 79–80, 99, 107; on Western Front, 94–95, 97

Felddivision, 1st (*Luftwaffe*) (FD [L]), 184n25, 195n37, 195n39; with Army Group North, Eastern Front, 78–81, 118, 121, 127–30, 138; collapse of, 147, 151, 195n40; morale, 182n11

Felddivision, 11th (*Luftwaffe*) (FD [L]): in the Balkans, 95, 111–16, 150–51; in Greece, 89–90, 187n59, 191n61; manpower, 75; strength of, 187n60; surrender, 115, 151

Felddivision, 12th (*Luftwaffe*) (FD [L]), 193n15; with Army Group North, 81–82, 118, 121, 123, 127–29, 131, 140–46, 151; Courland pocket and, 140–45; evaluating, 145–47; as standout formation, 81–83

Felddivision, 21st (*Luftwaffe*) (FD [L]): with Army Group North, 82, 118, 121, 123, 127, 130–31, 140–45, 151; Courland pocket and, 140–45; evaluating, 145–47; as standout formation, 81–83

Feldregimenter der Luftwaffe. *See* Luftwaffe field regiments

films, 1, 157n2, 165n34

Finland, 119, 121, 141

Flak units. *See* antiaircraft units

Flieger (Air) Divisions: 7th, 30–33; Mahncke with, 66

Fliegerkorps, XIII, 52

Forest Protection Corps (*Forstschutzkorps*, FSK), 38

FR der Lw. *See* Luftwaffe field regiments

Fraenkel, Heinrich, 25, 27

France, 8, 9–10, 74; Army Group Center in, 11; Caen, 101–3, 150; Case Yellow offensive into, 31; D-day, 100–101, 187n2; FD (L)s in, 87–89, 94, 96, 98–106, 125, 150, 153; German mess in, 95–99; guerrillas, 189n26; U.S. Army in, 101, 103–4, 108–9

Frank, Hans, 167n62

Frederick II, 9

French Expeditionary Corps, 110

Frevert, Walter, 38, 39

Frieser, Karl-Heinz, 168n77, 197n55

Fritsch, Werner von, 19–20, 26, 166n51

FSK. *See* Forest Protection Corps

Gangway, Operation. *See* Fallreep

German Army, The (Cooper), 161n2

German Generals Talk, The (Liddell Hart), 161n2

German Way of War, The (Citino), 161n3

Glantz, David, 161n2, 167n62, 178n50, 194n30, 196n44; on infantry divisions, 133–34; on Operation Barbarossa, 10–11. *See also When Titans Clashed*

glider-borne troops. *See Luftlande* Division

Goebbels, Joseph, 27

Goering (Overy), 168n74

Goering, Hermann, 168n74, 170n23; antiaircraft units and, 75; Basic Order Number 3 and, 54, 62; critics, 65, 155; Hitler and, 18, 22, 25–28, 51, 70, 155, 168n77, 174n1; interrogation of, 181n79; LwFDs and, 3, 15–17, 22–25, 27–28, 49, 51–54, 64, 69–70, 72, 148–49; at Nuremburg trials, 27; RFA and, 16, 38. *See also* Parachute Panzer Division

Goering's Grenadiers (Muñoz), 193n20, 195n39

Gollwitzer, Friedrich, 136–37

Goodwood, Operation, 5, 101–3, 125, 138, 150, 153, 189n32

Göring's Grenadiers (Muñoz), 173n57, 179n56, 190n54
Great Britain, 2, 9, 26, 36, 89, 151. *See also* Army, British
Great Escape, The (film), 165n34
Greece, 10, 115; FD (L)s in, 89–90, 187n59, 191n61; Operation Mercury, 26, 31–33, 169n7; partisans in, 41, 89, 112–13, 116, 191n61
Greek People's Liberation Army, 113
grenadier regiments: from 21st Panzer Division, 102; 424th of 126th Division, 125
Grier, Howard, 198n82
Groppe, Theodor, 166n48
Grossdeutschland Panzergrenadier Divisions, 63, 120, 141
ground war (1939–42), 29–30
Guards Rifle Corps, Red Army, 58; 1st, 44, 48, 173n63; 2nd, 44; 6th, 137
Guderian, Heinz, 10
guerrillas, 79, 83–84, 112, 113, 115, 189n26. *See also* partisans

Halder, Franz, 10, 20, 26, 168n77
Handbook on German Military Forces (U.S. War Department), 153
Hanks, Tom, 157n2
Haupt, Werner, 173n60, 182n8
Hauptquartier (Warlimont), 174n4
Heer, 73, 97, 148, 150–52, 155, 183n20
Heiber, Helmut, 161n2, 167n62
Henke, Gerhard, 113
Herbst, Emil, 39–40
"Hermann Goering" Division. *See* Parachute Panzer Division
Heydrich, Reinhard, 20, 39
Hilfswilligen. See Hiwis
Hill, Alexander, 178n50
Himmler, Heinrich, 20, 23, 39
Hindenburg, Paul von, 19
History of Fallschirm-Panzerkorps Hermann Goering, The (Kurowski), 170n23
Hitler, Adolf, 87, 95, 99, 167n62; assassination plot against, 20, 105; critics, 26, 57, 168n73, 176n25, 179n56; directives from, 38, 39, 97; Goering and, 18, 22, 25–28, 51, 70, 155, 168n77, 174n1; leadership, 7, 11–12, 23, 26, 123, 137, 139, 142–43, 149, 161n2, 163n18, 166n45, 168n73, 168n77; LwFDs and, 3, 15, 17–18, 24, 30, 34, 51, 54, 69, 70, 72–73, 91, 150, 175n15; Nazis and, 19–20, 22; OKW and, 5, 20–22, 96, 136, 167n57, 176n25; Operation Bagration and, 134–35; Operation Citadel and, 93, 94; storm divisions and, 107–8
Hitler, Dönitz, and the Baltic Sea (Grier), 198n82
Hitler and His Generals (Heiber and Glantz), 161n2, 167n62
Hitler's Army (Bartov), 183n20
Hitler's Northern War (Claasen), 169n3
Hitler's Soldiers (Shepherd), 161n2, 183n20
Hiwis (*Hilfswilligen*, Russian "volunteers"), 74, 76, 79, 94, 135, 183n12
Höcker, Oberst Hans, 104, 160n14, 190n38
Hollidt, Karl-Adolf, 66
Holocaust, 2
Hoth, Hermann, 10
House, Jonathan. *See When Titans Clashed*
Hungary, 114, 119, 120
hunting commandos. *See Jagdkommandos*
Husky, Operation, 93

infantry battalions: with 2nd LwFD, 62; with 3rd LwFD, 83, 85; with 4th FD (L), 118; with 4th LwFD, 85; with 5th LwFD, 67, 77; with 6th LwFD, 85; with 7th LwFD, 59; with 8th LwFD, 60; with 9th FD (L), 79; with 10th FD (L), 79; with 11th LwFD, 89; with 12th LwFD, 81; with 13th LwFD, 80; with 16th Army, 124; with 16th LwFD, 88; with 20th FD (L), 107; divisional strength discrepancy and, 57; infantry divisions and, 97; naval, 55
infantry divisions: Red Army, 43, 86, 126, 174n2, 176n26; U.S. Army, 108–9
infantry divisions, Germany, 3, 11, 15, 65, 75, 120, 127; 8th, 128; 11th, 195n33; 30th, 131; 32nd, 143; 34th, 108–9; 44th, 90; 65th, 90, 109; 83rd, 143; 126th, 48, 124–26, 128, 140; 129th, 84; 170th, 126; 197th, 137; 206th, 136, 137; 212th, 80, 128; 215th, 124, 140; 218th, 142; 246th, 62–63, 136, 137; 272nd, 102, 103; 336th, 60; 344th, 104; 356th, 110; 424th Grenadier Regiment with, 125; with bicycles,

infantry divisions, Germany (*continued*) 90, 91, 108; collapse of, 139; in France, 97–98; with II Army Corps, 44; III SS Panzer Corps, 124; LwFDs and, 77, 148; Red Army compared to, 133–34

intelligence: British, 102; German, 50, 56, 133, 149; Red Army, 56, 125; U.S. Army, 153

interrogation, 181n79, 189n32

Isserson, Georgii, 119

Italy, 3, 33, 55, 93, 112; FD (L)s in, 90–92, 94, 106–11, 150–51, 187n62; Operation Axis and, 36, 89

Iwabuchi, Sanji, 154

Jagdkommandos (hunting commandos), 40, 79

Jäger Divisions: 28th, 128, 130; 97th, 67

Jäger-Sonderkommando Bialowies der Luftwaffe (JSKB), 39–41, 48, 172n45

Japan, 154

Jeschonnek, Hans, 18, 23, 54, 69–70

Jews, 22, 38, 40, 48, 171n34

Jodl, Alfred, 18, 23

JSKB. *See Jäger-Sonderkommando Bialowies der Luftwaffe*

Juin, Alphonse, 110

Kampfgruppen (Battle Groups), 172n48; Bock, 128; Crisolli, 110; Pohl, 128; Scherer, 41; Schuldt, 128, 129; Speth, 128, 130

Keitel, Wilhelm, 18, 20, 23, 165n40, 166n53

Kesselring, Albert, 24, 191n58; in Italy, 55, 93–94, 108, 111; memoirs, 4, 167n66, 174n4, 179n56

Kholm pocket, 26, 41–45, 47–48, 121–22, 130, 172n48, 173n57

Kirchensittenbach, Friedrich-Jobst von, 145

Kirishima (Japan), 154

Kluge, Günther von, 105

Knight's Cross, 86, 106, 140–41, 142, 145

Konev, I. S., 63

Korovnikov, Ivan, 129–30

Kretzschmar, Wolfgang, 142

Kriegsmarine, 18, 98

Kroener, Bernhard, 178n43, 181n78

Kuban bridgehead, 152, 199n9

Küchler, George von, 123

Kurochkin, P. A., 44–45, 173n63

Kurowski, Franz, 170n23

Kutuzov, Operation, 93

Latvia, 141, 143

Latvian SS brigade, 128–29, 142–43; 15th Division, 131; 19th Division, 144

Lebensraum, 19, 38

Leningrad, 121, 124, 193n13, 194n30; liberation of, 117, 131; siege of, 5, 11, 78, 125

Leningrad Front, Red Army, 141

Leningrad-Novgorod offensive, 117, 119, 140, 146, 194n30; FD (L)s and, 125, 127–28, 130–31, 143, 147, 151, 193n20, 194n31, 195n37; LwFDs and, 118, 120–21

Liddell Hart, Basil H., 161n2

Lucas, James, 172n48

Luftflotten: 2, 17; 4, 52, 65; 5, 52

Luftlande (glider-borne troops) Division, 42, 69; 22nd, 30; *Sturmregiment*, 32–33, 37, 47, 52–53

Luftwaffe. *See* air force, German; *Felddivision*

Luftwaffe field corps (*Luftwaffenfeldkorps*, LwFK): I, 52; II, 52, 62–64, 83–86; III, 52; IV, 52, 70

Luftwaffe Field Division, 2nd (*Luftwaffenfelddivision*, LwFD): deployment, 50–51, 52, 57, 84; destruction of, 59, 65, 70, 71; disbanding of, 64, 180n77; with II LwFK, 52, 63–64, 83, 86; "luckless," 62–65, 71; in Rzhev salient, 50, 57, 59, 62, 64, 71, 105, 125, 138; training of, 53, 65

Luftwaffe Field Division, 5th (*Luftwaffenfelddivision*, LwFD): casualties, 59, 68, 76–77; deployment, 50–51, 52, 68; fighting retreat of, 70, 76, 77; manpower, 59, 68, 77, 199n9; in Southern Russia, 65–68; training, 53, 77

Luftwaffe Field Division, 8th (*Luftwaffenfelddivision*, LwFD), 178n41; deployment, 50–51, 52, 60; destruction of, 59–62, 63, 65, 71, 178n44; with I LwFK, 52; manpower, 59, 61, 66, 178n42; training, 53, 60, 177n35

Luftwaffe Field Division, 15th (*Luftwaffenfelddivision*, LwFD), 70, 72, 178n41, 180n60;

Index   223

deployment, 50–51, 52, 61, 68; destruction of, 68, 71, 178n44; manpower, 59, 61, 65, 66, 178n42; in Southern Russia, 65–68
Luftwaffe field divisions (*Luftwaffenfelddivisionen*, LwFDs), 8, 122, 159n12, 163n17, 165n14, 181n1; 1st, 52, 53, 58, 74, 183n16, 184n22; 2nd, 50–53, 57, 59, 62–65, 70–71, 83–84, 86, 105, 125, 138, 180n77; 3rd, 52–53, 59, 63–64, 83–85; 4th, 52–53, 59, 63–64, 83–85; 5th, 50–53, 59, 65–68, 70, 76–77, 199n9; 6th, 52–53, 59, 63–64, 74, 83–86; 7th, 50–53, 59–63, 65–66, 71, 177n33, 177n35, 178n42, 178n44; 8th, 50–53, 59–63, 65–66, 71, 77, 177n35, 178n44, 178nn41–42; 9th, 52, 53; 10th, 52, 53; 11th, 41, 52, 58, 89–90; 12th, 52, 81, 185n31; 13th, 52, 80–81; 14th, 6, 52; 15th, 50–52, 59, 61, 65–68, 70–72, 77, 178n44, 178nn41–42, 180n60; 16th, 52, 87, 88, 186n52; 17th, 52, 87, 88, 160n14; 18th, 52, 87, 88; 19th, 52, 90; 20th, 52, 91; 21st, 52, 58, 74–75, 81–83, 146, 158n9, 188n3; 22nd, 58, 75, 83, 158n9, 188n3; archival records, 4–5, 160n14; Army takes over, 73–74; artillery, 80, 84, 88; with bicycles, 58; casualties, 6, 50, 59, 61, 64, 68, 71, 76–77, 149, 185n31; collapse, 50, 54, 59, 62, 70; critics, 3, 50, 51, 65, 91, 148, 155, 165n38, 188n20; with dearth of academic analysis, 4; deployments, 3, 17, 25, 41, 50–57, 60–61, 68, 81, 83–85, 87, 89–90, 175n8, 177n33, 183n16; destruction of, 3, 6, 50, 58–63, 65, 68, 70–71, 178n44; disbanding of, 64, 180n77; dissolution of, 6, 25, 50, 61, 70, 77; Eastern Front and, 3, 5, 7, 33, 54, 58–60, 62, 67, 74, 85–87, 105, 117–18, 148, 151, 153, 195n39; equipment, 6, 49, 51, 53, 65, 71, 75, 181n79; failures on battlefield, 3, 49–50, 58, 61, 62, 64–65, 68, 149–50, 178n43; German officers with memoirs on, 4–5, 50, 167n57, 167n70, 168n73, 174nn4–5, 175n15, 179n56, 187n65; Goering and, 3, 15–17, 22–25, 27–28, 49, 51–54, 64, 69–70, 72, 148–49; Hitler and, 3, 15, 17–18, 24, 30, 34, 51, 54, 69, 70, 72–73, 91, 150, 175n15; with infantry battalions, 57, 59–60, 62, 67, 77, 80–81, 83, 85, 88–89, 124; infantry divisions and, 77, 148; Leningrad-Novgorod offensive and, 118, 120–21; manpower, 4, 23, 28–29, 49, 52, 54, 58–59, 61, 64–66, 68, 74–77, 82–83, 90–91, 149, 158n9, 174n2, 178n42, 199n9; Manstein and, 3, 4, 16–17, 50, 54, 71, 148, 155, 165n38, 169n1, 178n44; Meindl and, 5, 33, 52–54, 57, 68–70, 82, 91, 150, 169n10, 170n13, 187n65, 188n3; misorganization, 54–57, 58; morale, 68, 150; Nazis and, 24; in Norway, 3, 6, 52; OKH and, 150, 182n4; OKW and, 17–18, 69; organization and training, 50–54; panzer divisions and, 35–37, 56–57, 60, 69, 175n8; personnel changes, 74–77; redesignated as FD (L), 73, 75, 182n2; remnants incorporated into *Volksgrenadier* units, 25; reorganization of, 6, 69–71, 73, 76, 79, 148–50, 181n78, 182n8; secondary sources on, 159n10, 174n1; "solutions" and stigma, 68–72; as static units, 15, 81, 87, 98, 153; strength discrepancy, 57–59; supply lines, 55; targeting, 125, 138–39, 153, 195n39; training, 6, 49–54, 57, 60, 65, 69, 71, 77, 81, 83, 91, 146, 149, 170n13, 174n1, 177n35, 190n54; volunteers, 24, 52, 149, 155; weapons and, 49, 55, 58, 60–62, 64, 67, 71–72, 77, 80–83, 88, 176n26; on Western Front, 115
Luftwaffe Field Divisions (Ruffner), 159n10, 163n17, 168n73, 175n14, 183n12, 198n84
Luftwaffe field divisions, creation of (*Luftwaffenfelddivisionen*, LwFDs), 3, 5; *Alarmeinheiten* and *Bandenbekämpfung*, 37–41; Demiansk pocket and Division Meindl, 44–48; *Fallschirmjäger* and early war, 30–33; Flak formations in ground role, 33–35; FR der Lw and Kholm pocket, 41–43; in ground war, 29–30; Hitler and Goering, 18, 22, 25–28, 51, 155, 174n1; Luftwaffe personnel as solution, 16–17; manpower crisis and, 12–16, 68, 168n73; meeting of 12 September 1942, 17–18; origins, 7–8; Parachute Panzer Division and, 35–37, 68; tension in

Luftwaffe field divisions, creation of (*continued*)
German high command, 18–25, 148, 161n2, 166n50; the Wehrmacht and, 8–12
Luftwaffe field regiments (*Feldregimenter der Luftwaffe*, FR der Lw), 41–43, 45, 47, 173n57
Luftwaffe *Sicherungsbataillon* (LwSB, security battalion), 39–40, 172n40
Luftwaffe-Jäger-Regiment: 9, III Battalion, 199n9; 19, 126; 21, III Battalion, 112; 22, II Battalion, 112; 31, I Battalion, 186n52
Luftwaffenfelddivisionen. See Luftwaffe field divisions
Luftwaffenfelddivisionen 1942–45, Die (Denzel), 159n10, 174n2, 175n6, 176n26, 177n30, 181n1
Luftwaffenfeldkorps. See Luftwaffe field corps
LwFDs. See Luftwaffe field divisions
LwFK. See Luftwaffe field corps
LwSB. See Luftwaffe *Sicherungsbataillon*

Mackensen, Eberhard von, 107
Mahncke, Alfred, 65–66, 179n56, 187n65
Maigewitter (May Thunderstorm), Operation, 86
Malta, 26
Manila, Battle of, 154
manpower, Germany: Army, 119–20, 193n13; Army Group North, 122–23; Army Group South, 119–20; crisis, 5, 7, 12–16, 17, 28, 68, 148, 164n30, 168n73; FD (L)s, 73, 75–76, 79, 83, 86, 88, 91, 95, 99–100, 108, 118, 128–30, 144, 145, 189n27; LwFDs, 4, 23, 28–29, 49, 52, 54, 58–59, 61, 64–66, 68, 74–77, 82–83, 90–91, 149, 158n9, 174n2, 178n42, 199n9; OB-West, 98
manpower, Red Army, 12, 15, 58, 119, 123, 134, 144, 177n30, 193n13
Manstein, Erich von, 60, 105, 187n65; LwFDs and, 3, 4, 16–17, 50, 54, 71, 148, 155, 165n38, 169n1, 178n44; OKH and, 23. See also *Verlorene Siege*
Manvell, Roger, 25, 27
Mark I, 14
Mark II, 14
Mark III, 14
Mark IV, 100

Mark V Panthers, 100
Mark VI Tigers, 100
Market-Garden, Operation, 46
Mars, Operation, 50, 57, 62–63, 125, 178n50, 179n51
maskirovka (misinformation and deception tactics), 56, 72, 131, 133
massacres, 39, 154
Mauser Kar98k carbine, 39
May Thunderstorm, Operation. See *Maigewitter*
Mediterranean Front, 17, 26, 74, 90, 94–95
Meindl, Eugen, 160n14, 176n25; with Division Meindl, 5, 44–48, 52–53, 74, 82, 85, 130, 146, 188n3; *Luftlande Sturmregiment* and, 32–33, 37, 47, 52–53; LwFDs and, 5, 33, 52–54, 57, 68–70, 82, 91, 150, 169n10, 170n13, 187n65, 188n3; on morale, 76, 182n11; U.S. Army and, 169n10, 187n65
Mellenthin, F. W. von, 51, 71–72, 159n10, 174n5, 181n79
Mercury, Operation, 26, 31–33, 169n7
Mets, David, 162n6
Michael, Ernst, 125
Milch, Erhard, 69
Military Innovation in the Interwar Period (Murray and Millett), 162n6
Millett, Allan R., 162n6
misinformation and deception tactics. See *maskirovka*
"mission tactics." See *Auftragstaktik*
Model, Walter, 105, 132
the Mons pocket, 106, 150
Montgomery, Bernard, 102
morale, 24, 120; FD (L)s, 74, 76, 88–89, 99, 101, 182n11; LwFDs, 68, 150
Müller-Hillebrand, Burkhardt, 14, 54–55
Muñoz, Antonio, 173n57, 179n56, 182n8, 190n54, 193n20, 195n39
Murray, Williamson R., 162n6

Napoleon III, 9
Nash, Douglas, 158n7
National and Social Liberation, Greece, 113
National Republican Greek League, 113
National Socialism, 21, 24
Natzmer, Oldwig von, 120

navies: German, 13, 18, 21, 55, 96, 98, 142; Soviet Baltic Fleet, 121
Nazis, traditionalists and, 8, 18–25, 148, 161n2, 166n45, 166n48, 166n50. *See also* SS
NCOs. *See* noncommissioned officers
Nemesis of Power, The (Wheeler-Bennett), 161n2
the Netherlands, 8, 31–32, 46
Nevel, Battle of, 64, 70, 84
Niepold, Gerd, 197n58
Night of the Long Knives, 19, 35
noncommissioned officers (NCOs), 14, 39, 58, 100, 129, 154
North Africa, 8, 26, 34, 36
Northwestern Front, 44, 74
Norway, 3, 6, 8, 31, 52, 95, 152
Nuremburg trials, 27

Oberbefehlshaber-West (OB-West, army high command), 96, 98, 105
Oberkommando der Luftwaffe (OKL), 69, 96
Oberkommando der Marine, 96
Oberkommando der Wehrmacht (OKW, armed forces high command), 16, 48, 95, 174n70; FD (L)s and, 103, 109; Hitler and, 5, 20–22, 96, 136, 167n57, 176n25; LwFDs and, 17–18, 69; OKH and, 18, 21, 23, 96, 167n57
Oberkommando des Heeres (OKH, army high command), 3, 12, 17, 30, 56, 63–64, 70; Hitler undermining, 7; LwFDs and, 150, 182n4; Nazis and traditionalists, 8, 18–25, 148, 161n2, 166n45, 166n48, 166n50; OKW and, 18, 21, 23, 96, 167n57
OB-West. *See Oberbefehlshaber-West*
OKH. *See Oberkommando des Heeres*
OKL. *See Oberkommando der Luftwaffe*
OKW. *See Oberkommando der Wehrmacht*
Oranienbaum pocket, 79, 121–27, 129, 153
Ost (East) battalions, 79, 88, 153, 158n7, 183n12; as poorer quality soldiers, 2, 76, 98, 104; with POWs and "volunteers," 2, 16, 98
Overy, Richard, 27, 168n74

Panzer Army: 1st, 67; 2nd, 114; 3rd, 83–85, 133, 136–39, 141–42; 4th, 59; 6th, 114

Panzer Battles (Mellenthin), 51, 71, 159n10, 174n5, 181n79
Panzer Corps: "Hermann Goering" parachute, 25, 30, 35–37, 41, 48, 68, 149, 170n23; III SS, 124, 126; XIV, 108; XXXIX, 41–43; XXXXVIII, 60–61
panzer divisions, 28, 31, 97, 105, 120, 122, 161n3; 1st SS, 102–3; 11th, 36, 60; 12th, 63, 197n58; 19th, 63; 20th, 63, 136; 21st, 101–3, 189n27; 24th, 90; 26th, 109, 110, 111; 65th, 109; with Army Group Center, 132–33, 136; as cutting-edge, 8–11, 14, 15; in France, 98–99, 101–2; Lehr, 100–101; Luftwaffe and, 16; LwFDs and, 35–37, 56–57, 60, 69, 175n8; production and resupply, 2. *See also* Parachute Panzer Division
Panzergrenadier Divisions, 122, 133; 3rd, 110; 11th SS *Nordland*, 124; 29th, 110–11; 90th, 111; *Grossdeutschland*, 63, 120, 141
Panzergruppe West, 99
Parachute Corps, II, 169n10, 170n13
Parachute Panzer (*Fallschirm-Panzerkorp*, "Hermann Goering") Division, 25, 30, 41, 48, 149; history of, 170n23; LwFDs and, 35–37, 68
paratroopers, Allied, 46
paratroopers, Germany. *See Fallschirmjägers*
partisans, 38–40, 110, 114; in the Balkans, 90, 95, 115, 151; Greek, 41, 89, 112–13, 116, 191n61; guerrillas and, 79, 83–84, 112, 113, 115, 189n26; Russian, 37, 45, 47–48, 79–80, 83–86, 123, 136
Patton (film), 157n2
Patton, George S., 36, 105
Peschel, Rudolf, 86
Peschl, Walter, 137, 138
Petersen, Erich, 70
Pistorius, Robert, 138
Pohl, *Kampfgruppen*, 128
Poland, 8, 9, 14–15, 20, 37–40, 96
police, 14, 35, 39, 40, 65, 83, 139; 4th SS Division, 112; 65th Reserve Battalion, 42; bicycle battalion, 38
POWs. *See* prisoners of war
Prinz Eugen (Germany), 141
prisoners of war (POWs), 2, 16, 89, 98, 153; German, 137, 189n32; *Hiwis*, 74, 76, 79, 94, 135, 183n12; Red Army, 10, 11

Ramcke, Hermann, 69
Red Army: 1st Airborne Corps, 45–46; 1st Balkan Front, 137; 2nd Baltic Front, 122–23, 141; 3rd Baltic Front, 141; 3rd Belorussian Front, 137; 5th, 137; 11th, 44; 22nd, 63; 34th, 44, 173n63; 39th, 137; 41st, 63; 42nd, 124; 43rd, 137; 56th, 67; 59th, 129–30; 225th Division, 130; Battle of Nevel, 64, 70, 84; casualties, 12, 78–79, 140, 178n50; Courland pocket and, 198n82; with Dnieper-Carpathian offensive, 77; formation sizes, 163n19; infantry divisions, 43, 86, 126, 174n2, 176n26; intelligence, 56, 125; Leningrad Front, 141; manpower, 12, 15, 58, 119, 123, 134, 144, 177n30, 193n13; *maskirovka* and, 56, 72, 131, 133; myth of, 55–56; with Operation Bagration, 5, 118, 131–36, 139–41, 147, 151, 196n44, 197n58; with Operation Kutuzov, 93; with Operation Mars, 50, 57, 62–63, 125, 178n50, 179n51; with Operation Uranus, 56; with operational force buildup, 134–35, 164n21; POWs, 10, 11; Rifle Division, 44, 48, 56–58, 60, 121, 125, 130, 134, 137, 140, 173n63, 177n30; Shock, 41–42, 44, 47, 121, 123–24, 127, 131; surrender, 48; Tank Corps, 57, 61, 63, 84, 125, 126, 142, 144; targets of, 125, 130, 135, 138–39, 193n20, 195n39; training, 12; unleashed, 119–20. *See also* Leningrad-Novgorod offensive
Red Army and the Second World War (Hill), 178n50
Regiment General Goering, 35–36. *See also* Parachute Panzer Division
Reich Forestry Department (*Reichsforstamt*, RFA), 16, 38–40
Reichswehr, 12–14, 19, 164n21, 169n10
Reichswehr and Politics, The (Carsten), 161n2, 164n20, 166n45
Reinhardt, Hans, 136
Retreat from Moscow (Stahel), 163n15
Reymann, Hellmuth, 128–29, 195n33
RFA. *See* Reich Forestry Department
Richtofen, Wolfram von, 165n34
Rifle Divisions, Red Army, 56, 60, 130; at Courland pocket, 140; Guards Corps, 44, 48, 58, 137, 173n63; manpower, 58, 134, 177n30; Operation Mars and, 57; at Oranienbaum pocket, 121, 125
Röhm, Ernst, 19
Romania, 56, 60–61, 67, 119–20, 131, 140
Rommel, Erwin, 8, 26, 34, 97, 99–103
Ruffner, Kevin, 159n10, 163n17, 168n73, 175n14, 182n8, 183n12, 198n84
Rundstedt, Gerd von, 96–99, 105
Rupp, Ernst, 67
Russia, 74, 76, 94, 135, 183n12, 197n58; 5th and 15th LwFDs in southern, 65–68; partisans in, 37, 45, 47–48, 79–80, 83–86, 123, 136
Rzhev salient, 50, 56–57, 59, 62–64, 71, 105, 125, 138

SA (*Sturm-Abteilung*), 19, 35
Salerno, Battle of, 36
Saving Private Ryan (film), 157n2
Schaffner, Franklin, 157n2
Scheibert, Horst, 178n41
Scherer, *Kampfgruppen*, 41
Scherer, Theodor, 41, 43
Schmundt, Rudolf, 22
Schörner, Ferdinand, 132, 141
Schröter (*Feldwebel*), 152
Schuldt, *Kampfgruppen*, 128, 129
Schutzstaffel. See SS
Schwoppe, Heinz, 145, 198n84
security battalion. *See* Luftwaffe *Sicherungsbataillon*
Seeckt, Hans von, 13, 164n20
Senger und Etterlein, Fridolin von, 108
Seydlitz-Kurzbach, Walter von, 45–47
Shepherd, Ben, 161n2, 183n20
Shingle, Operation, 107
Shock Army, Red Army: 1st, 44, 47, 131; 2nd, 121, 123–24, 127; 3rd, 41, 42, 44; 4th, 44
Sievers, Karl, 99, 102
Soldat bis zum letzten Tag (Kesselring), 174n4
Soviet Union, 38, 120, 134, 141, 162n9; air force, 10, 17, 26, 133; northern offensive, 15, 78, 122; Operation Barbarossa and, 10–12, 15–16, 20, 26, 33–36, 135, 163nn18–19. *See also* Red Army
Spanish Blue Division, 78, 80

Speth, *Kampfgruppen*, 128, 130
Spielberg, Steven, 157n2
SS (*Schutzstaffel*): 3rd *Totenkopf* Division, 44, 46, 47, 48, 82; 4th Police Division, 112; 11th *Nordland* Division, 124; 19th Division, 140, 142, 144; 20th Division, 140, 195n33; air force, 23; battalion, 38, 124; III Panzer Corps, 124, 126; with Jews, 171n34; Latvian brigade, 128–29, 131, 142–44; Waffen-SS, 21, 24, 28, 30, 37, 55, 102–3, 124, 126
SS vs Wehrmacht (Groppe), 166n48
Stahel, David, 163n15
Stalag Luft III, 165n34
stalemate, 9, 21, 101, 107, 120
Stalin, Joseph, 132, 144
Stalingrad (film), 1, 157n2
Stang, Werner, 167n70
Staraya Russa, 42, 44, 121, 130, 146
static (*Bodenstandig*) units, 139; FD (L)s as, 76, 88, 94, 99, 103, 106, 109, 115, 121, 150; LwFDs as, 15, 81, 87, 98, 153
Stauffenberg, Claus Schenk Graf von, 20–21
Stewart, Ian McDougall Guthrie, 169n3
storm divisions (*Sturm-Divisionen*), 69, 91, 94, 107–8, 111, 165n38
Struggle for Crete 20 May–1 June 1941, The (Stewart), 169n3
Student, Kurt, 26
StuG-III assault guns, 60, 81
Stumbling Colossus (Glantz), 162n9
Sturges, John, 165n34
Sturm-Abteilung. *See* SA
Sturm-Divisionen. *See* storm divisions
suicide, 105
supply lines, 11, 45, 55, 86, 136
surrenders, 9, 32, 159n12; Germans, 31, 36, 87, 106, 115, 145, 151–52; Italians, 89, 112; Red Army, 48

Tank Corps, Red Army, 57, 63, 125, 142, 144; 5th, 84; 24th, 61; 152nd, 126
Totenkopf Division, 3rd SS, 44, 46, 47, 48, 82
traditionalists, Nazis and, 8, 18–25, 148, 161n2, 166n45, 166n48, 166n50
training: ASTP, 154–55; FD (L)s, 134; LwFDs, 6, 49–54, 57, 60, 65, 69, 71, 77, 81, 83, 91, 146, 149, 170n13, 174n1, 177n35, 190n54; Red Army, 12
trench stalemate, 9, 21
trench warfare, 87, 120
Tresckow, Joachim von, 100, 105–6, 182n11, 187n65, 188n20
Tukhachevsky, Mikhail, 119
Turkey, 111

Ukraine, 119, 134; Army Group North, 120, 132, 135; Army Group South, 120, 131, 132
United States, 2, 153, 155, 160n14, 163n18. *See also* Army, U.S.
Uranus, Operation, 56
U.S. National Archives, 160n14

Velikiye Luki, 44, 63, 85
Verbände der Luftwaffe, Die (Dierich), 175n8
Verlorene Siege (Manstein), 165n38, 167n57, 167n70, 168n73, 174nn4–5, 175n15, 178n44
Versailles, Treaty of, 12–13, 164n21
Victory Was Beyond Their Grasp (Nash), 158n7
Vilsmaier, Joseph, 1, 157n2
Vitebsk: 4th FD (L)s at, 83–85, 118, 136–39, 147, 151; 6th FD (L)s at, 83–87, 118, 136–39, 147, 151; 6th LwFD at, 74, 85, 86; FD (L)s and Third Panzer Army at, 83–85, 136–39; II LwFK at, 62, 64, 83–85
Völcker, Kaspar, 110
Volksgrenadier divisions, 2, 24–25, 28, 55, 139, 153, 158n7; 16th, 103; 18th, 106, 190n42; 19th, 109; 167th, 104, 190n38
Volkssturm units, 2–3, 153, 158n7
Von Arnim, Hans-Jurgen, 41, 43
Von Luck, Hans, 189n27
Voyenno-Vozdushnye Sily (VVS, Soviet air force), 10, 17, 26, 133

Waffen-SS, 21, 24, 28, 30, 37, 55; 1st Panzer Division, 102–3; III Panzer Corps, 124, 126. *See also* SS
Walimont, Walter, 187n65
war crimes, 2, 37
War Department, U.S., 153

Warlimont, Walter, 4, 17–18, 23, 165n40, 166n53, 167n70, 174n4
Warsaw Uprising, 37
"the war of operational movement." *See* Bewegungskrieg
weapons: captured, 90, 95, 107; FD (L)s, 79–80, 99, 107; losses, 64; LwFDs, 49, 55, 58, 60–62, 64, 67, 71–72, 77, 80–83, 88, 176n26; Mauser Kar98k carbine, 39; StuG-III assault guns, 60, 81; U.S. Army, 187n62
Weber, Gottfried, 127–28, 140–41
Wehrmacht Retreats, The (Citino), 162n9
Wehrmacht's Last Stand, The (Citino), 162n9, 192n6, 196n44, 197n55
the Wehrmacht, 192n6, 196n44, 197n55; *Death of the Wehrmacht*, 162n7, 162n9; mythos and reality of, 1–4; *SS vs Wehrmacht*, 166n48; zenith of, 8–12
Westermann, Edward, 34
Western Front, 5, 9, 74, 105, 133; FD (L)s on, 94–95, 97; LwFDs on, 115; *Ost* battalions on, 2, 16

Westphal, Wilhelm, 152, 199n9
Wheeler-Bennett, John W., 161n2
When Titans Clashed (Glantz and House), 159n10, 162n9, 163n15, 198n82; on German casualties, 163n17; Operation Bagration, 196n44; Operation Mars, 179n51; on Red Army, 163n19, 164n21, 177n30
Winkelried, Operation, 48, 82
winter crisis (1941–42), 26, 28, 37, 82, 149, 160n1, 163n14
Wintergewitter (Winter Storm), Operation, 60–61
Winton, Harold, 162n6
women, 38, 55
World War I, 9, 15, 21, 25, 65, 71, 169n10

Yugoslavia, 10, 41, 90, 95, 113–15
Yukhnov airbase, 37, 46–47, 53

Zeitzler, Kurt, 70, 136
Zhukov, Georgi, 56, 62–63, 178n50, 179n51
Zhukov's Greatest Defeat (Glantz), 178n50
Zwischen Don und Donez (Scheibert), 178n41

ABOUT THE AUTHOR

MICHAEL J. STOUT earned his PhD in European history in May 2022 from the University of North Texas. Since 2023 he has been a full-time professor at Grayson College in north Texas, in addition to working as an adjunct instructor since 2017 at several other locations, including the University of Texas–Arlington, Dallas College, and Tarrant County College, teaching U.S., world, and military history. He lives in Lewisville, Texas.

The **Naval Institute Press** is the book-publishing arm of the U.S. Naval Institute, a private, nonprofit, membership society for sea service professionals and others who share an interest in naval and maritime affairs. Established in 1873 at the U.S. Naval Academy in Annapolis, Maryland, where its offices remain today, the Naval Institute has members worldwide.

Members of the Naval Institute support the education programs of the society and receive the influential monthly magazine *Proceedings* or the colorful bimonthly magazine *Naval History* and discounts on fine nautical prints and on ship and aircraft photos. They also have access to the transcripts of the Institute's Oral History Program and get discounted admission to any of the Institute-sponsored seminars offered around the country.

The Naval Institute's book-publishing program, begun in 1898 with basic guides to naval practices, has broadened its scope to include books of more general interest. Now the Naval Institute Press publishes about seventy titles each year, ranging from how-to books on boating and navigation to battle histories, biographies, ship and aircraft guides, and novels. Institute members receive significant discounts on the Press' more than eight hundred books in print.

Full-time students are eligible for special half-price membership rates. Life memberships are also available.

For more information about Naval Institute Press books that are currently available, visit www.usni.org/press/books. To learn about joining the U.S. Naval Institute, please write to:

Member Services
U.S. Naval Institute
291 Wood Road
Annapolis, MD 21402-5034
Telephone: (800) 233-8764
Fax: (410) 571-1703
Web address: www.usni.org